A Political Suicide

For Kate and Isobel

A Political Suicide

The Conservatives' voyage into the wilderness

Norman Fowler

POLITICO'S

First published in Great Britain 2008 by
Politico's Publishing, an imprint of
Methuen Publishing Ltd
8 Artillery Row
London
SW1P 1RZ

10 9 8 7 6 5 4 3 2 1

A CIP catalogue record for this book is available from the British Library.

ISBN 978-1-84275-227-2

Set in Bembo by SX Composing DTP, Rayleigh, Essex
Printed and bound in Great Britain by Cromwell Press Ltd, Trowbridge,
Wiltshire

Contents

Introduction

The surviving band of Conservative MPs who returned to Westminster after the party's humiliating defeat in the May 1997 general election found their position in the new House of Commons radically changed. They faced overflowing government benches notable for the number of women they accommodated. They found that the front bench below the gangway, traditionally the home of the most senior Tory MPs, was occupied by the Liberal Democrats – the other beneficiary of the 1997 election. Worst of all, they found that the Conservative opposition was regarded as utterly irrelevant. Labour ministers' stock replies to questions were laced with references to the wasted Tory years. Labour backbenchers routinely jeered at the Tory front bench and joyously applauded the most banal rejoinders of their own leaders.

Before the election some Conservative MPs had reassured each other that 'it will not be as bad as the polls suggest'. The eventual results were every bit as bad. After eighteen long years in opposition, Labour, with its charismatic new young leader, Tony Blair, had swept into power with an unprecedented majority of more than 170 seats. Seven Conservative Cabinet ministers had been defeated and the vanquished prime minister, John Major, had immediately announced his resignation. For the Conservatives – up to then the most consistently successful political party in the democratic world – it was a spectacular fall from grace.

The only comparable defeats were those of 1906 and 1945 but in one vital respect the 1997 rout was to prove even worse. In each of the earlier catastrophes the Conservatives were able to recover much of their strength in the general election immediately following. The 1997 defeat was followed by results in the 2001 and 2005 elections which were just as dire. It has taken over a decade of gruelling opposition and five changes of leader for the party to become a serious contender again. Of course, after a long period in power any party must face the prospect of defeat but what set 1997 apart was the sheer scale of the public's rejection of the Tory cause.

So what had brought about such a defeat? Blair, and John Smith before him, had certainly made the Labour Party more electable than it had been under the avowedly left-wing leadership of Michael Foot and Neil Kinnock. But the real truth about the Conservative Party at Westminster in the 1990s is that it did not have the will to fight to retain power. There was an internal crisis which affected both the government and the parliamentary party. Some of those who had fought hardest for the Thatcher changes in the 1980s were prepared to put that achievement at obvious risk in the 1990s by allowing in a Labour government. Senior Conservative politicians who had decisively campaigned to secure Major's election to the leadership rapidly (almost overnight) turned away from him once he was in power. Progressively Europe became the dominating issue and the theory – deadly for a government with a tiny majority – was advanced that Europe was an issue 'above politics'.

The strains were evident before the 1992 election but following Major's unexpected success at the polls the sniping developed into full-scale warfare, with a number of Cabinet ministers pursuing their own personal agendas to the detriment of the government as a whole. Margaret Thatcher, following in the footsteps of Ted Heath but to much greater effect, undermined Major, her chosen successor. The parliamentary party disintegrated into factions. The Conservatives, traditionally seen by the public as broadly united – in contrast to the Labour Party of the 1980s – were now seen as deeply divided and unpleasantly quarrelsome. Against such a background there was no prospect of them retaining power in the 1997 election. They had committed political suicide: power was tamely handed over by a party with an all-too-obvious death wish.

In describing the events which led up to this debacle, let me make my own declaration of intent. This book is not an autobiography. It is a report on the decline and fall of the last Conservative government. It describes what I saw and can personally vouch for in my time as a Cabinet minister with Thatcher, as party chairman for Major and later as a member of William Hague's shadow Cabinet. It is a report based on political diaries I kept during the 1980s and 1990s. Without a diary you rely on recollection, which can be notoriously unreliable, or judgement after the event. The test I set myself in this account is that the events I witnessed should be reported honestly and frankly. There is no point in spending time gliding around important events or avoiding inconvenient truths which may cause embarrassment or irritation to the players. Looking back, I realise that my earlier book on the Thatcher years was written too early: for what none of us at the time could foresee was that Thatcher would have such an impact upon the premiership of her successor. Her departure from Downing Street in 1990 was not remotely the end of the story.

The further question for today is whether history is now repeating itself. Over the last twelve months we have seen Labour encounter many of the very issues which led to the downfall of Major's government. We have seen a new prime minister taking over from a leader who had won three elections in a row and who had been a dominant force for most of their time in power. We have seen the newcomer make a good start swiftly to be followed by a chapter of accidents in the 'black autumn' of 2007, reminiscent of 1992 and Britain's ejection from the Exchange Rate Mechanism. We have seen the government's reputation for economic competence undermined and another chancellor under pressure. Can we substitute Brown for Major, Darling for Lamont?

We have seen sleaze infect a party which once claimed that only the Tories were 'tainted' by it. We have seen another government at odds with its activists. The Conservatives had Europe; Labour have Iraq, which by most calculations is infinitely more serious but admittedly is not as politically potent. Above all we have seen a tired government struggling to start anew but instead meeting devastating electoral defeat in the local elections of May 2008. In 1995 Major suffered a comparable catastrophe and was never able to recover. Will the same fate now overtake Brown? The similarities are striking and certainly enough to prevent the Conservatives' suicide years being written off as simply a period piece. It is a cautionary tale with lessons for all the political parties together with the politicians.

1

The spirit of Thatcher (1979–86)

'The only people who can face inflation with equanimity are those workers with industrial muscle, those on inflation-proof pensions and those with land and property.'

Margaret Thatcher, Cabinet, Thursday 23 July 1981.

Margaret Thatcher survived as difficult an introduction to power as any prime minister has endured since the war. Like John Major a decade later she faced the worst position for any leader: a number of senior ministers who did not support some of the government's central policies. Her election in May 1979 had left everything to be proved. It was by no means clear that a few years later she would dominate British politics, towering over friend and foe alike, and many commentators believed that she was lucky to be in power at all. Had Jim Callaghan gone to the polls six months previously he would have won; at least, that was certainly the consensus among us Conservative shadow ministers, listening incredulously as in September 1978 the Labour prime minister announced his strategy of electoral delay. The following 'winter of discontent', when patients appealed for treatment and bodies went unburied, did for Labour and brought Thatcher to No. 10.

Britain's first woman prime minister faced trials of strength on every front. Union power may have been rejected by the electorate but that did not mean that the union leaders would quietly slip away. They had been used to having their own way for too long. The nationalised industries were accustomed to demanding more money rather than making do with what they had. Workers in industries which had been uneconomic for years were still sadly unrealistic in their aims. As transport minister I faced union officials in Liverpool, only to be told that the solution for the then bankrupt Mersey Docks and Harbour Board was for the government to take powers to direct shipping to the port. Opposition to the government was symbolised by demonstrations – some violent, some peaceful, some even silent – which stretched through the 1980s.

Inside Whitehall the change of government was viewed with some dismay. Departmental ministers had to outface an often reluctant civil service, who resented the new controls on their budgets. Public spending restraint meant changes in their programmes and difficult disputes with the nationalised industries that they oversaw. Doing away with regulations meant disposing overnight of the official expertise in interpreting them and abandoning the paternal good intention that lay behind them. Many civil servants wanted what they called a more consensual approach.

Inevitably the bloodiest battleground inside the government itself became public spending. For at the heart of Geoffrey Howe's economic policy as chancellor was the belief that all previous attempts by different governments to control inflation by imposing incomes policies had failed, often miserably, and the only sensible alternative was to control the money supply. It was a highly controversial approach, with 'monetarist' becoming a term of contemptuous abuse. For ministers it meant difficult budget decisions in their own departments and carrying out policies which were bound to be politically unpopular.

Inside the government it was the time of the 'wets' and the 'dries', a description which was nicely suggestive of the seafront battles between 'mods' and 'rockers' in the 1960s. The 'wets' were the doubters, led by Jim Prior and Peter Walker. Prior had a low boiling point and although an intelligent and thoughtful debater in private would all too easily explode in meetings with the prime minister. His step-by-step approach to industrial relations reform was attacked inside the party as being too timid by half, but in the event he had the satisfaction of successfully starting a process of lasting reform – in contrast to the failed 'big bang' attempts which had gone before. Walker's style was different. He was courteous and largely avoided public confrontation but he was also the minister from the left that Thatcher most feared. He was anything but a political soul-mate but he remained in the Cabinet for eleven years, not only because of his skill in handling crises such as the 1985 coal strike but also because the prime minister did not want him on the backbenches and particularly not teaming up with his friend Michael Heseltine.

The leader of the 'dries' inside the Cabinet, supporting Howe, was Keith Joseph, who by standing to one side in 1975 had left the way clear for Thatcher to successfully challenge Ted Heath for the party leadership. In opposition he had provided much of the intellectual coherence for the new direction that the government was now taking and in that process he was utterly supportive of the prime minister, both in public and in private.

My diary gives some flavour of the divisions around the Cabinet table during 1980 and 1981.

Thursday 31 January 1980. Cabinet. The subject is public expenditure. There is a second reading debate to begin with. The usual people argue against – Jim Prior, Norman St John-Stevas, Ian Gilmour – joined by Peter Carrington: a formidable group.* Their argument is that we are basically creating two nations. By going into social security and health we are hitting the poor. I argue that if we want to cut public expenditure then we have to cut social security as that is the budget which has grown and grown: from £14 billion in 1974 to £20 billion in 1980.† This is the first intervention on the side of the chancellor. Norman St John-Stevas has another go about the rich and the poor. John Biffen intervenes to say that if we wanted to stop subsidies for the rich then we should stop aid to the arts – most of which went to the rich. Norman says this is a thoroughly trivial argument – and then sits fuming, saying 'disgraceful', 'disgraceful' – while even Nick Edwards shouts 'cheap'.

The conversation goes to and fro. All known variations of savings are tried. Keith Joseph suggests that the Christmas bonus should go. I

---

* A brief description of some of the main characters in the book can be found on pages 217–223.

† I might have spoken more carefully had I known that less than two years later controlling social security spending would be my job.

support. Had we taken a vote it would have gone – but Cabinets don't vote. In the last analysis the prime minister decides. She decides against. So we don't help the children – we help the middle class by giving them £10 for Christmas.

The next into the firing line is Michael Heseltine. He has prepared an elaborate defence and suggests cutting mortgage tax relief. MT [Margaret Thatcher] immediately tells him that as long as she is prime minister that will not happen. After various other diversionary tactics he is roundly told by MT that she spends longer listening to him than any other minister. She believes that the housing programme should be cut and cut it will be. By this time we are all pretty exhausted. The meeting has lasted from 10.00 until well after 1.00. There is a last appeal for contributions – rather like the appeal at the party conference – and we break up. The tensions are obvious. There are a number of ministers who plainly don't believe in what we are doing on public expenditure. No real problems yet but if the going gets really rough…

Three weeks later the prime minister identified another problem.

Thursday 21 February 1980. Cabinet. Proceedings begin with a warning from MT. She says that Cabinet decisions are being leaked, as are the proceedings of Cabinet committees. Leaks are appearing in not just one paper but in all. We just cannot continue on this basis, she says.

But the leaks continued, as too did the arguments inside the Cabinet room.

Thursday 31 July 1980. A Cabinet which shows all the strains of the coalition between the radicals and the gradualists. The main subject is teachers' pay and what to do about the arbitration award, which has resulted in a 14.6 per cent increase. In the main those who run industries (like myself) believe we should interfere and reject it; against are those who think it is altogether too difficult – particularly in the last week of parliament. An order is needed, which must go through both Houses of Parliament. The argument is that we should not spring it on the Commons or indeed the Lords. How it is going to be better in the autumn after three months of educational lobbying goodness knows.

In the end those who argue that a stand should be taken prevail. As in most disputes, the 'sides' are not exactly as would be predicted from outside. Peter Walker is in favour of making a stand; Angus Maude [paymaster general] against. What becomes very clear is just how on edge Jim Prior now is. MT makes a remark about 'sound money'. Jim replies, 'I don't give a damn for sound money' – he is more concerned about the unemployment figures. MT is then forced to say that anyone who feels that he cannot support the government's economic policy should let her know. Silence from Jim and embarrassed silence all round. It is the last week in July but we all know it goes much deeper.* Jim will never get the kind of economic policy he wants with MT. He will be left defending the unemployment figures as they go beyond two million. The present position cannot last for ever. I suspect that Jim may leave not because he has not the character for the fight – he has shown great courage in his battles on the employment bill – but simply because he has not got his heart in it.

Four days later the decision was reversed.

Monday 4 August 1980. About turn. A meeting of 'E' (the economic committee of Cabinet) is in fact a full Cabinet. The prime minister has discovered that Christopher Soames has just completed a negotiation with the industrial civil servants which gives them 18 per cent. How then can the government plead 'national economic circumstances' to persuade both Houses that 14.6 per cent is too much for the teachers? Everyone agrees that we can't. Soames splutters with rage as he gets a broadside from MT and a very unhappy meeting comes to an end. MT looks very isolated with Willie Whitelaw coming to the aid of Soames. Soames claims he was given Cabinet authority to reach his agreement – although the details never came to Cabinet.

The reversal was immediately followed by the leak.

---

* July is a notoriously bad month at Westminster for taking decisions. Ministers are tired and looking forward to the long summer break.

Tuesday 5 August 1980. The papers are full of the 'defeat for Thatcher'. In spite of every appeal not to leak one or two have gone out and spilled a very incomplete story. Not a word about the real reasons – and a lot about MT being overruled.

There was even worse to come. In February 1981 the government suffered a humiliating defeat on plans to close fifty uneconomic coal mines and this was followed in March by Geoffrey Howe's third Budget. In retrospect it was a determining step in gaining control of the public finances but that was not how it seemed when the Cabinet were given the details a few hours before the statement. Howe set out the position very soberly. The public sector borrowing requirement was increasing at an unsustainable rate. To reduce it he intended to raise national insurance, put an excess profits tax on the banks, impose big increases in duty on petrol and cigarettes, and raise taxes by not implementing the requirement to increase personal allowances – all this in the middle of a recession with unemployment climbing.

The reaction was immediate. Jim Prior called the Budget disastrous and said it would make unemployment worse: he predicted (accurately) that unemployment would rise to more than three million. Francis Pym said he was expecting a Budget which did more for industry and among the other critics were Walker, Soames and Gilmour. Even Keith Joseph asked if more could not be done to bring private investment into public industry. Only the realisation that the Budget was now set and there was nothing anyone could do to alter it prevented a bigger explosion. Rarely can a chancellor have been sent into battle with less encouragement from his friends.

It was a criticism that was swiftly leaked to the outside world.

Monday 16 March 1981. There have been some quite extraordinary leaks. There was a leak on Friday which set out the position of all the Cabinet on the Budget and their reactions to it. Once the argument has been decided in Cabinet it is taken outside. Anyone who actually supports the government's economic policy is regarded as an eccentric.

By now, not only was the government under bombardment but

the prime minister was under personal pressure. She reacted by hitting out at both foes and friends. A few weeks after the Budget she called a small meeting of ministers responsible for nationalised industries. She was deliberately and personally confrontational from the start. She spared no one – not even Joseph, her mentor.

Tuesday 31 March 1981. She lectures everyone in sight. She lectures Keith Joseph and she treats Geoffrey Howe in a manner which can be most charitably described as patronising – and probably more accurately as contemptuous. She also has a go at me. She starts off by calling me 'dear', which does not go down well. Having heard a few of her views on the nationalised transport industries I decide that enough is enough and point out that she has got it wrong. If she looks at the four 'nationalised' industries in transport she will see that we have denationalised two of them. We have introduced competition into another for the first time in half a century. As for railways, which are her hate, we are denationalising the subsidiary companies and achieving more in manpower reductions than at any stage for a decade.* To be fair Margaret agrees that this is the case and Keith Joseph puts up a fairly good fight for his corner. Geoffrey gives the impression that he has seen this all before and does not intend to get involved in a slanging match.

There are some marvellous moments in which Margaret accuses all government ministers of not having the first idea about what is going on in their nationalised industries and not having any adequate accounts. She says that when she showed the accounts to Denis (Thatcher) he could not make head or tail of them. It is real 'Dear Bill' stuff. She says that no one has ever run anything – which is true but also applies to herself. Margaret really cannot continue to treat everyone in this extraordinarily aggressive manner. She has got to the stage at the moment when she will not listen even when there is good news. She wants to find the bad news. As we leave I talk to Keith

---

* The National Freight Corporation and the docks of the British Transport Docks Board were denationalised, while regulations preventing the development of inter-city coach services were scrapped. Among British Rail's subsidiary companies were the badly underinvested hotels – including the world-famous Gleneagles, which was open for only half the year.

Joseph. 'A bad meeting,' I mutter. To this Keith shook his head and replied, 'Ah, yes, but it must be far worse for Margaret.' By this he means that Margaret feels the defeats we have suffered in the nationalised industry area more keenly than anyone.

But according to my diary 'the worst Cabinet by a mile' in the early years of the Thatcher premiership came a few months later.

Thursday 23 July 1981. The chancellor is proposing that more cuts should be made in public spending so as to make room for tax cuts later on. It becomes clear very soon that he is going to run into very serious trouble. Quite exceptionally Humphrey Atkins starts the discussion. I have never heard Humphrey talk about economics before and he does not really talk about it this time. But what he does say has some truth in it. In Northern Ireland they are rather more worried about unemployment than they are about reducing taxation.

Humphrey is followed by Michael Heseltine, fresh back from Liverpool. Michael speaks emotionally about the position he has found there. He says there is a sense of hopelessness and this particularly affects the young. He is followed by John Nott. Now John is one of the supporters of the general economic strategy and pays some tribute to it at the start. The rest of what he has to say on the paper is entirely scathing. He says it is a hopeless paper. Basically, the chancellor should come back with a different and better one. Needless to say, if the so called 'dries' feel this way about the chancellor's plans then the 'wets' feel even more strongly. Francis Pym says that the package looks like the same old thing again. Ian Gilmour has a few well-prepared words to say about the decline and fall of the Conservative Party if we continue on the present path. Quintin Hogg says that the position reminds him of the Hoover–Roosevelt position before the last war, where, because Hoover had nothing to offer, the Republicans went into the political wilderness for thirty years.

Faced with such a wall of Cabinet criticism other leaders would have been tempted to attempt to take the sting out of the meeting. In contrast Margaret Thatcher was utterly defiant – finding time to single out farmers and landowners for particular counter-attack.

Margaret sums up. She makes no concessions to any part of the debate, which obviously has gone extremely badly. She says that all people are arguing for is the kind of reflation which we had in Heath's period of government and the last thing she wants to do is to preside over the kind of property boom that we saw then. She says that inflation is still one of the chief enemies of the country but then adds rather gratuitously that the only people who can face inflation with equanimity are those workers with industrial muscle, those on inflation-proof pensions and those with land and property. The last is directed particularly at Francis, who has argued that inflation is not the issue. Both Jim [Prior] and Francis look livid at the barb but they decide not to intervene again and Margaret closes the meeting. It really could not have been worse. It leaves the PM and the chancellor absolutely isolated.

So it is certainly true that Thatcher had to battle against attacks from both outside the government and within. Nevertheless it is wrong to believe that even in those very first years she was defended by only a tiny praetorian guard of true believers. It has always been misleading to divide the Cabinet rigidly into 'wets' and 'dries'. There was never a single ticket which covered every issue. It is true that at times ministers fought as if they were in different parties. At one meeting Jim Prior brought along Keith Joseph's election address and quoted from it to show why a proposed spending cut would be impossibly inconsistent. But as the political columnist Hugo Young pointed out, few if any of the Cabinet dissented from the broad priorities of controlling public spending and reducing both inflation and taxation. 'It was all a question of balance between them and of the rigour with which they were to be approached.'*

Even more fundamental, the *centre* of the Cabinet held broadly steady – as too did the centre of the party. Of course, there were acutely difficult meetings when the Treasury felt isolated and, of course, ministers did not proceed in unquestioning obedience. Given the scale of what was being attempted it would have been

---

* Hugo Young, *One of Us: A Biography of Margaret Thatcher* (London: Macmillan, 1989), p. 147.

amazing if they had. It is not what Cabinet government is, or should be, about.

The most important man of the centre by a long way was Willie Whitelaw, then the home secretary and later the deputy prime minister, whose influence in Cabinet easily surpassed either Joseph's from the right or Prior's from the left. Whitelaw was a big, larger-than-life man. A former chief whip and leader of the Commons, he knew Parliament through and through. He was a man of action and a natural leader – as I remember from my spell as a lowly parliamentary private secretary when he was secretary of state for Northern Ireland. He was a man you could trust, whose advice you would be wise to accept and whom you would follow into battle. He was very different in background and attitude to the prime minister but he was indispensable to her, particularly in those early years. But was Whitelaw a 'true' Thatcherite?

To ask the question demonstrates the absurdity of those right-wing commentators who today try to categorise former ministers into 'true believers' and the rest. Some of the self-proclaimed true believers were later shown to be the least effective ministers there were. Some presided over disaster. Indeed the very premise of 'true' belief is wrong. Thatcher did not have one set of unchangeable beliefs that took her through from 1975 to 1990. Her beliefs changed.

I remember our conversation in 1975 when she put me into the shadow Cabinet and her frank concern about her total lack of experience in foreign affairs. Learning about Europe was the priority, not setting out a radically new direction. In her first speech as leader in 1975 she argued against the referendum on remaining in the EEC. In 1979 she was elected on a notably pro-European manifesto, which charged Labour with failing in their negotiations because of a lack of belief in the European ideal. In 1985 she signed up to the Single European Act, which gave away more British sovereignty than any other European measure before or since and then, ignoring all opposition, steamrollered the subsequent legislation through Parliament. It was not until her Bruges speech of September 1988 – only two years before she fell – that she explicitly raised the spectre of 'a European superstate exercising a new dominance from Brussels'. But even then she still wanted influence. She did nothing to prevent Christopher Prout, the then leader of the Conservative group in the European Parliament, negotiating for the party's MEPs to become allied with the parliamentary group of the European People's Party, in spite of the aspiration in the latter's constitution for a united Europe.

The truth is that many of the most important changes were carried out by ministers who, although not regarding Thatcher as some kind of mystical goddess, more importantly shared her view that Britain had drifted for too long and cried out for reform and change. I had not voted for Thatcher when she defeated Ted Heath in the leadership election and rather feared that this woman with her easily lampooned middle-class accent might not be the election winner that her skilful campaign manager, Airey Neave, had promised. Nevertheless I believed that if we failed as a government to curb the unions, reform industry and bring down inflation then the national outlook was bleak. I resented Britain being regarded as the sick man of Europe and hoped that once more we could have some influence in the world. Of course, I had every reason to be grateful to Margaret Thatcher. She had put me into her first shadow Cabinet – guided, I suspect, by Keith Joseph, who I had been working with for the previous six months. In 1979 she promoted me straight into the Cabinet as minister of transport, although I had no ministerial experience whatsoever, and at Transport I was able to carry out some of the first privatisation measures of the new government.

Privatisation is today seen as one of the hallmarks of the Thatcher years but that is not how it was at the beginning. Even the term, which Thatcher personally hated, was not widely used. The 1979 manifesto contained only two new pledges in this area: my proposals to take the National Freight Corporation and the British Transport docks out of state ownership. But these did not come about as the result of any edict from the centre. I was not a reluctant minister being pressed to be courageous. My fight had been to get the pledges into the manifesto at all and make them firm commitments for the incoming government. In 1979 the fear was that such radicalism might frighten the voters.

The July 1981 meeting marked the low point of the new government but the process of recovery was slow. As Parliament broke for the summer recess the opinion polls showed Conservative support at a mere 30 per cent − 7 points behind a Labour opposition led by Michael Foot. The pain of the last two years had been obvious enough but the gain was less so.

A reshuffle in September 1981 brought into the Cabinet Cecil Parkinson, Nigel Lawson and Norman Tebbit and excluded some of the 'wets', such as Ian Gilmour and Christopher Soames. But there was no immediate change in our fortunes. In January 1982 I lunched with Hugo Young. 'He clearly believes that our chances of winning the next election are not at all good,' I said in my diary. 'He is prepared to concede that there may be a theoretical chance of this happening but not much more.' It was not until three months later at the start of April, with, ironically, the Argentinian invasion of the Falklands, that the government's electoral position started to improve.

The irony arose because initially the occupation of the Falklands was seen as a political disaster. On Friday 2 April 1982, the day of the invasion, there were two special Cabinet meetings. In the morning we tried to find a convincing argument to explain why we had been caught unawares; in the evening we found intelligence reports (rapidly removed) which said that the best assessment was that the Argentinians would now reinforce their troops and that they would be very difficult if not impossible to dislodge. Some of us remembered the 1956 Suez operation and the difficulty of getting our forces the short distance from Cyprus to Egypt. Here we were proposing to travel thousands of miles to the other end of the world and defeat an entrenched army of occupation. And yet that is exactly what happened. The operation was a clear triumph for the utter professionalism of the British forces − but also for Thatcher's determination not to agree to fudged compromises. In one Commons exchange the former Conservative minister Enoch Powell (then an Ulster Unionist) had reminded the prime minister that she took some pride in her description as 'the iron lady'. In the next weeks, he added, the nation 'will learn of what metal she is made'. He received his reply. The recapture of the Falklands brought a triumphant end to the first period of her premiership and victory in the ensuing election.

By the mid-1980s Thatcher had established beyond doubt her authority over the Cabinet and the party. It was the purple patch of her premiership but even so the government still faced profound challenges. The 1984 Conservative conference at Brighton saw the most direct of these, when the IRA tried to assassinate the Cabinet. In the early hours of Friday morning, 12 October, I was woken in my room at the Grand Hotel by a loud cracking bang and the noise of what seemed to be stones or bricks falling. It sounded as though there had been an explosion in the building. When I reached the main staircase the gravity of the attack began to become clear.

The scene reminds me irresistibly of a stage play of the 1914–18 war. There is smoke and dust. In the grey murk a line of people are moving down the staircase. No one is hurrying and few are talking. There is Jock Bruce-Gardyne,* who confirms it is a bomb. Jock is fully dressed and is carrying two suitcases. But Keith Joseph is in his dressing gown and carrying his red box in one of the sacks in which they are delivered. Another of the group is Patrick Jenkin, who is literally in nothing more than his dressing gown. 'I always sleep like this,' he says.

At the bottom of the staircase we are directed to the back of the hotel and are soon out in the road. It is still dark but even so, looking up at the Grand Hotel it is possible to see what has happened. The explosion has caused a partial collapse of the façade of the hotel on the fourth and fifth floors. There is a U-shape cut out of the building. As Michael Jopling says, with damage like that it is difficult to see how injuries and even deaths can have been avoided.

In a few minutes we are pushed back along the front by the police. By this time I have joined up with both Michael Jopling and Nigel Lawson, who has appeared in an old sweater. None of us think much of the invitation to go into the Metropole. Having just escaped from one hotel there is no particular appeal in setting up in the one next door. Sure enough, about a quarter of an hour later the order comes to evacuate the

---

* A journalist who became a Conservative MP and minister and who died prematurely in 1990 at the age of sixty.

Metropole. It is an interesting commentary on security precautions that we have half the Cabinet wandering about on the Brighton seafront. Not even the chancellor of the exchequer rates protection.

Our trio decide eventually to try our luck at the Bedford. We find a settee and settle down. Coffee is provided by the hotel and they are even prepared to give away rooms. Personally I am going to stay up. On another armchair is a man in jeans who says his company owns the Grand. We politely enquire about the insurance. After about an hour I make my way back to the Metropole. Rumours are rife. It is believed that the prime minister was evacuated safely but there are a number missing – George Younger is mentioned, as is Norman Tebbit, and no one has seen John Wakeham.

The Metropole announces that Grand Hotel refugees can have breakfast with them in a special room. I get through to Fiona and tell her what has happened before she hears it on the radio. Breakfast is rather a touching sight. Not only are there all the Grand Hotel residents, still clothed exactly as when they left, but the early shift of the Grand Hotel have come to serve us. There are about five waiters for each table. A message next comes through that Marks and Spencer are opening their store early.

A grimmer message concerns the Tebbits. Eric Ward,* who has been to the hospital, says that Margaret is particularly badly injured. There is still no news of John or Roberta Wakeham.

The decision has been taken that the conference will go on. We go to the back of the conference centre and up to the speakers' room behind the stage. Willie Whitelaw is there and so too are Leon Brittan and Geoffrey Howe. Willie is furious about the BBC television pictures of Norman Tebbit being rescued from the rubble, which he says were photographed in very close detail. The stories of the night were interrupted by the news that the prime minister has arrived and is sitting on the platform. We hurry down – a rather depleted Cabinet. The audience rises to its feet as it sees some familiar faces. We then have a short service – a period of silence – and straight on to the debate on Northern Ireland. The conference is subdued and people listen with one ear to the predictable contributions on the problems of the province which have overspilled so violently to Brighton.

---

* A long-serving Conservative area agent.

The eventual casualty list showed five dead, including Roberta Wakeham, who Fiona had breakfasted with only twenty-four hours before, and Tony Berry, the MP for Enfield Southgate. Of the other casualties the most serious was Margaret Tebbit, who in the years since has confronted her injuries with great courage, and John Wakeham, who made a remarkable recovery. The impact of the bomb on the families affected was obviously profound; the impact upon the political debate was utterly counter-productive. If anyone wanted further proof of the savagery of the IRA they had it here.

The year-long miners' strike, which ended in March 1985 ('Mr Scargill's Insurrection', as the Thatcher memoirs have it),* was a more familiar political challenge. The leader of the mineworkers took on the government hoping for the same success that his union had achieved in 1981 – only to find that this time coal stocks for the power stations had been built up and the government was ready for the often violent confrontations which followed. With the Cabinet solidly behind her there was never any prospect that the prime minister would fold. Strangely, she was at greatest risk of forced resignation during the Westland helicopter row – by most measures the least important crisis of her premiership.

The dispute concerned the future of the small Westland company, based in Yeovil, which happened to be Britain's only manufacturer of helicopters. Facing possible bankruptcy, the company wanted to merge with the American firm Sikorsky. This was vigorously opposed by Michael Heseltine, now the defence secretary, on the grounds that there should be a European solution. The position of the Department of Trade and Industry, now under the control of Leon Brittan, was that this was a decision for the company to take, not for the government to impose. And so in the last months of 1985 the dispute began – but in a way that by now was in danger of becoming the modus operandi inside the Thatcher government.

There were no long debates on Westland in full Cabinet. Instead the rival cases were considered first by a small group of

* Margaret Thatcher, *The Downing Street Years* (London: HarperCollins, 1993), pp. 339–78.

directly involved Cabinet ministers, in a meeting chaired by the prime minister, and then eventually by the economic committee of the Cabinet. At no stage did Margaret Thatcher take the obvious step of having a face-to-face talk with Heseltine in an attempt to sort out the differences. The one and only time Westland arrived at full Cabinet was the morning Heseltine dramatically snapped his folder shut and walked out. Ministers left the Cabinet Room to the hall outside, leaving Thatcher alone with Willie Whitelaw and the chief whip. After a pause of a few minutes we trooped back to our places. George Younger, who had started the meeting as Scottish secretary, was made defence secretary in a battlefield promotion; and a search party was sent out to find Malcolm Rifkind with the news that he was the new Scottish secretary.

That was not the end of Westland. Attention now turned to a letter from the solicitor general, Patrick Mayhew, which had become public. Mayhew had been asked to advise on Heseltine's view that an American solution would harm Westland in the European market and make involvement with some European military projects 'incompatible'. Mayhew's advice was that there were 'material inaccuracies' in the case Heseltine was putting forward. The question became: who had leaked the law officer's advice? Michael Havers, the attorney general, was insistent that the issue should be pursued. The answer seemed to be that the leak had taken place with at least the knowledge of two of the prime minister's closest advisers, Bernard Ingham and Charles Powell. The water was now lapping very dangerously at the doorstep of No. 10; just before the ensuing Labour censure debate on Monday 27 January 1986, Thatcher is reported to have mused that she might not be prime minister 'by six o'clock tonight'. In the event Neil Kinnock's assault on her was so rambling and general that she walked away largely unhurt – the chief casualty remained Brittan, who had been forced into resignation some days earlier.

Thatcher survived and as the 1987 election approached she could tick off a list of achievements to put before the British public. The economy had visibly strengthened and inflation had fallen. Industrial relations had been transformed and, following Arthur Scargill's last hurrah, the policy of the elected government was no longer subject to union veto. Privatisation had now reached undoubtedly major companies such as British Telecom and British Airways. Even unemployment looked as though it might be on a consistently downward path. Abroad Britain's standing was high and the country had entirely discarded its reputation as the sick man of Europe.

But what of the prime minister herself? This was the woman who dominated the 1980s and whose shadow would hang over British politics for most of the 1990s. How did she handle the people who worked most closely with her? How did she make and seek to make policy? What was her working style? A few extracts from my diaries give some answers to those questions. I do not pretend that they are more than a sketch; a full-scale portrait would take an entire book to paint.

In the autumn of 1981 I had moved from Transport to take over the double-headed department – the Department of Health and Social Security. I remained there for six years – longer than any of my post-war predecessors on either side of the department and frankly longer than was in the interests of my political career. I became typecast but whatever else I had a very good view of the Thatcher approach to social policy.

One of her constant fears was that ministers would 'go native' in defence of one of the big public services such as health or education. Her attitude, and her view of her ministers' position, were graphically illustrated at what was intended to be a health seminar meeting at No. 10 in September 1983. I, together with Ken Clarke, then my minister of health, sought to defend our budget against the combined assault of the new chancellor, Nigel Lawson, the chief secretary to the Treasury, Peter Rees, and, of course, the prime minister.

Friday 16 September 1983. It becomes clear from the start that Margaret is not going to keep to our agenda. Her agenda is a letter that she has received from a consultant she met who happens to be extremely critical of the NHS and its administration. MT keeps going for about half an hour on the inefficiencies of the health service while Ken and I seek to play out the storm. Strangely, however, it tends to suit our book. Neither the chancellor nor the chief secretary can get a word in, although Peter Rees does begin several times on a sentence which seems to indicate that he would favour higher health service charges. As he never gets to the end of the sentence we never find out. MT repels all boarders.

There is a revealing aside during the discussion. At one point when we are being criticised for not tightening the screws sufficiently I remark that it would be a great mistake if she was to think that in the health service I was regarded as a friendly and overgenerous figure. She replies to the effect: 'That is just as well. I wouldn't employ you if you were.'

Health was not her only concern. Social security policy also loomed large, particularly when – as in February 1985 at a Downing Street lunch – she had just returned from a visit to the United States. A trip to the US always boded ill.

Monday 25 February 1985. The PM has returned determined to take action to move us more to a self-help country. Although it is a tedious thing to observe, the UK is not the USA. Values are different: people here place greater value on public services and on a welfare system which at least prevents them from falling into poverty. I agree with her that we need more of the American entrepreneurship. The difficulty is how to do it. At lunch MT is in no doubt. Social security benefits are standing in the way of recovery. She has been shown a chart in Washington which relates new jobs to the length of unemployment benefit. In the US it lasts for only six months and thus people are 'encouraged' to get jobs. She will brook no argument and there are of course colleagues who broadly agree with her. The message is that we are just tinkering with social security – she wants real action. I defend almost alone and at one stage warn her that an indiscriminate attack on the welfare state will put us in opposition for a decade. It is a truly awful lunch.

And then there was the issue of AIDS, a new and largely unknown public health challenge. What we did know was that there was no vaccine, no cure and no drugs. It was a death sentence. The only policy was to warn the public of the dangers and my instincts were for a major public education campaign using all the power of modern advertising.

This was some way from Margaret Thatcher's initial position. On 6 March 1986, the head of my private office received a peremptory note from the prime minister's principal private secretary, Nigel Wicks, on one of my advertising proposals. The note said:

> The Prime Minister has emphasised that she still remains against certain parts of the advertisement. She thinks that the anxiety on the part of parents and many teenagers, who would never be in danger from AIDS, would exceed the good which the advertisement might do. In her view it would be better to follow the 'VD' precedents of putting notices in doctors' surgeries, public lavatories etc. But to place advertisements in newspapers which every young person could read and learn of practices they never knew about would, in her view, do harm.
>
> Your Secretary of State will now wish to consider how to proceed in the light of the Prime Minister's firmly held views. He may wish to consider showing the Prime Minister an amended advertisement which omits the parts which, in the Prime Minister's view, would be likely to offend.

You might think that the sum of these sketches was a woman who it was difficult if not impossible to work with. Not so. Every one of the sketches has to be qualified. Her tactics of direct confrontation often shocked those who came up against them for the first time. Even a bruiser like Ken Clarke said he felt like taking a 'hot shower' after one of our early confrontations on the National Health Service. Clarke became a veteran of the scraps but others never adapted. My own view was that, although she often went storming over the top, it could bring out the best in her ministers. Of course, not everyone shares my view but personally I enjoyed her direct confrontational style. The adrenalin rose and you gave of your best. She put you under pressure but it enabled you to argue back. But then, as she suggested in her memoirs, I was a natural defender. It was not for nothing that I gained my school colours as a goal keeper, a wicket keeper and even a centre half at hockey.

She was also right to fear that ministers could 'go native' and simply act as spokesmen for their departments. In case anyone thinks that was my position at social security I would only say that my most senior adviser on the social security side virtually dissociated himself from the review I carried out in the mid-1980s on the grounds that I insufficiently appreciated their achievement.

In this area Thatcher was in practice much more cautious than her words might suggest. She well understood the politics of the position and would distance herself from some of the most purist, but least political, Treasury proposals, much to the annoyance of successive chancellors and chief secretaries. I remember being involved in one particular dispute with the Treasury shortly before the 1987 election. Eventually after a series of meetings I won the battle. 'Well done,' said Thatcher quietly and privately as we were about to meet at the next Cabinet meeting – before delivering a collective warning that the contingency reserve for the next year had now all been used.

As for AIDS, I did not change the advertising approach; rather I developed it so that in the autumn of 1986 we not only launched a high-profile advertising campaign but also sent warning leaflets to every household in the country. Our approach, encompassed in the slogan 'Don't die of ignorance', was the very opposite of her initial reaction. She was never a great supporter of the campaign or my later visit to the United States, where I was photographed shaking hands with an AIDS patient who died several weeks later – a simple act later made truly memorable by Princess Diana. She did, however, allow herself to be persuaded that this was a policy area where she did not need to be involved and instead allowed policy to be decided by a special Cabinet committee under Willie Whitelaw.

So it is true that at times Thatcher stormed away, sought to lecture her ministers and pursued indefensible or oddly eccentric lines of argument based on a letter she had received or a person she had met. It is also true that if ministers were silly enough not to respond then she would walk all over them. But that was only one part of her style. If you were in a hole, defending government policy – as I was in 1982, dealing with a lengthy health strike – she would support you without equivocation. In the main she would avoid the usual, tired advice that 'it is all a matter of presentation'.

In Cabinet itself she was generally formal. Unlike Tony Blair she rigidly followed the custom that ministers should be addressed by their official titles: Chancellor of the Exchequer, Foreign Secretary, Secretary of State for Social Services. Christian names were only used in 'political' Cabinets, where civil servants were absent and ministers were plotting, for example, the issues to be raised in an election. The formality sometimes went further. I noted that when I was called, literally from the middle of a full Cabinet meeting, across Westminster Bridge to St Thomas' Hospital to be at the birth of my second daughter Isobel she made no mention of the fact as I left the room – let alone wishing me good luck. That was not because she lacked kindness in such matters: friend and foe agree that she was notably kind in personal issues. It was that her respect for the institution of the Cabinet was such that she rarely allowed private lives to intervene within it.

But in one respect life at No. 10 did change radically. Like Blair, the longer she stayed as prime minister the more control she wanted. From the start she had preferred to pursue her aims in discussion with small groups of ministers rather than full Cabinet. My diary is full of pleas by one minister or another to be made part of the process. By the mid-1980s she wanted not just a check on what was happening in the individual departments but, increasingly, to determine the policies ministers pursued. Progressively she began to place more and more reliance on her special advisers to the partial exclusion of her ministers. It was the beginning of a new form of political governance. Unless ministers were careful they risked being second-guessed, not by other ministers in Cabinet committees, which was how government had always worked, but by advisers answerable only to the prime minister.

I came smack up against this new way of doing things in a dispute of June 1986. It received no publicity but was an obvious forerunner of a later row centring on the chancellor of the exchequer that was to rock the government. Some months earlier I had asked the then deputy managing director of Sainsbury's, Roy Griffiths, to carry out a management review of the NHS. As a result we introduced managers into the health service: an obvious and long-overdue change which was predictably opposed outright by the Labour Party and the unions, including the British Medical Association.

Thatcher herself distrusted the NHS. She regarded it as a nationalised industry in the social service area but up to 1987 was very cautious about change given the overheated political debate of the time. At one point I proposed that we should make it a separate commission or corporation managed separately from the Health Department. 'No,' she replied after a little thought. 'If we do that they will say we are going to sell it off.' And there is no doubt that would have been exactly the charge. Instead she wanted a much more direct say in how the NHS was run. I had suggested that Griffiths should be appointed my adviser on the health service; her plan was that he should be brought in as the 'prime minister's adviser on the health service'. I strongly disputed this. I was not prepared as health secretary to be second-guessed by an adviser at No. 10 who appeared to have all the authority of the prime minister. The argument went to and fro. Griffiths badly wanted to have the status and Thatcher badly wanted him to have that position. In an angry meeting late at night at No. 10 I said that if this were to go ahead then I would resign. It was the only time that I ever used the explicit resignation threat face to face in fifteen years' service with Thatcher. But it was effective. Griffiths became my adviser and not the prime minister's.

I was lucky. We had just come through Westland and the loss of two Cabinet ministers. The election was only a short distance off and by any standards the NHS was politically one of the most sensitive policy areas. Nevertheless my experience was the clearest warning of what was to come. Advisers with relatively little experience of government were to be given increased importance over ministers who by now had very substantial experience. The Cabinet survivors from the early days had now survived everything from violent demonstrations and strikes to acts of terrorism. They were not likely to take kindly to this new development. Here were the seeds of destruction of the Thatcher government.

2

The turning point (1987)

'In eighteen months' time we will be very unpopular as a government.'

Margaret Thatcher, 10 Downing Street, Saturday 13 June 1987.

On the morning of Saturday 13 June 1987, the post-election reshuffle began. Margaret Thatcher had just won a third successive general election victory, the only prime minister in the twentieth century to have achieved that record. She was in a position of power that no Tory prime minister had enjoyed since the days of Churchill – and infinitely stronger than the position of Tony Blair after his third victory almost twenty years later. Since 1979 her governments had passed legislation that had transformed the industrial relations position, privatised a succession of state-owned industries, repaired the public finances and restored Britain's reputation overseas. She now intended to finish the job and to initiate a period of radical reform in social policy. It was to be the turning point of the Thatcher administration.

Customarily all the comings and goings of a reshuffle had been through the front door of 10 Downing Street. The promoted beamed while the dismissed were expected to put on a brave face and vow undying loyalty to the leader. This script had been spectacularly torn up a few years earlier by the Cabinet minister Ian Gilmour, who following his sacking had confided to the cameras in Downing Street that the government was 'steering full speed ahead for the rocks'. It was then remembered that there was a perfectly good and anonymous side entrance to No. 10 via the Cabinet Office in Whitehall.

This was the route that John Biffen, the most prominent of the casualties that day, took to hear his fate. Since 1983 he had been leader of the Commons and in that role had been counted a notable success. But he had signed his own political death warrant when in a television interview, following local election reverses in 1986, he had publicly called for a 'balanced ticket' rather than leaving the next election to an alliance of Thatcher and the party chairman, Norman Tebbit. The prime minister was enraged at the attack and her first instinct had been to sack him straightaway* but she was persuaded to stay her hand. In 1987 there was to be no reprieve. Biffen was judged a risky ally in the fight for the brave new world that was now to be planned.

Thatcher's new priorities had their roots in her earlier career. She was determined at long last to properly challenge the educational establishment, which had frustrated her back in the early 1970s when she had been education secretary in Ted Heath's government. She was resolved to successfully reform the rating system, which, as she had pointed out when a shadow minister in the October 1974 election campaign, bore particularly hard upon the elderly widow who paid the same as the working family next door. Meanwhile her experience as prime minister had added other priorities such as the National Health Service, where she could never understand why the government received so little credit for what she considered was the vast amount of money lavished upon it.

It was a very personal agenda but more ominously it was also an agenda where she was not playing to her strengths. Thatcher was seen as a warrior, not a social reformer. Yet here she was preparing to embark on a programme which very substantially raised the stakes. The public had been waiting for years for a government to successfully tackle union power but the schools, the universities, the NHS were not seen as public enemies. They were also guarded by public service unions which on all past performance would be entirely unscrupulous in fanning fear.

In the afternoon, with the thunder of a summer storm rumbling in the background, it was the turn of the promoted, the transferred and in one case the resurrected to go to No. 10 and learn their fates. We were all dropped by our drivers at the front door

---

* Years later I gathered that for twenty-four hours I was to be his replacement.

and at one point there were no fewer than six ministers crowded into the small waiting room diagonally opposite the Cabinet Room – John Moore, John Major, Ken Clarke, John MacGregor, Paul Channon and myself. A later arrival was Cecil Parkinson, who was to be restored to the Cabinet after his spectacular resignation four years earlier when his affair with Sara Keays became public. (Had that not happened the chances are that at this point Parkinson would have been seen as the man most likely to succeed to the leadership.) One by one we were called up the staircase, lined with pictures of former prime ministers, to the large study where Thatcher took so many of her meetings: at one end a large writing desk, at the other comfortable sofas and chairs.

However radical Thatcher's plans were, no one could accuse her of being in triumphant mood. There was undoubted relief that the campaign was over. She had never liked elections and 1987 had not been one of her best. She had been badly scared a week before polling day when the Tory lead in the opinion polls had been temporarily reduced, and her mood had communicated itself to some of those around her. In one extraordinary scene Lord Young, who had been working directly to Thatcher, had grasped Tebbit, the chairman of the official campaign, by the shoulders and shouted, 'Norman, listen to me. We're about to lose this fucking election. You're going to go. I'm going to go. The whole thing is going to go.'[*]

Not surprisingly Thatcher wanted to move on. She wanted to demonstrate to friend and foe alike that more, much more, needed to be done in transforming Britain. It was this determination that communicated itself most directly to the ministers she saw in a succession of friendly but relatively brief meetings during the afternoon. The task was not yet completed; the pace of change was to increase.

For eight years Thatcher had been persuaded or had decided to put to one side obviously contentious issues like rating reform and health. But after the election the government had a massive 100-seat majority. Neil Kinnock in his first election as Labour leader

---

[*] Lord Young, *The Enterprise Years: A Businessman in the Cabinet* (London: Headline, 1990), p. 222.

had been easily defeated and the SDP/Liberal Alliance reduced to a mere twenty-two seats. On the face of it, it seemed a triumph – although if you looked more carefully the picture was not quite as rosy. In Scotland and Wales the Conservatives now held only a small handful of seats while in cities such as Birmingham, Manchester, Liverpool, Leeds and Newcastle Tory MPs were becoming a rare breed. Nevertheless any thought of eventual electoral catastrophe seemed utterly fanciful. Governing had become a familiar and natural way of life. Several up-and-coming ministers – Major was one, Michael Howard another – had never known what it was like to be in opposition. There would never be a better time to introduce legislation which would inevitably face hard battles in both Houses of Parliament. It was now or never.

The fundamental fault with this strategy was that the radical reforms Thatcher wanted were often largely unprepared. The plan was to introduce the legislation as early as possible, endure the public pain, and then move on in time to recover for the fourth election. The flaw was that the need for speed conflicted with the requirement for workable reform. The successful changes in the labour laws had been carefully prepared and introduced step by step. In education there were months of detailed Cabinet committee work still to come; in health not even the principles had been settled, let alone the detail. With the community charge – or the poll tax, as everyone other than government ministers would soon call it – there were major questions still to be settled. They could hardly be more important. Change would not only affect every household in the country but would come up against the certain strong opposition of the Treasury, who preferred the old and tried method of raising local money.

The new path had other political consequences. For years Thatcher had proclaimed that the NHS was 'safe in our hands'. The new way ahead was unknown: there was only off-the-record guidance and the occasional speech which suggested that something radical was afoot – a suggestion which proved to be false, at least for those who were hoping for a new system based on private insurance. All was uncertainty with rumour and counter-rumour – as potentially fatal for governments as for stock markets. The government would need skill and luck not to trip flat on its face.

But June 1987 was not a time for faint hearts. There was no obvious end to this period of Conservative power and what mattered in the immediate aftermath of the election was who was in the new Cabinet and who was out. Thatcher's belief that the job was not yet finished led inexorably to a further decision of immense political significance. Although she had been leader of the party since 1975 she intended to continue. Unlike Tony Blair almost twenty years later, who also won three victories, she had absolutely no intention of moving over, or being moved over, to let in a new leader. On the contrary, she was determined to continue for the whole of the new parliament and stand down only after what she planned to be her fourth election victory. This belief also coincided with another even firmer view that there was no one else who was yet fitted to take over from her. There was no heir apparent like Gordon Brown to Blair but even she recognised that, as she put it that weekend, she could 'not go on for ever'. Very tentatively she began the process of long-term succession planning.

In the election campaign there had been a revealing moment when she called for two new 'young faces' to be put on television – John Moore and Ken Clarke. With the election over it was these two who she saw as the leading but eventual contenders for the succession. She would allow them to show their paces. There were no guarantees and other young candidates for the leadership might emerge. They would have to fight it out. But on one point she was absolutely clear: she intended to skip a political generation. The natural order of succession was to be destroyed.

At the time the favourite eventually to succeed was Moore, the then transport secretary. Not only was he regarded as an excellent presenter but he was also close to Thatcher in terms of political belief. He was 'the favourite son', a position previously occupied by politicians as varied as John Nott, Cecil Parkinson and John Biffen. The position came with something of the curse of being chosen Young Businessman of the Year. Moore's own background suggested he would get an industrial department in the post-election reshuffle, rather than my old job as social services secretary, heading a department which, as it controlled both the NHS and the entire social security organisation, was under constant parliamentary, professional and public bombardment. Afterwards when we compared jobs downstairs in No. 10, Moore appeared decidedly lukewarm about his new department. Although ministers frequently gave their views on tackling the 'extravagance' of the social security system or 'getting a grip' on the health service I had never noticed a long queue anxious to take my job.

My obvious successor was the second candidate for the eventual leadership, Ken Clarke. He had unprecedented experience on both sides of the department, having served as my health minister in the difficult period at the beginning of the 1980s and also in opposition as a social security shadow minister. More than that, he was a robust minister and a skilful debater: no mean qualifications for a department which was at the centre of some of the bloodiest public and political debates of the time. The difficulty was that Thatcher had never entirely trusted the political instincts of this Tory self-evidently from the liberal side of the party. In particular she now hankered for a radical solution, so far entirely undefined, to the health service. As Clarke had said to me just before the election, 'you and I have a lingering affection for the welfare state. That may not be required.' The result was that Clarke went to the Department of Trade and Industry, not as number one, but as deputy to Lord Young. He was to continue the role he had filled at the Employment Department: Young's representative at the despatch box of the House of Commons.

Moore and Clarke were the initial front runners for the eventual succession but there was another man among those waiting to be seen that Saturday afternoon. John Major was the undoubted outsider in any book. He was only forty-four and almost entirely unknown. His ministerial career had started two years earlier when he came to work for me as the most junior of ministers in an unfashionable department. My main contribution to his career came in 1986 when I asked that he should be promoted to minister of state for social security. In the same reshuffle of ministers I also asked that Edwina Currie should be given her first government job as a junior health minister inside the department. (No, I did not know of their affair.) At the time Currie was much better known than Major and to her credit won her promotion by stout defences of the government's social policies in late night Commons debates.

Major had proved both persuasive and utterly reliable in the social security role, his conciliatory manner disarming his Labour opponents. But frankly I was surprised to see him waiting at No. 10 for what was obviously to be his first Cabinet job. In the natural order of things he was junior to experienced and able middle-rank ministers such as Tony Newton. But Major had impressed the chancellor, Nigel Lawson, at an election press conference, although even then luck had played its part. He was not the chancellor's first choice to be his deputy as chief secretary to the Treasury. Lawson had originally wanted John Wakeham but Wakeham's long-held ambition had always been to become leader of the House of Commons, which he was now able to achieve in place of Biffen.

Lawson then remembered Major, and the MP from Huntingdon was catapulted (to his surprise and customary doubts about whether he would be able to master the new job) into the political front line. Strictly speaking, chief secretary is the most junior post in the Cabinet but in practice it is one with very substantial power. In the Thatcher government the annual battles between the chief secretary and the spending departments not only determined the priorities of the government but also heavily influenced the political reputation of the combatants.

On the face of it the appointments of Moore, Clarke and Major could be seen as just sensible team building but that would be entirely to underestimate the impact of the Thatcher plan. The prime minister was certainly bringing on a new generation of politicians but by the same measure she had judged that the two leading members of her team – the foreign secretary, Geoffrey Howe, and the chancellor of the exchequer, Nigel Lawson – had reached their political ceilings. It was also crystal clear that she would do her damnedest to defeat the plans of her most determined and publicly popular would-be successor, Michael Heseltine.

Heseltine, of course, expected nothing else. Relations between the two had never been easy. Very early on Thatcher had noted

his popular success as a conference orator. At the 1975 party
conference we shadow Cabinet ministers had walked onto the
stage one by one as we took our seats for the final session.
Heseltine received a rapturous reception as he appeared. The next
year the decree went out that the shadow Cabinet would form an
orderly crocodile and receive a collective welcome.

Thatcher had been appalled when in 1976 Heseltine had
grabbed the mace in the chamber of the Commons and flourished
it at celebrating Labour members who had just emerged successful
in a crucial debate. Nevertheless she recognised that Heseltine was
not only an outstanding conference orator but also an effective
minister. In the early 1980s she had reluctantly confided to a
Cabinet colleague that Heseltine was her 'natural' successor. It was
not a feeling that lasted very long. Heseltine, like Thatcher, may
have been a conviction politician but it was precisely those
convictions – like his advocacy of a reduction of mortgage tax
relief – which brought him into conflict with the prime minister.
In 1986 relations finally collapsed altogether when Heseltine
walked out of Cabinet in the Westland row. Since then his
position had been that, although he would never stand against
Thatcher, he was determined to succeed her when she retired.
Thatcher was sending out the clearest signal not only that he
would have a long wait but that new faces would be in the
leadership frame when the time came.

Howe and Lawson, on the other hand, might have expected
more sympathetic consideration. Howe in particular had every
right to believe that he was a serious contender for the succession.
In opposition he had been the architect of the economic policies
that the government pursued. In government as chancellor of the
exchequer he had taken and stood by all the difficult decisions in
those early years when public spending plans were being cut back
and VAT was being increased. More than that, he had to see off
the challenges to his economic policy inside the Cabinet itself and
the continual complaint from spending ministers (myself included
when I took over the health and the social security budgets) that
his public spending economies could be attained only at massive
political cost. Of course it was evident to anyone who had
attended more than a couple of meetings between Howe and the

prime minister that temperamentally they were miles apart. Thatcher had always been impatient with Howe's deceptively plodding style and suspicious of his traditional one-nation instincts. The point she never seemed to understand was that without his determination and skill she would have failed.

Equally Lawson was a long-standing ally. In her memoirs Thatcher dismisses out of hand any claim of his to the leadership: 'Nigel Lawson had no interest in the job – and I had no interest in encouraging him.'[*] In fact, Lawson, apart from being intellectually one of the cleverest men in the Cabinet, was an effective politician – albeit sometimes brutal. It is disingenuous to believe, as the Thatcher memoirs suggest, that Lawson's only ambition was to be the longest-serving chancellor of the exchequer of the twentieth century. It was an open secret that he wanted to leave the Treasury months before his eventual resignation and his ambitions (justifiably) included the Foreign Office.

It is also fanciful to believe that Thatcher's plans remained secret. For, as friend and foe will agree, she was entirely incapable of dissembling on such personal issues. To give a small example of my own: prior to the 1987 election my relations with the prime minister had been generally good. We fell out for reasons I will come to shortly. Some weeks after the election I was invited to one of the regular lunches she gave for ministers at No. 10. Thatcher came up to me with the old welcoming smile on her face – a smile which froze the instant she recalled my new 'dog house' position. You certainly could not complain that you did not know where you were with the prime minister. Moore, Clarke and Major knew that they were in with a chance of serious advancement. By the same measure it should have become clear to Howe and Lawson as the months went by that according to the prime minister's plans they were not contenders.

In the aftermath of the election Howe and Lawson were not the only members of Cabinet with a problem of political ceilings. In age I was in the same bracket as Moore and Clarke but I had been in the Cabinet from the start. Transport had seen my salad

[*] Margaret Thatcher, *The Downing Street Years* (London: HarperCollins, 1993), p. 755.

years, when I had carried out the first privatisations of the new government long before the Treasury took a serious interest. I had even been named the Adam Smith Institute Man of the Year. But for six long years I had been making and defending both health and social security policy in the cold climate of strict public spending control.

Thatcher's judgement was that I was 'better at publicly defending the NHS' than radically reforming it. That rather depends on what you mean by reform. Over the years I had fought the longest strike in post-war history to prevent all the money intended for patient services going in wage increases. I had introduced the contracting out of ancillary services, new policies of cooperation with the private sector, and the introduction of general managers into the woefully undermanaged service. Each of these policies was fiercely resisted by Labour but each was later endorsed by the Blair government. I had fought the pharmaceutical companies to reduce the drugs bill through the use of generic drugs. While in public health I had run the high-profile campaign to stop the spread of HIV/AIDS, which was much criticised at the time by many who basically thought that homosexuals should be left to their own fate but which led to a fall in new infections of HIV as well as other sexually transmitted diseases.

It is true that I was cautious about the many half-baked proposals for introducing compulsory private health insurance, but so for that matter was Thatcher. It was only after her third victory that her thoughts turned seriously to that kind of solution – and even then the reform process was rescued by Clarke, who shared most of my views on the health service, rather than those on the right pressing for a two-tier service. My view remains that the National Health Service should continue as the basis of health care in Britain and that the private sector should have an accepted part in developing it. Twenty years later that became once more the official view of David Cameron's Conservative Party – but in the aftermath of the 1987 election such attitudes were distinctly out of fashion.

Even worse, I and the health service were blamed through guilt by association for the worst moment of the 1987 election – 'Wobbly Thursday'. The press conference planned for Thursday

4 June at Conservative Central Office was mine on social security, but when we met for the usual 8.30 a.m. pre-meeting briefing it was clear that there were other things on the prime minister's mind. An opinion poll in the *Daily Telegraph* showed that the Tory lead had reduced to 4 points and Central Office's own polls also showed the lead narrowing. No poll showed Labour in the lead and that very night a poll in the *Guardian* reported a rock safe 10-point Conservative lead. But Thatcher was deaf to any advice that she should wait to see what that poll revealed and instead embarked on an all-out assault on her own election team.

The lesson of the polls, she said, was clear. She needed to be on television more. She was shaking too many hands. She had just returned from the West Country, where she had shaken hundreds of hands. Shaking hands was not going to win the election. It would be won on television. At this point a Central Office official scuttled away with orders to get the prime minister onto David Frost's Sunday morning show. She next turned to the party chairman, Norman Tebbit. The message needed to go out: 'Talk about the strength of the economy.'

At last she started to read my social security press release. 'It's so bad you couldn't have written it,' she exclaimed. 'No one knows what "an increase in real terms" means.' She returned to her theme. We were not getting our message over. We needed direct language. We needed more of Maggie on television, not ever more hands to shake. My reaction to Thatcher in this mood had always been to argue back but this time it was to absolutely no avail. She was not responding to argument. To his credit Tebbit tried to be a calming influence. 'It's better that she works out her frustrations on us in private,' he told me as we prepared to walk down the stairs to the press conference. The trouble was that we had not succeeded in absorbing all the punches. Once my social security presentation was over the questioning became more general. She replied at enormous length to a question from Irish television. She was like a greyhound who had been kept on the lead for too long. Her views came bubbling out. She had the cameras and she was going to make the most of them. With the first question this did not matter but with the next it most certainly did.

Tony Bevins, a political reporter who was then working for the *Independent* and was never to be underestimated, floated a question more in hope than expectation that he would receive a frank reply. How could she be trusted with the National Health Service when she took her own medical care privately? There was a perfectly good two-sentence reply to this frequent challenge: 'Dedication to the health service does not mean turning your back on the private sector. Neither of the other two main parties proposes to abolish the right to private medicine.' Instead Thatcher, forgetting the effect that her words would have on those waiting for operations, baldly defended her right to go to hospital 'on the day I want, and the time I want, and with the doctor I want' – but added that if she was really ill she would consider turning to the NHS.

The following day's press was highly critical. Private health insurance became the issue of the next days. Labour rejoiced as they dusted down all their old arguments on the Tories' plans to privatise the health service. The government was painted as the friend of the private sector, which only the minority could afford, and the enemy of the health service on which the majority of the nation relied. It was not until Edna Healey, the wife of the Labour politician Denis Healey, was revealed as using the private sector that the row subsided.

My view on the press conference was quite plainly that the prime minister had made a mistake. Her view was that I had failed to present the government's health case. Whatever the virtues of the respective arguments, one point was beyond dispute. She was the leader and she made the decisions on who her ministers should be. In the immediate aftermath of the election a leader in the *Sun* advocated my execution together with Peter Walker and John Biffen. It was a sure sign in those days that a move to the Cabinet door was under consideration.

Years later Willie Whitelaw guardedly told me that in the exchange of views on the new Cabinet I needed 'some support'. When I saw the prime minister she paid tribute to the 'superb' job I had done over the last six years, which was a good start but, even so, not conclusive. Peter Bottomley tells a typically self-deprecating story that he had been promptly dismissed after the

initial hymn of praise. In my case, however, I was to be moved
sideways to a business-linked department which she knew I
wanted, the Department of Employment. As luck would have it
on my first outing a few days later I was able to report that
unemployment had dropped below the three million mark and in
each of the next thirty months I was able to announce further falls.
'Make the most of it,' said Nigel Lawson at one point. 'We won't
see the like in our lifetime.'

In our discussion at No. 10, Thatcher soon moved off the tasks
of the Employment Department – it was not one of her post-
election priorities – and onto the new parliament. Although our
personal relations were never to be quite the same we talked easily
enough that afternoon. She was sad that Norman Tebbit – 'my
beloved Norman' – was standing down in spite of her efforts to
persuade him to stay. It was one of the big surprises of the
reshuffle. The campaign was not counted a great success –
although Thatcher herself was partly at fault, by creating an
alternative campaign under David Young – but it had been
victorious. Tebbit was entitled to his reward. Instead he decided
to step down and devote himself more to his wife, Margaret, so
cruelly injured in the bomb blast at the Grand Hotel in Brighton.
Tebbit had always been a strong voice in Cabinet and his
resignation deprived the prime minister of a close ally who would
have been of undoubted help in the tumultuous months to come.

As for the dismissed Biffen, Thatcher said that her main
complaint was that he had done little outside Parliament to
promote the government. Biffen's criticism of her before the
election still rankled. She hoped that the new leader of the House,
John Wakeham, would be an easier colleague – although 'we will
have to teach him to speak'. But the most important part of the
conversation was about the immediate parliamentary agenda.
Change in education and reform of the rating system would
require lengthy and highly controversial legislation. She
recognised the risks. She knew that any changes to the rating
system or in education and health would be bound to be
controversial. There was no chance of getting the changes
through without fierce debate inside Parliament. Her eyes were
entirely open to the political price she might have to pay. 'In

eighteen months' time', she told me, 'we will be very unpopular as a government.'

It was not just the public who needed to be convinced. The government's majority in the Commons might have looked comfortable enough but that did not mean all the Conservative Party was facing the same way. The position of Biffen, the most prominent casualty of the post-1987 election reshuffle, was a case in point. His significance was that he was no figure from the liberal left of the party. A disciple of Enoch Powell, he was a Eurosceptic and a monetarist with an almost touching faith in the workings of the market. On the face of it he seemed a complete Thatcher soul-mate: indeed back in 1976 I had been moved out of the shadow Cabinet explicitly to make way for him.

He had become alienated by what he saw as the strident style of the prime minister. 'I will not be screamed at in that way by that woman,' he told one journalist after a particularly bruising confrontation when he was still in government.* But the differences went deeper. Biffen had become a doubter on a number of government policies – most notably the poll tax – and he was now free to express his doubts. He was not alone. There was a growing band of former ministers on the back benches displaced by the regular reshuffles over the last eight years.

Reshuffles had always been an integral part of the Thatcher approach. She did not enjoy the process of sacking ministers – on one or two occasions she did not have the heart to continue – but they enabled her to give the impression of momentum. As her period in power became longer her concern was that the press would say she was running out of steam. A reshuffle of ministers was the easiest way of answering that charge, although each series of changes brought its own price tag. Unlike in the United States, former ministers did not ride into the sunset. They remained members of Parliament, free to roam the back benches. With their political careers usually ended (some for no good reason) they would not automatically respond to calls for loyalty when the going became rough. There were even a few – quite apart from

---

* Quoted in Edward Pearce and Michael White, obituary, *Guardian*, 15 August 2007.

Michael Heseltine – who bided their time and dwelt on the thought that ultimately it was the Conservative parliamentary party which decided who was to be the leader.

For Thatcher, however, the challenge of introducing new policy against a background of scepticism and hostility was nothing new. She had outfaced the unions and withstood violent strikes and angry demonstrations. Inside her own party she had emerged successful in the struggle with the economic 'wets'. The fights may have been bitter but she had prevailed. She had seen it all before and she had emerged victorious.

3

Reshuffle and resignation (1989)

'Norman, I don't want to see the government falling apart.'

Margaret Thatcher, 10 Downing Street,
Tuesday 19 December 1989.

At the beginning of February 1989, eighteen months after Margaret Thatcher's prediction to me of government unpopularity, the writ was issued for a by-election in the super-safe Conservative seat of Richmond in North Yorkshire. The previous member had been Leon Brittan, who, in spite of a promise that he would return to the Cabinet, despaired of that happening before the millennium. Thatcher wanted no reminder of Westland, which had almost led to her own demise and remained nervous of any fresh investigation into the affair. Instead Brittan was offered an appointment as one of Britain's two European Commissioners in Brussels, where he achieved a notable and deserved political recovery. His replacement as candidate was a young man in his late twenties who had made his reputation as a schoolboy in a famous speech at the 1977 Blackpool Conservative Party conference.

When I went to Richmond I was intrigued to see William Hague in action. All the reports were that he had seen off the by-election pack of journalists, who had been only too ready to devour this young prodigy. You could quickly see why he was never going to be easy meat for the newspapers. Hague was bright, fluent, and well informed. With no great skill of foresight I marked him down in my diary as 'an undoubted future political star'.

It was just as well that the local party had chosen such a quality candidate. Without him the by-election could easily have been lost. Even so, when the result was announced the Tory majority had been reduced from almost 20,000 to 2,600. David Owen's Social Democratic Party were runners-up; had they and Paddy Ashdown's Liberal Democrats settled their differences and agreed a common front there is little doubt that the Conservatives – even with Hague – would have lost. It did not help that the by-election came in the immediate aftermath of Edwina Currie's resignation from the government, following her remarks that much of the nation's egg production was infected with salmonella. This had certainly not endeared ministers to the farming community but in truth the Richmond by-election was just one of the pointers to the unpopularity of the government that spring.

For the first time since the election the opinion polls were now putting Labour ahead and as the year progressed the gap between the parties grew wider, with Labour opening up a massive 20-point lead. It needs to be remembered that by the time of Thatcher's downfall the Conservatives had been behind in the polls – and well behind at that – for an uninterrupted eighteen months. In test after electoral test in the last two years of her premiership the government failed. In the 1989 European elections Conservative support fell to 34 per cent, the lowest point the party had achieved until then in any twentieth-century national election. In the Mid Staffordshire by-election in March 1990 a Conservative lead of 14,600 was turned into a Labour majority of almost 9,500. In the local authority elections two months later the Conservatives lost control of eleven councils – although the scale of this disaster was partly masked by the party chairman, Ken Baker, skilfully pointing to success in Westminster and Wandsworth. In the Commons members in marginal seats (and even in seats which, viewed objectively, were not marginal) were beginning to become seriously nervous. The nervousness was increased in the autumn when the apparently safe Tory seat of Eastbourne was lost to the Liberal Democrats. Some Tory MPs had known nothing but uninterrupted success since 1979. It was now becoming apparent that this was not just a political armchair ride.

So what had gone wrong? Thatcher's prediction of trouble ahead had come about with a vengeance. Education reform had met with the vocal opposition of the teaching unions while the health change process seemed close to shambles. In spite of the rhetoric little progress had been made in the months after the election. The most significant political development had been the decision to divide health from social security in Whitehall and the demotion of John Moore to head just social security. However much she valued the ideological support of figures such as Moore she would never place the government at risk to preserve a friend. For Moore it marked the end of his leadership prospects, and indeed of his political career. He had been dogged by ill health and politically had made the profound mistake of signalling 'radical' health change in the press before anyone, including himself, had much idea of what such change was going to entail. The health unions distrusted modest change, let alone revolution, and happily reverted to their customary black propaganda about the destruction of the health service as we know it.

The policy which had caused the greatest grief, however, was Thatcher's own personal flagship. The election manifesto had promised a scheme which would 'abolish the unfair domestic rating system and replace rates with a fairer community charge'. But the plans ran into trouble inside the party early on. In an end-of-year report I commented on the close of an ill-tempered two-day debate just before Christmas 1987:

> Poll tax has few friends. As I sat on the steps of the Speaker's chair for Michael Howard's wind-up, it was clear that there was no great enthusiasm on our side. Most of the party seem to be distancing themselves from the bill. The matter is not helped by the fact that half the Cabinet have their reservations. It is very much MT's own tax and this of course is the danger. She is in an exposed position if things in the party should turn nasty.

By the beginning of 1989 the community charge, now almost universally known as the poll tax, was succeeding in putting together an extraordinary opposition coalition of the Militant Tendency and the middle class. Disagreement led to demonstration and eventually to violent protest on the streets of London. Even those who had sympathy with the idea of greater fairness found the ground cut away from under their feet. The losers from the new system were all too obvious while many of the gainers had to wait two or three years before seeing any advantage. Had extra resources been devoted to bringing in the new system then the outcome might have been different, but Nigel Lawson was opposed to the change and, as I knew to my cost when changing social security in 1985, Treasury opposition puts a substantial roadblock in the way of implementing any new policy.

The depth of Lawson's opposition was later graphically described by Geoffrey Howe. In September 1989 Lawson sent a note to Howe, a few weeks before he resigned from the government, in which he said that money spent on making the community charge 'slightly less appalling' was 'bad value for money' and would also be 'money spent to save her face'. He added, '[I] do not regard that as a worthy cause. Do you?' Howe's reply was more conciliatory: 'Her face? Well, yes – certainly. But our bacon as well, surely? Though even there we have to compare prices.'* Even given the chancellor's attitude the government collectively should have undertaken a much clearer analysis of the initial impact that the new tax was going to have. With the social security review we had laboured long into the night to eliminate as many losers as possible. With community charge the Cabinet committee deciding policy was given remarkably little information on this obvious piece of politics. The policy was the policy and the consequences flowed.

As the reform process faltered there was also a shift in the public mood. In 1979 and in the years that immediately followed the public demand had been for a strong leader – but times had changed. By 1989 new voters were coming onto the electoral roll who could scarcely remember the winter of discontent. Rather than a brave fighter Thatcher was increasingly seen as autocratic and inflexible. She was portrayed as not in tune with the new times; uncaring; and, most damaging of all, dated. More than a decade later Tony Blair suffered a similar fate as his period in office

---

* Geoffrey Howe, *Conflict of Loyalty* (London: Macmillan, 1994), p. 603.

extended. The fresh young man with energy and new ideas became seen as a tarnished figure reliant on 'spin' and a close bevy of committed supporters. Perhaps we should simply recognise that in an age of news around the clock and constant exposure on television the natural shelf life of any political leader is no longer than ten years.

Thatcher certainly recognised the dangers. For the tenth anniversary of the 1979 election her orders were explicit. The occasion could be marked but any celebrations were to be low key and under no circumstances triumphalist. The risk otherwise was that the 1989 anniversary would simply underline the message that the government had been in power for too long and it was time for a change.

On Wednesday 3 May the 1922 Committee, the committee that represents all backbench interests, organised a lunch for the entire parliamentary party at the Savoy. It was a jolly enough affair with the committee's chairman, Cranley Onslow, presiding ('contrary to predictions there will be no raffle') and with Ted Heath seated at the top table. Although even then there was one notable absentee. The traffic on that day was exceptionally heavy so after the lunch I abandoned my car and walked back to the Department of Employment. In one of the traffic jams Max Hastings, the editor of the *Daily Telegraph* and no favourite of either Thatcher or John Major, leaned out of the window of his car. He was being driven back to his office having had lunch elsewhere with Michael Heseltine.

The press the next day compared the Cabinet photograph of 1979 with the equivalent ten years later. There were few of us still there – Howe, George Younger, Peter Walker and myself. At Cabinet that morning Howe, the senior survivor, started the business with an impressive tribute. Over the last ten years, he said, the authority of government had been restored, the economy brought back to health, and Britain's position in the world re-established. The short celebrations culminated that evening in a private dinner for all Cabinet ministers and their spouses at No. 10 – the first time, we were told, that such a gathering of couples had taken place at Downing Street for 250 years. Howe again made a generous speech and Thatcher's response included a much-applauded tribute to her husband: 'If ever I am tempted to say something nice about the BBC Denis soon persuades me against.'

On Friday it was back to business with a bump. At lunchtime the news came through that the party had lost the Vale of Glamorgan by-election with a swing to Labour of more than 12 per cent. Worse was to come. Not only were the results of the European elections the next month bad but the campaign itself was widely and justifiably regarded as dreadful. To the outrage of the party's MEPs, crude and puerile advertising warned the public against a 'diet of Brussels'. It may have mirrored the latest Thatcher view but it was entirely at odds with the sensible pragmatic approach that had been followed in most of her period of government, a pragmatism which was best illustrated in 1985 by the introduction of legislation which, by incorporating the Single European Act into UK law, accented a massive extension of majority voting in the European Union. Although amnesia seems to have struck down some members of the Cabinet who agreed this policy, I can recall clearly enough the reason that we agreed. It was the quid pro quo to give us a single market without tariff barriers. Lord Young was the measure's devout salesman and among the Cabinet who agreed this step (and the later parliamentary guillotine to push the legislation through) were Norman Tebbit, Nick Ridley, and of course, Thatcher herself.

As the summer progressed, the government's standing with the public failed to improve while internally the position was no happier. It was now obvious that Thatcher was relying on the people she employed directly and answered to her. The influence of unelected advisers such as her foreign affairs specialist, Charles Powell, and her chief press officer, Bernard Ingham, became markedly greater and the influence of her ministers proportionately less. The most common complaint of Cabinet ministers was that Thatcher was running the government as a court. Even Willie Whitelaw, looking back at his time as her deputy, used the term. 'I was never much of a courtier,' he told me at one conference as he waited to speak. Some other Cabinet ministers managed the role better. Young was the prime example of the successful courtier, while another who succeeded was the education secretary, Ken Baker – but in a rather different way. The meetings of the Cabinet committee on education presided over by the prime minister were at one level the best entertainment in Whitehall as Thatcher took on her old department. Irrespective of the many missiles directed at him Baker always ended the meetings smiling and placatory.

More seriously, education reform illustrated the new way of working inside government. One instance came during a discussion in the Cabinet committee examining education policy. The subject was the teaching of English and Thatcher strongly disputed Baker's paper. 'Does anyone disagree with me,' she asked, 'apart from the secretary for education?' It was not said in jest and it became the way that the government was organised. She knew what she wanted and did not want to be delayed, let alone left in a minority. The pre-meeting briefing between the prime minister and her advisers could often be more important than the actual meeting with her ministers. Cards were marked before a minister presenting his or her case had uttered a word. If any difficulty was predicted allies were recruited before the meeting took place. Young ministers knew that the way forward was to be as helpful as possible to the prime minister. The whole tilt of government went to the advisers. When Thatcher spoke of 'her people' too often they were the civil servants and her special advisers.

It was a point illustrated only too well when in February 1989 I put forward a proposal to privatise the Jobcentres. These were the offices that sought to get unemployed people back into work. The government had made little progress in privatising civil service functions and the Jobcentres were an obvious candidate for transfer. In my view civil servants had no expert knowledge of outside industry and were some distance away from its workings. Inevitably the proposal was fiercely resisted inside the Department of Employment and allies were sought in Whitehall – but the crucial stumbling block was the prime minister.

Wednesday 8 February 1989. A crucial meeting of EA* on the future of the Jobcentres. Everyone supports the principle of what I am proposing but then come the niggles. The chancellor is worried about

* A sub-committee of the main economic committee.

the financial details but the main point comes from MT herself. She is very concerned that nothing should be done to give the impression that we are being hard on our own employees. My case of course is that we are not – that the good ones will have a better and more prosperous future in the private sector. But I am also proposing that if a civil servant goes from the public sector to the private sector and stays in the same job then he shouldn't be paid redundancy. MT is very unhappy about this and appears to believe that we should pay redundancy on the grounds that their job has changed. But as Cecil Parkinson points out on this basis all his electricity workers should have had redundancy as well – so too should my NFC [National Freight Corporation] staff when they moved. MT tries to argue that the civil service is different but I don't think really takes many with her. This is, however, all bad news. The chancellor is visibly cooling to the proposals as he hears MT go on. The last thing he wants to see is a big redundancy bill to be financed by him. Walking out, John Major says that MT is always worried about the position of civil servants. On this issue, he says, she is not at all the iron lady.

A few months later, in September 1989, I came up against the power of the No. 10 special advisers when I introduced a further paper at EA with proposals to tackle strikes in essential services. Having observed Ken Baker's battles I made some effort to discover in advance the prime minister's views. The message back from No. 10 was that there was no hint of disagreement but that proved to be spectacularly dud advice.

Before allowing me to introduce the paper the prime minister indelibly marked cards. 'We have just had a meeting,' she said. 'I am very concerned about these proposals.' The identity of the shadowy group who advised her but did not dare speak its name was never revealed but the result of the guidance was unmistakable. Most of the ministers at the meeting, including one who had come ready to extend the proposals to his own department, either remained silent or jumped overboard with depressing plops. To his credit Geoffrey Howe argued in favour but Thatcher next tried to sum up on the basis that the majority of the committee were opposed to the proposals. I objected on the grounds that both Baker and Ken Clarke had written in support. A new doctrine was then expounded. It would be unwise, the prime minister said, to continue with a proposal when there was obvious disagreement within the government. Such a working rule might have been politically sensible but it would have left the poll tax legislation safely in a Downing Street drawer.

Thatcher's reliance on her own trusted advisers in preference to her ministers was bound sooner or later to bring her into conflict with her Cabinet. The more senior the minister, the greater the resentment. It was one thing for the prime minister to question, argue and disagree in open meetings – she had always done that. It was quite another to have policies vetoed as a result of meetings at No. 10 to which ministers were not invited. Ministers were sidelined even when the policy decisions went to the heart of their responsibilities.

A spectacular example of lack of consultation between No. 10 and the responsible ministers came in June 1989 with the preparations for the important European summit meeting in Madrid. Nothing better showed the new way. The first meeting between the prime minister, her foreign secretary and her chancellor of the exchequer to prepare for Madrid took place just six days before the summit – and only then at the insistence of Howe and Lawson, who not surprisingly believed that, as future policy on the Exchange Rate Mechanism was at the centre of their responsibilities, they had some right to be consulted. The full-scale meeting of advisers had taken place the day before at No. 10 and the prime minister was in no mood to accept the proposition that a definite time target should be put on Britain's entry into the ERM rather than relying on the by now slightly ludicrous formula that we would enter 'when the time is right'. Provoked, Howe and Lawson threatened joint resignation, which would have rocked the government to its foundations, but this crisis was averted by Thatcher reaffirming 'the United Kingdom's intention to join the ERM' – subject of course to conditions. An open split was avoided but the gulf between the prime minister and particularly her foreign secretary was now unbridgeable. On the flight to Madrid the prime minister's party and the foreign secretary's party sat in separate parts of the aircraft with a drawn curtain between. All communication was via Charles Powell. At the summit meeting itself the British foreign secretary had no more knowledge of what the British prime minister was about to say than his French or German counterparts.

The next month, as yet another reshuffle loomed, all eyes were on Howe. If there was to be any movement in the top positions of government he seemed the man most in danger. Personal relations between him and Thatcher were now at an all-time low – which given their previous state was saying quite something. Yet Howe, perhaps not recognising how bad they had become, and relying on an assurance from the chief whip, David Waddington, that his job was secure, continued blissfully unaware of what was in store.

On the morning of Monday 24 July 1989, the reshuffle began. To Howe's amazement and anger Thatcher offered him the leadership of the House of Commons, which, although a position of importance, did not have the status or power of the Foreign Office or the Treasury.* In the negotiations that followed Howe was half offered the Home Office; perhaps the prime minister forgot that she already had a home secretary in Douglas Hurd who might have some ambitions to be foreign secretary rather than whatever other job she had in mind for him. That certainly was not the Foreign Office. For the man who had been earmarked for the Foreign Office was the largely unconsidered minister who had been waiting patiently in the Downing Street waiting room two years previously to receive his first Cabinet job, John Major.

If I had been surprised at his initial promotion into the Cabinet it was as nothing compared to the day he became foreign secretary. By chance on that day Major and I were both lunching at the Ritz with different *Daily Telegraph* journalists. By now some of the details of the comings and goings were leaking out. The unfortunate John Moore, two years previously widely regarded as the next leader of the party, had been removed from the

---

* It has nevertheless been a post popular with prime ministers. A few years later when discussing the sacking of the then chancellor, Norman Lamont, Thatcher observed that he should have been offered the job of leader of the House, while Tony Blair also moved his foreign secretary, Jack Straw, out to the same post.

government altogether.* The place as chief contender for the succession was now taken by Ken Baker, the new party chairman. Cecil Parkinson was to be transport secretary and John Gummer agriculture minister. At this point Major had heard nothing – although virtually every political commentator had tipped him for promotion. And even Thatcher herself had teasingly hinted in a Cabinet committee meeting before the reshuffle that a change was expected: 'I read in the papers that you are being tipped for great things.' Talking to me before I left the restaurant, Major said prophetically, 'There is something missing in the reshuffle so far.'

Indeed there was. During the afternoon I ran into Major in a division in the Commons. He asked me to come with him to the Speaker's courtyard outside, where our cars were parked, and told me that he was the new foreign secretary. 'I hope I can do it,' he said, using exactly the same words as when he had been appointed Treasury chief secretary. He added, in another typical Major response, 'I will need all the help I can get from my friends.'

As it happened his stay at the Foreign Office was brief and not at all his happiest period in politics. Meeting him six weeks later, when we were both flying to the United States, I was struck by how downbeat he was, even to the point of leaving politics altogether and taking a job in the City. 'There is only one job I have ever wanted and that is chancellor of the exchequer,' he said as Concorde sped to New York.

The irony of the reshuffle was that it satisfied almost no one at the very top of the government. In a few hours Thatcher had removed Geoffrey Howe from the job he loved; promoted John Major to a job he was amazed to get and never enjoyed; left Douglas Hurd nursing some injured pride at having his own job hawked around; and deprived Nigel Lawson of the only other job that was open to him by promoting his number two into it. The July reshuffle, intended to show the government fighting back, had been transformed into a political disaster.

Amidst it all one point was clear. If the intention was to keep Howe on board then he needed to be handled with kid gloves. I

* Although at one stage his political prospects were exceptional Moore never complained at his treatment.

spoke to Howe on the night of the reshuffle. Unhappily he described the events of the day and how it had been that after several hours' consideration he had returned to No. 10 to say that he would become leader of the House only on condition that he would be also deputy prime minister and the chairman of Cabinet committees. He wanted the position once so successfully occupied by Willie Whitelaw. Thatcher had responded that no one could take that position but with bad grace agreed. Almost immediately the briefing from Downing Street was that Howe's position as deputy prime minister was in name only.

Even at this stage – several hours after the announcement of the changes – Howe was wondering whether he should have refused the new job and resigned. It had been a very close call and he justified remaining (not least to himself) on the grounds that resignation would have harmed the whole party. He had been part of the revolution for the last fifteen years and did not want his resignation to derail the government. In retrospect the most significant feature of our conversation that night was that, in spite of the shock and distress of his removal, Howe's major pre-occupation was where his removal left European policy. Whether foreign secretary or leader of the House he was fundamentally at odds with Thatcher and was prepared to fight his corner.

This was the danger sign that even at this stage most of his colleagues did not pick up. Europe may have dominated Conservative politics in the 1990s but throughout much of the 1980s it was more of a smouldering fire. It was an issue capable of igniting but inside the parliamentary party the debate was by and large left to the enthusiasts on either side. I had noticed that at our 1987 pre-election briefing for all candidates there had been no question to the foreign secretary on Europe and in the campaign itself the subject was scarcely mentioned. But for Howe it had become an issue of almost transcending importance. He was committed to a fully engaged, constructive policy on Europe. His view of Thatcher was that she was a not particularly well-disguised follower of Enoch Powell, inherently hostile to community membership. He was strongly critical of her strident tone. Howe had his cause and nothing much to lose in pursuing it to the end.

For the time being, however, he remained on board and the government stumbled on – but with one very significant difference. For the first ten years of the Thatcher government ministers had been employed on what in business would be called twelve-month rolling contracts. There were absolutely no guarantees of continuing employment. On the Thursday after this latest reshuffle the prime minister told the Cabinet that 'barring accidents' this was the team that would go into the election in two or three years' time. It was a quite exceptional statement for her to make. Up to this point job security for Cabinet ministers was an entirely unknown concept; the theory was that the threat of sacking kept us on our toes. It was a change which spoke volumes about the political failure of the reshuffle but which proved notably unsuccessful. Three months later the first 'accident' destroyed the prime minister's plans.

In late October newspaper stories reported a serious rift between Nigel Lawson, the chancellor of the exchequer, and Alan Walters, the economic adviser to the prime minister. I had first come across Walters in the very early years of the Thatcher government when he had argued unsuccessfully against further electrification of the railways and for reducing the rail network. Since then he had been in the United States and only recently returned to No. 10.*

There was an inbuilt tension in the eternal triangle of prime minister, chancellor and prime minister's adviser. By now Lawson had been in the job for six years and was not inclined to join in a daily battle for the prime minister's ear. He was the chancellor and that was that. The issue that brought the row to crisis point was an article Walters had written for an American journal which comprehensively rubbished the ERM. Had Walters written the article while in appointment there was no question that he would have been dismissed. But the prime minister clung to the defence that it had been written before he had taken up his post – although published since. The sub-text was that she agreed with every word of the article. My diary takes up the story.

* Later in his career Walters stood against the Conservatives as a parliamentary candidate for the Referendum Party.

Thursday 26 October 1989. After lunch I go over to the House for Prime
Minister's Questions. MT is challenged on Walters but defends with
some well-prepared formula which falls a step short of whole-hearted
support for Nigel Lawson or indeed condemnation of Walters:
'Advisers advise; ministers decide.' At the department we go back to
work on the social chapter. During the break at 6.00 pm Graham
Roberts (one of my deputy secretaries) comes in looking thunderstruck
and saying, 'The chancellor has resigned.' According to the news Nigel
has gone on the issue of Alan Walters. Our meeting is abandoned and I
go over to the House. By the time I arrive the House has been
suspended and a statement promised on the position. I meet Norman
Tebbit. He has been asked by the whips to say something helpful. Have
I any ideas? Frankly I do not. The resignation is a disaster. It is scarcely
credible that we have lost the chancellor of the exchequer on such an
issue. The immediate criticism in the lobbies is of Margaret Thatcher.
How can she have allowed the position to get to this point? It is quite
ludicrous. The opposition of course can hardly believe their good
fortune. It has the hallmarks of Westland all over again.

Later that evening I went further and was more heartfelt.

My major thoughts tonight are that this really must be the beginning
of the end of the Thatcher years. She may hang on. She probably will
but she will never again get the affection that she once had. She has
chosen to support her advisers and turn to her officials. She can hardly
expect the friendship of her political colleagues. The question is not
whether she will go but when.

The immediate fallout, however, was nothing like as dramatic. In
the reshuffle Douglas Hurd was appointed to the Foreign Office
although the prime minister's first instinct had been to appoint
Cecil Parkinson. David Waddington became home secretary and,
most notable of all, John Major was switched and achieved his
original political ambition as successor to Lawson at the Treasury.
As for Lawson, his resignation speech the next day was restrained
and his enemies began to surface. Could you really expect the
prime minister to give into the blackmail of a threatened
resignation? Was he not just looking for an excuse to go? Was he

really that good? 'Nigel on his bike at last,' mocked the *Sun*. 'The best possible news for the economy.'

Margaret Thatcher seemed to have successfully survived another crisis. Beneath the surface, however, the prime minister was not as confident about the stability of her government and by implication her own position. I learnt this as I progressed through the rather tortuous process of my own resignation. I had been planning to go for several months – but as my last act as a government minister I was determined to abolish the notorious National Dock Labour Scheme, which was preventing development of the ports and casting planning blight on the land around them.

It was a sign of Thatcher's caution in the first years of her government that this utterly indefensible and locally damaging piece of legislation had been allowed to continue. Lawson was convinced to the last that she would pull the rug on my plans and that her fears of a national dock strike, which had so damaged Ted Heath, would prevail. In fact, although she was clearly nervous about the prospects I was left to plan and run policy without interference. On Thursday 6 April 1989 the Cabinet met at 8.30 a.m. (an exceptionally early hour so that Thatcher could go on to welcome the Soviet leader, Mikhail Gorbachev, to London) and the white paper was approved.

> The statement is at 3.30. Secrecy has been maintained – an almost unique achievement. The house is packed and particularly packed on our side. The notice went up on the screen at 1.00 that there would be a statement on the scheme and I assume everyone thinks I have something to say. John Wakeham is doing Prime Minister's Questions before me and brings the house down by explaining that Margaret Thatcher cannot be here because she is 'making herself available' to Mr Gorbachev. The laughter goes on and on. Just before I get up Michael Meacher* tries a point of order but is slapped down by the Speaker and told to raise it later. My statement is given the loudest cheer I have ever heard from our side. They cheer when I say that the scheme is to be abolished and when I say that the bill will be introduced tomorrow the reception is deafening. When I sit down

---

* My long-standing shadow – whose place was eventually taken by Tony Blair.

there is another enormous cheer and the waving of order papers – the first time that one of my statements has provoked quite that response! Our members rise one after another to welcome the news, as does the spokesman of the Liberal Democrats, Jim Wallace, although not the unofficial one, Simon Hughes. Labour attack but not with much force, although Eric Heffer rambles on about the Tories being lower than vermin.

The fear remained in the weeks following that the unions would call a strike but the surprise of the first statement helped us. We kept the initiative and the scheme, originally intended to tackle the pre-war problem of casual working, was abolished without serious disruption. It is a revealing footnote that although the repeal was regarded as one of the more popular acts of the government in the post-1987 period, it rates no mention in the Thatcher memoirs. The policy was not invented at the No. 10 court. Nevertheless today if you go to vibrant ports such as Bristol you can see the effect of taking regulations off – one of the most beneficial parts of the Thatcher legacy. With the scheme abolished and Lawson's resignation now behind us I could now move to my own departure.

So why leave at a point when, as Michael Heseltine remarked, I had been given a virtual job guarantee? One of my reasons for leaving has been much used since and nowadays is almost automatically taken as disguising the real reason for departure. In my resignation letter I had written, 'I have a young family and for the next few years I should like to devote more time to them while they are still so young.' This was entirely reasonably shorthanded by the media to 'spending more time with my family'. I can only say that although it was not my only reason for leaving it most certainly was one of the reasons. Both my young daughters had been born while I was a Cabinet member; any minister who also takes his constituency seriously will confirm that this leaves you precious little time to contribute to and enjoy the other parts of life.

My diary contains regular laments on the impossibility of leading a balanced life and my reliance on Fiona. When we were married in 1979, a month after I had gone into the government, I inherited a small step-son, Oliver. So when in March 1981, during dinner at a little Italian restaurant in Chelsea, Fiona gave me a small bronze of a youth carrying a baby to mark the impending arrival of our first daughter, Kate, I already had some idea of what would be involved – together even then with some fears.

> *Friday 27 March 1981.* I have been broken into children by Oliver and that has been a tremendous experience. My only fear is that I am a rather distant figure. I hustle off to work in the early morning and crawl back late at night. At weekends I am often away and on Sunday I am normally trying to catch up on the boxes. But this life cannot go on for ever. The resolution I must make is to make time. Children have an unqualified right for time to be spent on them.

The birth in 1984 of my second daughter, Isobel, increased the feeling that I was both missing out and should be doing more. But the pressure of government work – particularly managing both health and social security – meant that a balanced life was still as elusive as ever. By September 1987 I was writing in my diary:

> I have not spent enough time, devoted enough energy, thought enough about Fiona and her needs. I have left her to run the family and organise virtually everything. What does she get in return? A rather exhausted politician who over the past eight years has put politics first and foremost. (*4/6 September 1987.*)

The following May I wrote, 'I am conscious of the fact that I flit in and out. Fiona is the anchor and because she is so good everyone of course relies on her.' And then a few months later, in August 1988, I added bleakly, 'Unless I am careful I will half-miss the children growing up.'

I never regretted my decision to leave the Cabinet but I have never pretended that rejoining the family was my only reason. My resignation letter also spoke of my aim to enter business. When I came down from Cambridge I had not considered it as a serious option. In the early 1960s industry had a woeful reputation for conflict, but that was not the real reason. My father had been a middle manager in a sizeable engineering company. What struck

me about his life was just how hierarchical it all was, with separate
dining rooms for different grades. He was exceptionally pleased
when he reached the highest of these eating places but less pleased
when he attended a company theatre production only to be
ignored by those one step up. We forget just how ludicrously
stratified a society we were. Divided by job and divided by class –
as my army National Service before university had shown me. I
wanted none of that and so what better job than journalism,
which for all its faults was neither bureaucratic nor class ridden?

Thirty years on industry seemed to me very different. Nissan,
for example, made it a rule in its Sunderland plant that everyone,
managers included, should wear the same blue overalls and eat in
the same canteen. Industrial warfare had given way to a new wave
of entrepreneurship. It had become exciting. At the National
Freight Corporation, which I had privatised, the management
buy-out had rewarded not just the top management but the men
driving the lorries and the women working in the warehouses.
There had been a substantial revolution brought about very
largely by the Thatcher governments.

And what about the possible financial rewards of leaving
government? My record as an accumulator of wealth was less than
impressive. I had spent my entire journalistic career on the *Times*,
which may have been a revered newspaper but was beyond
question the worst payer on Fleet Street. As a political candidate
in Nottingham in the late 1960s I had struggled to afford two
bases. When my Nottingham South constituency was earmarked
to disappear in redistribution, I had spent two years nursing my
new constituency of Sutton Coldfield – while continuing to look
after my Nottingham constituents, who did not go their separate
ways until the 1974 election. As a shadow minister I made a little
from journalism but basically lived on my parliamentary salary for
five years. On joining the Cabinet I had never been paid so much
in my life but even then it was hardly on the scale of George
Soros. When I came out of government our accounts were over-
drawn. Our car was a Ford Sierra bought at a discount as a
demonstration model. And our holidays were largely confined to
the Isle of Wight, although I make no complaint of that – it was
one of our better choices.

Yet by any objective standard we were comfortable enough. We had done what so many others had done in our part of Fulham at the end of the New King's Road – bought a house and watched with some amazement as it appreciated. My very first house in Fulham, just down the street from Helen Mirren, was bought for less than £10,000 and would now be marketed for well over £1 million. I will not pretend that today I do not enjoy the freedom that a little money provides but it has never been a great motivator. Contrary to popular perception, most politicians are simply not that interested. In this they are unlike many career businessmen, who measure their status by what they are paid. I remember listening with complete lack of interest to an MP who was leaving the Commons describing to me his obviously generous payment package. The challenge and occasional satisfaction of politics is in trying to change things, not in how much you are paid.

For all that is said about Margaret Thatcher's woeful man management of her ministers, her responses to my news were impeccable. We met first at midday on Monday 20 November 1989 in the familiar study at No. 10. The head of her private office, Andrew Turnbull, had withdrawn and we were entirely alone. She looked younger than her sixty-four years and she had lost tiredness around her eyes which followed the Lawson resignation. I set out my reasons for standing down and she responded in a wonderfully over-the-top way.

'Norman, it is a blow. You're such a good communicator. I had hoped to go on with the same team to the election. You are not ill, are you?'

'No,' I replied, 'I have never felt fitter.'

'Well, that is a relief. I had thought you had come to say you were going into hospital for a period. How old are you?'

'Fifty-one,' I replied.

'Yes, I have seen it before. You have the chance of a fresh career and you want to take it. It was the same with Grey Gowrie and John Nott. You will be very successful.'

'I certainly want to do something in industry but I want to stay in the Commons.'

'That's good,' she said doubtfully, almost certainly thinking that she already had quite enough ex-Cabinet ministers on the back benches. 'It will be a blow,' she repeated. 'You know I am accused of having too many old Etonians in my Cabinet. There's Douglas [Hurd] and now Tim Renton.* I didn't know he went to Eton. It doesn't come into my reckoning but our Cabinet needs people like you who made it by their own ability. We both made it up in that way.'

When Margaret Thatcher wanted to charm she could charm. My experience gives some clue to why so many Tory MPs and ministers, in spite of all the disagreements, retained affection for this remarkable woman – and why it was such a catastrophic misjudgement for her to absent herself in Paris in the last days of the leadership election the following year rather than use her formidable powers of persuasion with Tory MPs in Westminster.

Looking back, she said, 'It's rather ironical that now it is only Geoffrey Howe and Peter Walker who have been here from the beginning.' There was a pause. 'Have you thought who could take your place?'

My reply was that Michael Howard was the obvious choice and would be good on industrial relations law. I added a point about my then shadow minister with more foresight than I imagined. 'Tony Blair is a lawyer and he could certainly counter him.'

She did not respond immediately but returned to a point that was obviously troubling her. 'I know that you said you wanted to stay in the Commons. If you want to go to the Lords that is entirely possible.'

'No,' I repeated. 'I would like to stay in the Commons.'

We talked on for another ten minutes. She then came back to my successor. She was not convinced about Howard. 'Michael Portillo might be a better choice,' she said. She regarded Portillo at that time as a kindred spirit while she underestimated Howard and saw him more as a skilled barrister. In the event – and with the strong advice of the whips' office – she plumped for Howard.

Two weeks later Sir Anthony Meyer, a wonderfully *ancien régime* 'stalking horse' candidate very much on the liberal left of the party, staged what was widely described as a maverick bid for

* The new chief whip.

the leadership. In the event the bid was easily repulsed but even so sixty Tory MPs were dissatisfied enough to vote for this unlikely candidate or abstain. The following week I received a call from No. 10 for another meeting with the prime minister.

We met again on Tuesday 19 December, just before Cabinet, and Thatcher came straight to the point. Once again the compliments flowed. 'Norman, I have been giving a great deal of thought to our last conversation. I have spent a great deal of time thinking about it. I really have thought and thought about it. I wonder if you would stay on until July. There are many things to do. You have the industrial relations legislation and all the training. You are going to be so hard to replace. No one else has your combination of qualities.'

As it happened, I had been warned that this would be the approach and my reply was that I did not think it was a good idea to hang onto office when I had decided to leave. Up to this point Thatcher had been trying to persuade, almost woo, a minister to do her bidding. Then for a moment the mask slipped. 'Norman,' she said urgently, 'I don't want to see the government falling apart.'

This was the first time in either of our discussions she had expressed such a fear and to me – in spite of my immediate reaction to the Lawson resignation – it seemed almost fanciful. 'There is no question of the government falling apart,' I replied and repeated that I did not think it was a good idea to continue once I had decided to go. This time my point was accepted – 'I can see you have made up your mind' – and we settled down to discuss the timing of a friendly divorce.

I first remembered Margaret Thatcher as a shadow Cabinet minister lining up with her tray in the small cafeteria in the bowels of Westminster and I had seen her develop into the immaculately groomed national leader with a world reputation. In the fifteen years I had served with her we had had our disputes but these were easily cancelled out by the excitement and achievement of that period – and sometimes even the humour. In spite of the problems of her last years at No. 10 she was outwardly more relaxed and prepared at Cabinet to lighten the mood. 'We welcome the foreign secretary on one of his visits to this country,' she said, calling Geoffrey Howe for his foreign affairs report. After a visit to Poland at the height of the Solidarity movement's popularity she reported back to Cabinet that she had seen a banner in Gdansk which read, 'Well done, Maggie. You beat Arthur Scargill. We are against Communists also.' In February 1989 discussion in Cabinet focused not only on salmonella in eggs but also on a new scare concerning soft cheese. It led Nick Ridley to observe mournfully that raw eggs and soft cheese were about the only things he ate. Thatcher responded that as he was not pregnant he would probably survive.

For all that, she was of course right about the dangers of the government 'falling apart'. Yet few thought so at the time. Ministers and journalists gossiped about the end of the Thatcher years but at this point even Michael Heseltine, who had most to gain, thought that there was only a 5 per cent chance of her standing down before the next general election. She still attracted enormous affection bordering on devotion inside the constituency parties. Most of the ministers who had seen her at her best as well as her worst retained personal loyalty to her. She was not unassailable but as 1990 began very few members of her Cabinet thought that she was in imminent danger.

4

The fall of Thatcher (1990)

'It is a moment of history.'

Michael Heseltine, Saturday 24 November 1990.

On Thursday 1 November 1990 Geoffrey Howe finally resigned from the government. Ironically, ERM membership had now been achieved under John Major's chancellorship but Howe had been pushed beyond his point of personal endurance by Margaret Thatcher's Commons answers to questions following her statement on the European Council at Rome. Free from the prepared script she gave her frank unvarnished views on Britain in Europe: namely that Britain already had surrendered enough, that the European Commission was 'striving to extinguish democracy', and that the ideas of its president, Jacques Delors, for further integration were utterly unacceptable. 'No! No! No!' she shouted in reply to a question. For Howe Britain's role in Europe was an issue of dominating importance but his letter of resignation in no way matched Thatcher's passion and was amply stocked with compliments to the prime minister's 'strong leadership' and sentiments about how it had been 'a privilege and an honour for me to have contributed to that success'. Perhaps for that reason the importance of this latest catastrophe was initially underestimated. The assumption was that – like Nigel Lawson – Howe would reasonably quietly fade away. A serious leadership challenge seemed unlikely – but Thatcher herself was taking no chances.

My personal insight into her tactics came a few days after Howe's resignation. On the afternoon of Tuesday 6 November I was sitting in my new backbencher's office in the House of

Commons clearing up some papers. The House itself was not sitting. Howe had resigned on the last day of the old session and we were now on the eve of the Queen's Speech, when a new session would open and hopefully a better chapter for the government. The phone rang. It was Peter Morrison, now the prime minister's parliamentary private secretary, calling from Downing Street. Could we meet privately for a talk, he asked.

I had first known Morrison twenty years before when he was seconded to me from Central Office and took charge of my personal campaign in the first election I ever contested, in Nottingham. In those days Morrison was a tall, energetic, slim figure who kept up a ferocious pace throughout, whether in the slums of the Meadows, the Clifton housing estate or the blue-chip streets of West Bridgford. We started early at factory gates or schools and finished late in clubs or pubs. In between we ran from house to house canvassing. In those days he was in every way unlike the picture later drawn of him by Alan Clark during the leadership election: feet on desk, sleeping after a boozy lunch. Of course I agree that the intervening years had taken their toll but equally Morrison was no one's fool and certainly cannot be held mainly responsible for his leader's fall.

'This is a meeting which is not taking place,' Morrison said as we settled down in his small room behind the Speaker's chair. He (meaning Thatcher) was planning forward. Party rules now allowed the leader, even a leader in office, to be challenged at the beginning of each parliamentary year. Under the rules nominations would open on Thursday 8 November and if a contender came forward an election would have to take place within the following twenty-eight days. The decision of when in that period the election was held rested with the leader of the party. She obviously hoped that no contender would come forward but if one did her plan was to give the pretender as little time as possible to organise a campaign. Morrison intended to see the chairman of the backbench 1922 Committee, Cranley Onslow, and set a date for the election earlier than anyone expected, on Tuesday 20 November – only twelve days from the opening of nominations. If there was a campaign it would be short and sharp. The whole aim was to get the election over and return to the business of governing the country as soon as possible.

Morrison said that Thatcher would have liked the former defence secretary George Younger to run her campaign again as he had done when she had countered the challenge of Anthony Meyer a year before. But Younger, who was trusted on all sides of the party, had taken up a position as chairman of the Royal Bank of Scotland. It was unlikely that he would have the time to organise a campaign and instead was pencilled in as its 'president'. The idea was that in his place I and Michael Jopling, another former Cabinet minister now also on the back benches, would be the joint chairmen of this new campaign team. She would like this if we did, Morrison said.

Why us two? I never asked the question, even though on the face of it there were more obvious kindred spirits to gather in the votes – not least Norman Tebbit. I imagine the answer was that we were both seen as being in the centre of the party, where any election would be won or lost; we were still regarded as friends; and Jopling as an ex-chief whip had a fair knowledge of where the buried bodies were. There was one feature of the plan which I ignored. In the corporate sector 'presidents' and 'joint chairmen' are usually the badges of a once successful company which has lost its way and has no clear idea of what to do to recover.

My assumption was that if there was an election any possible challenger would be of the stalking horse variety. Michael Heseltine was my choice as the eventual successor but his consistent and often repeated position had been that he would not stand against the prime minister while she was still in office, a position I entirely supported. In any event he had not done himself any good by an ill-judged and opportunist intervention following Howe's resignation. In a letter to his constituency association in Henley he called for a return to collective responsibility within the government – a call which was swiftly disowned by the officers of his association on the grounds that it already existed. I could not imagine Howe himself mounting a challenge and after that even the political commentators were hard pushed to name a credible candidate. It was in no one's interest that a stalking horse candidate should do well and I agreed to meet with Morrison and the others he was bringing together at his home in Pimlico that weekend.

When I look back at my conversation with Morrison, one point is clear enough. By the time we met for the meeting 'which isn't taking place' – but which was duly leaked to the Sunday press the following weekend – the strategy was in position. Thatcher and her advisers had decided that if there was a contest then the best course was to bounce the parliamentary party, who were the only electors, into re-electing her. In the event it proved to be a disastrous mistake. It was all too quick. It prevented the constituencies, where her support remained overwhelmingly strong, from bringing their influence to bear on any doubting MPs. And it left the campaign flat footed and fumbling when Howe made his devastating resignation speech only seven days before voting.

Added to this, the whole intent of the campaign planners appeared to be to taunt the one credible candidate, Heseltine, into standing. There was nothing to be gained by increasing the drama of the nomination period but instead the aggressive guidance from No. 10 targeted him with both barrels. The message was a clear 'put up or shut up'. It was a message faithfully relayed in a paper notably loyal to Thatcher – David English's *Daily Mail*, which specialised in arresting front-page headlines. On Monday 5 November (the day before my meeting with Morrison) the *Mail*'s front page asked what it termed the key question regarding a possible Heseltine challenge:

DOES HE HAVE THE COURAGE?

You did not need to know Heseltine very well to realise that temperamentally he would be unlikely to let such a challenge pass. This after all was the man who had defiantly gestured with the mace at Labour backbenchers in the House of Commons as they started to sing 'The Red Flag'; and this was the man who had walked out of Cabinet.

On Sunday 11 November Heseltine himself rang me at my constituency home. It was clear that what was really influencing him was the 'put up or shut up' campaign. He would have no credibility left if now he did not take up the gauntlet. Rather than keeping him out of the contest No. 10 were forcing him into a corner. Later that day I rang Morrison and withdrew from the campaign team. My reason was simple. Any leadership campaign consists of two elements: the first is to expound the virtues of your candidate; the second is to attack your opponent. I was not prepared to join a campaign which would obviously target Heseltine – as in fact it did in a crude and silly way, painting him as a 'socialist' in Conservative clothing. As it happened Michael Jopling also withdrew. He had been abroad with a select committee when Howe had resigned and was still in South Africa when approached by Morrison. His reply was that he was a friend of Howe and, although he would probably be a Thatcher voter, he would need to consider the position. He was outraged to find his name in the Sunday press before he had replied. He withdrew immediately. Poor Morrison lost two campaign managers in one day.

In newspaper articles and interviews I continued to argue as strongly as I could against a leadership contest but any hope of that was spectacularly destroyed over the following forty-eight hours. On the Monday evening Thatcher spoke at the lord mayor of London's Guildhall banquet. Her message was again challenging. She would take on all comers: she would relish the contest. 'I can assure you there will be no ducking the bouncers, no stonewalling, no playing for time,' she said, using the language of cricket. 'The bowling's going to get hit all round the ground. That is my style.' Perhaps these tactics were decided at the Morrison dinner I had pulled out of on Sunday night. Perhaps Thatcher and the No. 10 court believed that a characteristic piece of fighting oratory was what was needed to rally the backbench troops. Perhaps it was thought that Heseltine was weak and this was the opportunity for a knockout blow which would settle the issue once and for all. Whatever the reason, Thatcher's comments made Heseltine's already probable intervention practically certain.

The next day, Tuesday 13 November, put the issue beyond doubt. Howe at last had the opportunity to make his delayed resignation statement in the Commons. The television pictures show me perched behind him as he carried out one of the most devastating demolition jobs that Westminster has ever seen. The nearest comparison was the use by Leo Amery of the devastating Cromwellian injunction 'In the name of God, go' against Neville

Chamberlain in 1940 after the disastrous British expedition to Norway.

I had entered the chamber basically to wish Howe luck before he made what most of us expected would be a 'more in sorrow than in anger' speech, just as Nigel Lawson (sitting next to him) had done eighteen months previously. What I did not know was that Howe had studied both Amery's speech and the 1963 speech of Nigel Birch following the Profumo scandal. In a devastating attack Birch had called for Harold Macmillan to stand down, using the words of Robert Browning (from his poem 'The Lost Leader') to predict 'never glad confident morning again'.

Not yet entirely knowing the ways of the back benches, I was unaware that since the introduction of television cameras members had been 'doughnutting' themselves around a speaker they knew would be in the news. Neither Jonathan Aitken nor David Sumberg, the MP for Bury South, showed any inclination to move up, so risking their elimination from the camera shot. The result was that the television pictures show me perched rather precariously behind Howe with an exceptional view of his typed notes which laid out his case.

All the pent-up feeling of fifteen years came pouring out. He painted Thatcher as anti-European in thought and deed. He attacked the background noise of her public relations machine, which meant more than the substance of carefully worked-out statements of policy. Devastatingly he accused Thatcher of damaging the negotiating position of her ministers, matching her cricketing metaphors. 'It is rather like sending your opening batsmen to the crease only for them to find, the moment the first balls are bowled, that their bats have been broken before the game by the team captain.' For too long he had wrestled with a conflict of loyalties – a conflict between personal loyalty to the leader and what was right for the country and the party – and it was now time for others to consider their own response.

In my diary I wrote:

The effect is devastating. It is difficult to exaggerate the impact on those listening to the attack. I come out of the chamber feeling shell shocked and I think that is the predominant feeling. Some make instant comments. I say nothing. There is nothing useful or helpful to say. Geoffrey has fired a number of torpedoes. They are well aimed and Margaret is now really holed. She is not yet sunk but it is as nasty a position as I can remember.

The next day Heseltine announced that he would stand.

Many of us now faced our own conflict of loyalties. My own position was an example. Heseltine's previous stance had been that he would not challenge Thatcher in office. He had been goaded into changing. I counted myself as one of his supporters but I had served with Thatcher for fifteen years and did not want to see her premiership, which had achieved so much that I supported, end in this way. In the event it was this loyalty I considered most important. On the Friday I wrote to Heseltine, telling him that I would not be voting for him. I said that at this stage he would doubtless be getting many letters pledging support. I was afraid that I was withdrawing mine.

On the Sunday Heseltine rang me again. He said that my letter was a big blow. He went on to say how well his campaign was going; how it was certain that there would be a second ballot; how in that ballot he would win; how the support was flooding in; and how he would be at No. 10. It occurred to me, not surprisingly perhaps, that he was really saying that if I had any further serious political ambitions then I should join up. My reply was that in personal terms it might well be that what I was doing was totally against my interests but I still intended to do it. He ended by saying, 'Well, I suppose at least you are being honest.' I fear, however, that in leadership elections that quality is not always placed highest on the scale.

The next day, Monday 19 November, at the beginning of the fateful week of the election itself, MPs came back to Westminster from their constituencies. Most local associations, like my own in Sutton Coldfield, were rock hard for Thatcher – although Tory supporters generally were much less certain. But the speed of the whole election process was now operating against Thatcher's interests. There was insufficient time for pressure to be applied locally on the wavering and no time at Westminster for every method of persuasion to be employed let alone exhausted. If two years later the whips could deliver the Maastricht vote, the

Thatcher campaign managers and their friends in government should have been able to achieve victory for the most successful Tory leader in post-war history.

Incredibly, at this crucial moment Thatcher decided to absent herself from the battlefield. The prime minister travelled to Paris for a conference to mark the end of the Cold War. Although it sounded important there were in reality no decisions to be taken. As foreign secretary, Douglas Hurd accompanied her and he suggests in his memoirs that her 'tearoom techniques' would have had no effect in gaining MPs' votes at this stage.* I think that judgement is wrong. Her personal authority was such that it is inconceivable that she could not have won the few votes necessary for outright victory, while all past history suggests that her absence overseas emboldened her critics. So why on earth did she do it? Perhaps her election advisers thought that seeing her among the world leaders would underline her status. Perhaps they thought that the cancellation or cutting short of her visit would send out the wrong signals of panic. Perhaps they even thought they had it in the bag. My own theory is that she believed her record should speak for itself rather than that she should go grubbing for votes among her backbenchers. She had lost the appetite for yet another party fight. Exhaustion was beginning to set in.

Confirmation that these were indeed some of the factors comes from the memoirs of two of the insiders in the Thatcher campaign. Ken Baker, the party chairman, reports that she decided she would run her campaign as 'a national and world leader' – just as Ted Heath had done unsuccessfully in 1975. Baker urged her to stay in London and not travel to Paris. Later she told him that although she recognised that he had told her to ring up MPs and spend time in the tearoom, 'that's not for me after eleven years'. Baker says that at a dinner at Chequers on the Saturday before polling, Peter Morrison reported that their canvas showed she would win 230 to 240 votes while Heseltine would be below 100.† In his memoir Lord McAlpine takes up the story. After most

---

* Douglas Hurd, *Memoirs* (London: Little, Brown, 2003), p. 401.
† Kenneth Baker, *The Turbulent Years: My Life in Politics* (London: Faber & Faber, 1993), pp. 389–92.

of the dinner party had left (including Baker and Morrison) she was left alone with two close supporters, McAlpine himself and Gordon Reece. To them she confided, 'I have heard all this before. This is exactly what they told Ted.'*

On the morning of the vote itself I ran into Geoffrey Howe in one of the Westminster corridors. He was obviously conscious that not everyone in the party now regarded him as the revered elder statesman. He looked at passing colleagues for a friendly smile but not all were prepared to play. The Scottish MP Nicholas Fairbairn had written Howe a friendly note after his resignation letter but had followed it with a ferocious attack following his resignation speech, accusing him of treachery to the party. Fairbairn showed me Howe's reply, in which he had simply said that good advocates resorted to abuse only when their case was weak. Even by Westminster standards Fairbairn was an eccentric but there was no disguising that feelings on Howe's speech ran very high. In our conversation Howe returned to his European case: namely that Thatcher's views on Europe were of the kind that would have prevented us going into Europe when the decision was first taken at the start of the 1970s. He also added a less familiar point. She had had the opportunity of forming an administration of all the talents but failed to keep her ministers. Certainly one point could not be contested. The only minister now left from the 1979 Cabinet picture was Thatcher herself.

The result came through as I was being interviewed by ITN. My instant reaction proved notably inaccurate. Thatcher had a majority of fifty-two but the election rules required an overall majority plus a 15 per cent margin over the next candidate to avoid a second ballot. This left her a frustrating four votes short; had two Tory MPs changed their vote she would have been safe. Alistair Burnet asked me whether Thatcher would stand on the second ballot. I replied that she would and she would win.

The first serious indication I received that not only would Thatcher fail to win but that she might not even stand came early the next morning. I had been appearing virtually daily on BBC's

---

* Alistair McAlpine, *Once a Jolly Bagman: Memoirs* (London: Weidenfeld & Nicolson, 1997), p. 266.

Breakfast Time programme and when I returned home I received a message to ring my successor as employment secretary, Michael Howard, who had rung at 7 a.m. When I rang back, virtually Howard's first words were, 'We are in a mess.' He did not think that Thatcher, even given that she was fifty-two votes ahead, would have enough support to win in the second round. The prospect was for a second-round election in which Douglas Hurd and John Major would come in to challenge Heseltine. Howard's view was that if Hurd looked like winning then that would bring in Norman Tebbit. Major on the other hand would take the Tebbitites with him. 'Would you be prepared to be John Major's campaign manager?' he asked. Given my earlier too hasty agreement to help lead the Thatcher campaign I said in effect that I would think about it. It was yet another conflict of loyalties. Although I was closer to Major than any of the other candidates I had supported Heseltine at a time when the prospect of Major would have seemed fanciful.

When I arrived at the House of Commons later that morning it was quite clear that Howard's assessment was correct. There was widespread gloom on the Tory tables in the tearoom. MPs who had voted for Thatcher at the first ballot were now switching. I wrote in my diary, 'Goodness knows what the logic of their position is. How can you vote for Margaret Thatcher one day and then against her five days later in a contest with the same alternative candidate?' The answer seemed to be that loyalty to the leader had determined many MPs' first votes but that a leader who could not win clearly on the first round in an election of MPs was fatally weakened. I noted that 'sensible people such as Michael Jopling, Francis Maude, Norman Lamont and William Hague think that she is finished'. Perversely my own view remained that she should stand again and tough it out. That was also Tebbit's view, whom I met in the lobby later that afternoon.

At 4.15 Tebbit was saying that she would stand. The 'men in the grey suits' – the backbench grandees of the 1922 Committee – had given an unclear and uncertain message. Their assessment had been that the election was not lost but it could be close. 'What's the alternative?' asked Tebbit. 'Douglas won't beat Michael. John Major would have a better chance but it is by no means certain.' In the division lobbies I met David Lightbown, a no-nonsense whip and one of my West Midlands neighbours, who told me that nine out of twelve whips thought that Thatcher would win and believed that she should fight on.

I next met Ken Clarke in the members' lobby. Tebbit had said that his plan was that Clarke should be Thatcher's new campaign manager. That was not remotely Clarke's idea. He was slightly red in the face, a sure sign of anger taking over. He told me that there was no chance whatsoever of his doing that. He was seeing Thatcher later in the evening and intended to tell her to go. She could not survive, he said, and if she stood it would prevent anyone else from the Cabinet standing as well. There was no prospect of any other Cabinet member standing as long as Thatcher remained a candidate.

By ten o'clock the scene had changed to the Cabinet corridor in the House of Commons, a row of small offices on the first floor behind the speaker's chair. Making my excuses from the opera that night, I had returned to the Commons and settled down with John Wakeham. He told me that the Cabinet had been asked one by one to give their views on whether if she went to a second ballot Thatcher could win. The overwhelming advice – some of it tearful – was that she could not. Only one or two, such as Ken Baker and Cecil Parkinson, felt that she should fight on. Most of the remainder believed that she would be defeated or felt that the party should have a greater choice and that Hurd and Major should be allowed to stand. As we left the room we ran into Clarke, Chris Patten and Norman Lamont in the corridor. Clarke said that if she did not stand down he would raise it at Cabinet in the morning. 'Perhaps this is the way we should have been acting ever since Nigel Lawson resigned.' By that he meant that the Cabinet should have stood up to her more and not allowed her to get away with her statements on Europe. Patten was also determined to see her go. There was an atmosphere of the deepest crisis.

As I was leaving Lamont asked if he could have a word. We were talking before Thatcher had actually stepped down but that outcome now seemed certain. He knew that Howard had approached me to head Major's campaign. What was my view now? Major had been a friend since our days dealing with pensions and social security; our views were broadly similar. Nevertheless my attitude remained the same. My earlier commitment to Michael Heseltine would have to take precedence. Friendship apart, I also felt that Heseltine had the experience and appeal necessary for a new leader, while Major would be an unknown quantity as leader and would benefit from a longer period as chancellor. One result of my refusal was that Lamont himself headed the Major team and was later rewarded by being appointed chancellor of the exchequer.

At an emotional Cabinet meeting on Thursday 22 November Thatcher announced her resignation – and two new candidates entered the fray, Hurd and Major. The party outside Westminster was now in a high state of indignation at the fall of Thatcher. They had woken up too late to what was happening – and been given too little time to make their voice count. Heseltine was now widely seen as the villain. He had destroyed Thatcher but the oldest political rule in the book is that the assassin very rarely inherits – although it has to be said that Thatcher herself was an exception to this rule.

Mid-morning on the Saturday Heseltine rang once more. Would I join others such as Nigel Lawson and Geoffrey Howe who were declaring their support for him, he asked. 'It is a moment of history,' he said excitedly. My reply was that, moment of history or not, I was seeing my executive on the Monday and would issue a statement then. Heseltine's view was that that would be too late to influence the vote. My response to that was that the contest was not my idea and in my strong view everything that I had forecast would now happen. The result of the challenge was that Major would be elected leader. I hoped he realised how high were the feelings in the party. Heseltine's optimistic reply to that was that these would soon disappear, just as had happened after Ted Heath's defeat in 1975. I replied that there was an essential difference: Thatcher was highly popular with the party in a way that Heath had never been.

Back in London that night I received a call from Downing Street and Peter Morrison. Any doubts that Thatcher was instrumental in helping install Major as her successor were entirely dispelled by that call – which was doubtless repeated to other target voters. Morrison's message was that what would make it 'alright' for Thatcher was the election of John Major. I listened but when he threatened to develop on the theme of Heseltine's socialistic instincts told him that Heseltine was a friend. An hour later I received a call from Warwick Lightfoot, my old special adviser, who also wanted my support for Major. Again I declined.

On the Monday morning as I left for Westminster I met a lady in wellington boots who was exercising her dogs in the park opposite my house. She revealed herself as Douglas Hurd's first wife, Tatiana. She could not really believe that Douglas wanted to be prime minister and hoped that he would not be too hurt if he failed. My private view was that he would come a distant third. My view also was that he would not be too upset and my strong suspicion was that he was only taking part because he was expected to take part. He was ideally suited to the post of foreign secretary and later proved to be one of Major's indispensable ministers.

In the library corridor of the House of Commons I met Geoffrey Howe and predicted to him that Major would win. It was not exactly a surprising forecast; any Tory MP worth his salt could see how the contest had progressed. Nevertheless Howe seemed taken aback. He thought such a decision would be extraordinary. 'He has not the experience,' he said. 'He has never raised interest rates.' For Howe this was obviously the acid test of a chancellor of the exchequer. He obviously felt that a change to Major would be an enormous jump into the dark. Perhaps it was but I assumed sourly at the time that he must have worked out some of the possible consequences of his devastating speech. In fact I suspect he was surprised – although not necessarily disappointed – at the impact of his resignation speech.

At lunchtime both Hurd and Major appeared in the tearoom. Hurd and his supporters took one table, Major and his team another. I was, symbolically, on a table between the two. Lunch finished, I crossed the corridor to the library and wrote a letter to Major. I had now a different conflict of loyalties but I felt that I could not abandon the Heseltine cause now that Thatcher had left the field. My letter to Major explained the position but added, with more foresight than I imagined at the time, 'You will find many friends in the aftermath of what I expect to be your victory. Inevitably there will be problems ahead and conceivably some may come after the next general election. If at that stage I can be of any assistance you only have to ask.'

For me the next events happened quickly. I travelled to Sutton Coldfield to speak to a crowded meeting of my association and told them frankly at the end that I intended to vote for Heseltine. Being the exceptional constituency they were they accepted that this was a decision for the member of Parliament – although undoubtedly most of the executive would have preferred Major. That night I publicly declared for Heseltine but the position had long been settled. The eventual result showed Major with 185 votes, Heseltine 131 and Hurd 56. A few minutes later Heseltine was shown conceding defeat and the election was over.

The implications of the leadership election were immense. It led to a decade and more of bitterness among Thatcher's closest followers. The wounds did not heal as they had after Heath's overthrow fifteen years earlier. A new battle began for the soul of the Conservative Party. But all that was for the future. The question that absorbed the party and public alike in the immediate aftermath of the election was: just why did she fall?

The European issue of course played its part; it could hardly fail to do so, given Howe's devastating resignation speech. But the leadership was not decided on Europe. Many passionate pro-Europeans, such as Ken Clarke, Chris Patten and John Gummer, voted for her out of loyalty in the only round in which she was a candidate. It is simply one of the great fictions of the 1990 leadership contest that Thatcher was defeated by Tory MPs who preferred the Euro-enthusiasm of Heseltine and Howe to the by now open scepticism of the prime minister.

The factors that really spelt her doom were the perceived failure of her policies, notably the community charge; her alienation from ministers and MPs as she withdrew into the company of those who were either her employees or her unquestioning followers; the presence on the back benches of a growing army of dispossessed; and, most of all, the party's abysmal showing in the opinion polls, where Labour were consistently shown 20 points ahead. Many Tory MPs now feared for their political lives – rightly, as it happened – and even some of her most faithful right-wing supporters would confide, 'I wonder if she is past her sell-by date.'

Yet even all this could have been overcome. There was immense personal loyalty to Thatcher. Of course some deserted her when the leadership election came but many others swallowed their doubts, rallied and voted for her. Ken Clarke in typical mode said to me before the election, 'I would feel an absolute worm if I argued for her in public and voted against her in private.' Doubtless some did exactly that but what really sank her was her disastrous breakneck election tactics. She needed to mobilise the constituencies and do everything in her power to muster her support in the Commons. She did neither.

Of course, this was not how it should have ended. If Tony Blair was able to organise a world-wide farewell tour then Margaret Thatcher certainly deserved more than a tearful and forced exit from No. 10. In my diary I wrote on the day of her resignation:

> Why, oh why, did she not have the sense to stop and step down gracefully after, say, ten years? It would have been a much better way to end than being forced out in this unceremonious way. Of course now the mood will change. MT will become a national hero and will remain so until the end of her life.

Doubtless that reaction is too tinged with sentimentality. Happy endings are not that common in politics. Too many politicians stay on for too long. While, of course, in strictly political terms it can be argued that the Conservative Party got it right. Even if Thatcher had won, it would have been only just. Her authority would have been shattered. To put it at its mildest, it was very unlikely that she would have won the next general election, which needed to be held by the autumn of 1992. That task she bequeathed to the then youngest prime minister of the twentieth century, John Major.

5
False dawn (1991–2)

'A word in your shell-like.'

Norman Tebbit, 7 November 1991.

At the beginning of 1991 I was firmly anchored on the back benches. I had refused offers to be the campaign manager of both Margaret Thatcher, who was a national hero all over again, and John Major, who was now prime minister. In the second round of voting for the party leadership I had supported Michael Heseltine, who was now heartily disliked by a large part of the Conservative Party. It was not a winning hand if I was intent on a political comeback but fortunately that was not my aim. By a stroke of luck I had become chairman of the Birmingham Post group of newspapers after a management buyout and joined two other boards. At home the family were becoming accustomed to my presence and I was enjoying the new life. Politically I intervened in occasional debates but I had to admit that here I wanted something more. If I was to be a backbencher I might as well be an active one.

By the autumn it was clear which issue would dominate the internal politics of the Conservative Party for the next few months. The forthcoming negotiation by European ministers at Maastricht was the acid test of Major's first period as premier. Maastricht raised issues designed to raise the temperature of any self-respecting sceptic: proposals for a single currency; the adoption of a social chapter which could reverse many of the British labour reforms of the 1980s; a 'federal' structure for Europe with the prospect of a common defence policy and a common immigration policy. The question was whether this reasonable man would be able to stand up to the pressure of his European colleagues in the same way as his outspoken predecessor. The parliamentary party might have said that they wanted a new, less strident style of European negotiation but most of all they wanted to see success.

Major had made a good start to his premiership. The first Iraq war had been successful, and the United States and Britain avoided becoming embroiled in either the occupation of Baghdad or what would have been a 'turkey shoot' as allied troops destroyed the retreating Iraqi army. The alliance, which included Arab nations, had been preserved; the authority of the United Nations resolution had been strictly observed; the advice, more popular then than today, that the allies should 'go on and finish the job' had been ignored. At home the opinion polls had improved and the new prime minister had put together a strong Cabinet team. Douglas Hurd remained foreign secretary and Ken Clarke had moved to the Home Office. I was told later that it had been a 'toss-up' between Norman Lamont and Clarke for the Treasury with the vote going to Lamont on the grounds that he had been Major's campaign manager and was better 'house trained' (meaning more amenable) than the more obvious candidate. Politically the most significant change had been to bring back Heseltine to head the Environment Department, with the task of replacing the poll tax.

So far so good – but Major, a keen student of political history, needed no reminder of the capacity of the European issue to split political parties. Twenty years earlier the Conservatives had been the party of Europe, although even then there had been internal opposition. Ted Heath and his chief whip, Francis Pym, had taken out all the persuasive stops to push through the original European Economic Community legislation in 1972. Doubting back-benchers who it was judged could be bullied were scooped out of the corridors of the Commons and placed in front of the prime minister. At that time Labour were opposed to entry and in the years that followed there was no doubt which party showed the more obvious divisions on Europe. For twenty years the vast majority of Eurosceptics and outright opponents were to be found on the Labour benches. In 1975 Harold Wilson avoided a manifesto commitment to withdraw from the EEC only by offering a referendum. In a remarkable political convolution the official policy became to stay but Cabinet ministers who disagreed, such as Barbara Castle and Peter Shore, were allowed to campaign for an exit. Later in 1981 Michael Foot once again committed the party to withdraw and in so doing was instrumental in persuading Roy Jenkins, Shirley Williams, Bill Rodgers and David Owen to break away and form the Social Democratic Party. Most Labour MPs, however, remained where they were, including Tony Blair and Jack Straw, who only later discovered their enthusiasm for Europe.

With Labour hopelessly divided it was easy for the Conservative Party to claim to be consistent and right. This certainly was the message of Thatcher's first and victorious election manifesto of 1979. The manifesto criticised 'the frequently obstructive and malevolent attitude of Labour ministers' towards Europe and promised that 'the next Conservative government will restore Britain's influence by convincing our partners of our commitment to the Community's success'. Even in her second term of office the prospect of surrendering power to Brussels was not a total road block.

Agreement to the 1985 Single European Act gave away more exclusively British sovereign power than any other European measure before or since. Majority voting (meaning loss of sovereignty) was not the only price we paid. The authority for the commission to bring forward the measures that it did at Maastricht came straight from that Act, which committed Britain to 'progressive realisation of economic and monetary union'. It was part of Major's inheritance for him to deal with as best he could.

The pragmatic European policy that Thatcher had initially pursued when in office had suited me well personally. I was in favour of Britain's membership of the EEC on the economic grounds that the single market could give us new opportunities to both export and attract inward investment. Politically my view was, just as we had said in our 1979 manifesto, that Europe had the potential to give Britain more clout in international affairs. But my support was hardly unqualified. I did not believe in political integration and thought that some European leaders were pushing the pace to an extent which was both wrong and counterproductive to their case. I was not a Eurosceptic in the sense that

I use it in this book: sceptical of the whole idea of a European community, opposed to even considering the prospect of a single currency, opposed to Maastricht and even prepared to take that opposition to leaving the union altogether for some undefined free trade area. Equally I thought the idea of 'Europe right or wrong' was daft.

I also had another belief which most of my Europhile friends thought distinctly quirky. My first election address in Nottingham in 1970 had called for a referendum on Britain's entry into the EEC – and I still believe that had we introduced referendums to decide the decisive issues on Europe then some of the party's problems would have been avoided. Conservative governments would have won referendums both on Britain's entry into the EEC and on joining the single market but we all exhibited an unappealing lack of confidence in our case. As a result we spent too much time whipping the party into the division lobbies and too little time trying to convince a wider public. We believed that winning a parliamentary vote was the same as winning public support.

My experience as a minister had done little to strengthen my European faith. As transport minister I had haggled for hours at Brussels about a handful of extra lorry permits which enabled British road haulage to compete equally in Europe. As employment secretary my view was that the social chapter threatened to undo some of the major reforms we had carried out in the labour market. Since returning to the back benches I had been content to keep my distance from the European debate at Westminster, which in my view lacked balance and was too often dominated by zealots – but all that changed in the autumn of 1991.

On the Conservative back benches there were two organised groups intent on pursuing their own brands of belief. On the right was the 92 Group – unaffectionately known by its opponents as the Black Hand Gang. It was mainly inhabited by self-professed right-wingers who were often sceptical not just about Europe but about the way society had developed with more crime, more one-parent families and less discipline. Their organising leader was George Gardiner, who suffered from a disadvantage that he could do nothing about – he looked conspiratorial even when following the most innocent of pastimes. He later left for the Referendum Party – one of a number of Tory MPs at the heart of the European debate in the early 1990s who eventually decided they were in the wrong party – but in his heyday Gardiner was an astute and successful manipulator. On the centre-left was a more loosely organised group going under the curious name of the 'Lollards', whose director of operations was Peter Temple-Morris (who eventually crossed to Labour). The Lollards included undoubted Euro-enthusiasts but many had the same cautious view of Europe as I did.

The great coup of the 92 Group had come the previous year when Hugh Dykes, the then chairman of the European back-bench committee (who was later to join the Liberal Democrats), had been defeated in an election to that post by Bill Cash (who remained with the Conservatives – just unconstrained by the party's policies). Few in the party had shed any tears over Dykes's demise, where he was regarded as fervently and eccentrically Euro-enthusiastic as Cash was Eurosceptic. A tearoom hope was that both could be marooned together on a desert island. More seriously it had become obvious since the change of leader that the European committee had been transformed into the party's anti-European committee.

In October Temple-Morris, who had once been my vice chairman at Cambridge of the Conservative Association, came to see me. He had two proposals. The Lollards had considered the future and believed that after the general election there would be a vacancy for chairman of the 1922 Committee. Their proposal was that I should stand for election to the committee with the aim of going for the chairmanship later. My response to that was that I was not interested. Having escaped from the conformity of government I had no wish to impose upon myself the conformity of being the spokesman for all backbenchers. The second proposal was more intriguing. How about standing against Cash for the chairmanship of the European committee?

That was a different matter. I did not believe that Cash and co. were representing the Conservative Party view on Europe and all too often appeared to be attacking the policy of Major and Hurd, which I supported. There was no point in having already difficult negotiations made even more difficult by attacks from behind. So I was interested but by no means determined. Nevertheless the word was out that I might be challenging and that meant that the right had to decide their tactics. One way forward was for them to dump Cash and get Norman Tebbit to stand in his place. The result would be a high-profile contest between two ex-Cabinet ministers.

During a division on the evening of 7 November I ran into Tebbit in the division lobby. 'A word in your shell-like,' he said in best Mafia style. We went through to the corridor behind the speaker's chair, the political equivalent to a walk in the car park. He said that he had been under a great deal of pressure to stand for the chairmanship of the European committee but he had resisted it. In his view there should not be an election at all until after Maastricht – although he was silent on how, under the constitution of annual elections for backbench committees, this wonder was to be achieved. He also believed that ex-Cabinet ministers should not stand for backbench committees – ignoring examples such as Bill Deedes, who when we both joined the House in 1970 had been the elected chairman of the home affairs committee. But Tebbit's real message was this. If he found that another 'heavyweight' was standing he would have to reconsider his position.

'Does that mean if I stand you will stand also?' I asked.

'I would have to consider standing,' he replied. 'You will be seen as Major's man. Just think what would happen if I won,' he smiled threateningly.

The Tebbit conversation was followed up during the next twenty-four hours by a series of other overtures. All kinds of people were sent forward to try to persuade me not to stand. Their advice was accompanied by high praise for my abilities, character and standing. A long-serving Tory backbencher, Toby Jessel, said how 'disappointed' he would be and another veteran sceptic, Teddy Taylor, said that he had far too high a regard for me to think that I would want to stand. From the whips' office my genial but bluntly persuasive Midlands neighbour David Lightbown also advised me not to stand. Far from the whips organising my campaign (as one or two papers later suggested), the only advice I received from the chief whip, Richard Ryder, was not to underestimate the opposition. It was by no means certain, he said, that I would win an election in the whips' office, whose members at that stage, apart from Lightbown, included David Heathcoat-Amory, David Davis and Neil Hamilton.

As far as I was concerned the campaign of quiet persuasion was entirely counter-productive. Rather than dissuading me it persuaded me that I really had no other option. Backing people into corners is not a good tactic, as had been shown a hundred times more dramatically with Michael Heseltine. On Tuesday 12 November I announced my candidature before the television cameras to a meeting of rather bemused Nottingham women who had not kept up with the minutiae of our backbench manoeuvrings. A few hours later the news came through that in spite of the sabre rattling Tebbit had decided not to go through with his threat. Back in the Commons I found that he had contented himself with denouncing me as a 'recycled Cabinet minister' but all the huffing and puffing could not disguise the fact that he had walked away from the contest. Even had he stood I do not think he would have won, although I readily concede that if the election had been after the 1992 general election, with the new intake of MPs, he almost certainly would have succeeded. As it was the contest was a straight fight between myself and Cash.

In our canvassing it became clear that not everybody was intending to vote simply on the issue of Europe. Several Eurosceptic backbenchers, including Tony Marlow and Patrick Nicholls, quietly pledged their support for me, as did Terry Dicks, another confirmed right-winger, who wanted to ask Tebbit why, if he felt so strongly on Europe now, had he voted in favour of the Single European Act. But not all the canvassing went the same way. Bob Hughes, my campaign manager, came back to me after a meeting with the Tory MP Geoffrey Finsberg. 'What have you done to him?' he asked. 'He won't vote for you under any circumstances.' The answer was that I had asked him to be moved from the DHSS, where he was misplaced as one of my junior ministers. I had hoped for some other job for him but in fact he was moved out of the government altogether. He blamed me for his dismissal and I could not complain. As Margaret Thatcher had found to her cost in the leadership contest, sacked ministers do not easily forgive.

The election the next day was one of the most extraordinarily crowded backbench contests that I ever saw in the Commons. For some reason Cash and his committee had organised it in one of the smaller committee rooms. There was a massive turnout, including both Ted Heath and Geoffrey Howe, and we all tried to push into the tiny room. Not unfairly Tebbit lifted himself onto a table top to protest at the chaos, although some of us thought that this only confirmed our view that the existing committee might have had some difficulty in running a decent fish and chip shop. Twenty minutes later the result was announced: not only had I won but my supporters standing on the same ticket were also elected. Talking to the press afterwards I offered a comment on the latest somersault by Labour on Europe. 'That's the first time for a long time we have heard the chairman of the European committee talk about the Labour Party's policies,' a reporter commented afterwards. A rather sourer comment came from Tim Eggar, who had been my minister of state at the Employment Department and knew my views on the social chapter. Half in jest (but only half) he said, 'If you are a moderate on Europe then God help this party.'

A week later Major set out the position he would take at the European Council meeting in a special Commons debate. Although the language he used was determinedly less strident than Thatcher's, in substance he set out exactly the kind of position that his predecessor might have taken a few years previously. He would fight on the social chapter and there was no prospect of him signing up to the single currency – although he was not going to say that the idea of a single currency was so objectionable that he would not even talk about it. It was as good a speech as he made in the first two years of his premiership and made even better in contrast to Neil Kinnock, who seemed entirely at sea. But the star of the debate in terms of media coverage was not Major but Thatcher. In a typically robust speech she ended by calling for a referendum on any move to join the single currency. 'Let the people speak,' she declaimed. Although I had sympathy with the point, it was not exactly the motto I felt had been above our heads in the Cabinet Room when she was prime minister and discussed these matters. At the end of the debate there were a number of significant abstentions when the motion to approve the government's strategy was put to the vote. They included all the former officers of the backbench committee plus Tebbit – but not Thatcher, who decided at that point not to publicly rock the boat.

As a backbencher it is unusual to gain any insight into the workings of government but back in London on the second day of the Maastricht council, Tuesday 10 December, I caught a glimpse. Up to then the news had been confusing. The *Evening Standard* had begun the day with a headline saying Major was on the brink of triumph but as the editions went by the front page changed to a prediction that the council was on the brink of collapse. At 6.30 that evening a special meeting was convened at 12 Downing Street by the chief whip, Richard Ryder. Present were Michael Heseltine; Chris Patten, the party chairman; John MacGregor, the leader of the Commons; John Wakeham, now the leader of the Lords; Francis Maude, from the Treasury; and myself. Ryder explained that the meeting was a result of a phone call from the Foreign Office minister Tristan Garel-Jones in Maastricht. In effect he had asked: if the negotiations collapsed on the social issues, would that be defensible in terms of British public opinion?

Patten's view was that we would be in real difficulty if they all broke down on these issues and Heseltine was even stronger. His view was that although we could defend retaining our immigration checks we could not stand out on issues like maternity rights and the disabled. I found myself the discordant voice. My view was that Major had made a great deal on how unacceptable the social chapter was. He had said so publicly and the briefing from No. 10 had made his opposition even clearer. I said it was essential that he should preserve his own position and this must not be seen as a personal defeat for him. Both MacGregor and Maude nodded in agreement on that. The discussion was interrupted by a call from Sarah Hogg, the head of the prime minister's policy unit, in Maastricht and Ryder summarised the conflicting advice. At the time my uneasy feeling was that there was no one guarding Major's own position but on this occasion I did not need to worry. At about eleven o'clock the news came through that the prime minister had stuck to his guns and appeared to have won a great victory. Britain had opted out of the social charter and it had been accepted that we would not be joining the single currency. The 'federal' word, regarded by the sceptics as code for a 'United States of Europe', would be excluded from the treaty. According to the usually cautious Major it was 'game, set and match' for Britain.

Following the 1992 general election the very mention of the Maastricht name was enough to provoke catcalls and hisses at party conferences. But that was not how it was seen in the immediate aftermath of the negotiation, inside or outside the party. The overwhelming feeling was that Major had secured a deal which preserved British interests but also kept us as a firm player in Europe – and without the kind of personal rancour that Thatcher invariably provoked. That was certainly the view of the newspapers that later took pride in their Eurosceptic colours.

The *Times* called the negotiation 'an emphatic success for John Major and his new European diplomacy'. The *Daily Telegraph* leader was headed 'Out of the summit and into the light' and their European Community correspondent, one Boris Johnson, reported, 'In almost every sense it was a copybook triumph for Mr Major, the stuff of Foreign Office dreams.' The *Daily Mail* front-page headline shouted, 'MAJOR WINS BY A KNOCK-OUT!' Its leader was headed 'Good for Europe, great for Britain'; of Major it said, 'He went. He stood firm. And he prevailed.' The *Sun* described how 'Major played the winning hand in Europe' and its political editor, Trevor Kavanagh, wrote, 'A lot of surprised people learned the hard way yesterday that it's a dangerous mistake to underestimate Gentleman John Major.'

As for Parliament, when Major entered the Commons chamber on his return he was given a hero's welcome with Tory MPs enthusiastically waving their order papers. Well, was not Chamberlain also feted when he returned with a piece of paper from Munich? A Labour MP who took the point and shouted out 'peace in our time' was laughed out of court. During the exchanges Thatcher sat silently in her corner place on the back benches, a fixed smile on her face. Perhaps she was reflecting that had she still been in office and achieved the same result her advisers would have proclaimed it a triumph. At Cabinet on the Thursday there were further songs of praise for Major with, among the chorus, the later Eurosceptic leader Ken Baker.

Years later a tribute to Major's negotiating success came from a determined and skilful sceptic, Michael Howard, after he had taken over as Conservative leader. Howard's view of the European Union was that it was not necessary for every nation within it to sign up to exactly the same policies and regulations. He particularly wanted to renegotiate the Common Fisheries Policy. But surely that would be impossible, he was told. Not at all, said Howard. Maastricht showed that a British government could opt out of policies that other nations in the union wanted to pursue.

By most political standards Major had scored a formidable political success and established himself as his own man. With a majority of more than 100 and with parliamentary opinion strongly in favour of what had been achieved there seemed little difficulty in pushing the legislation through. The die-hards would of course oppose it but there would have been no doubt about the eventual outcome. But Major faced one formidable obstacle. The very latest time the next general election could be held was the autumn of 1992 but the likely election date was April – a mere four months ahead. The room for manoeuvre was severely limited. The party chairman, Chris Patten, wanted the decks cleared and certainly did not want the election to be preceded by legislation – including the social chapter opt-out – which could be exploited by both the Labour opposition and the open rebels on the Tory side.

Disastrously for Major's premiership, the decision was taken that there was no option but to put the Maastricht legislation to one side as unfinished business. It turned out to be a fateful decision – although few recognised it at the time. Had the business managers pushed through the legislation in the same way as Thatcher had forced through the Single European Act legislation, or Gordon Brown later guillotined the Lisbon treaty legislation, the story of the next years would have been very different. At the start of 1992 there was an overwhelming majority for Maastricht. Nine months later – particularly after the Danish referendum which initially rejected the treaty – the government was forced to fight for every vote on every issue.

With the legislation shelved the party went to the 1992 general election proclaiming in its manifesto not only support for Maastricht but also: 'The Conservatives have been the party of Britain in Europe for 30 years. We have argued when argument was necessary; but we have not wavered nor changed our views. We have ensured that Britain is at the heart of Europe; a strong and respected partner.' They were brave words – strikingly similar in tone to the words of Thatcher's first manifesto. There was only one trouble. A significant number of the candidates fighting the election in seats that the party would win did not remotely agree.

Back in 1987, at my office at Elephant and Castle, Major and I had discussed our prospects as we waited for that election to be declared. He confidently expected us to win the third election but then suddenly asked, 'Whoever has heard of a party winning four elections in a row?' At that stage he was no more than looking ahead to what he feared might be his reduced chances of reaching the Treasury. Major was always an ambitious politician and he always looked ahead. Now with almost incredible irony he was to attempt the task that once he had considered impossible.

In spite of my refusal to be his campaign manager in the leadership election and my vote for Michael Heseltine, our friendship had been slowly restored. At the beginning of 1992 I was asked by Chris Patten to take on a role as adviser and 'travelling friend' to the prime minister during the campaign. Each week at Central Office there was a planning meeting. One of the issues was whether instead of rallies we should have 'Meet John Major' events, where the prime minister would sit on a stool, chat to the audience positioned around him and take questions. This was an American idea imported by the party's new communications director, Shaun Woodward, who had once been an editor on the television programme *That's Life!* and later became a Labour minister. Woodward's view was that Major was no orator and the more informal setting (evidently used to advantage by George Bush Senior) would play to his strengths. I argued strongly against the proposed format and in an effort to convince me I was taken to York to watch a dress rehearsal. It only served to confirm my doubts when a solicitor asked a series of deeply technical questions on conveyancing. I gave Major full marks for apparently knowing the answers but wondered what any news programme could possibly do with the exchange. My nightmare was that Neil Kinnock would be televised at enthusiastic rallies night after night while Major would be pictured quietly and patiently answering questions from invited audiences.

Parliament dissolved on Monday 16 March and there followed day after day of early-morning alarm calls; press conferences at Central Office; fast cars to RAF Northolt using ways through London which until that moment were entirely unknown to me; tours the length and breadth of Britain; and finally the evening rallies or the much inferior 'Meet John Major' events, which eventually we managed to eliminate.

Looking back, Major won the election for two main reasons. A highly effective advertising campaign run by Maurice Saatchi warned the public against the tax and spending increases which it was claimed would follow a Labour victory: 'Labour's Double Whammy – More Taxes, Higher Prices'. It was a charge that Labour were never able to answer convincingly; here again Kinnock's lack of confidence in issues economic worked against him.

The second reason was Major's own personal performance. He took strength from direct contact with the electors – something that many politicians talk about but few actually feel. He had to be prised away from the crowds that had come out to see him. He noticed how Kinnock was being carefully driven from one photo opportunity to another and kept as distant as possible from both a questioning press and anyone other than a selected member of the public. Major's idea to counter this was the soapbox, which took him back to his youth and brought old-fashioned politics back to the campaign – much against the judgement of Conservatives such as Edwina Currie who believed that this was not what a prime minister should do. In fact it was exactly what a prime minister fighting to get his party elected for a fourth term should have done. He needed to somehow underline that the government had not lost contact with the public that it served, that it was not remote from the people. He needed to underline that the country had a new leader who was different in both style and approach to his predecessor, that he was relevant to the 1990s in the way that Thatcher had been relevant and essential for the 1980s.

The contrast with his predecessor was palpable. There was a genuine humility about Major. He realised he was lucky to be leader; above all, his attitude was that he did not want to let anyone down. At the briefing meetings he listened courteously to his ministers and if anything was too courteous. At one briefing with the press waiting downstairs Norman Lamont's advisers withdrew the figures they had initially provided to counter John Smith's shadow Budget. There was the opportunity for an explosion but there was none. A couple of days later the corrected figures were published but the debate had moved on.

Behind the scenes Major was not always as forgiving. At Edinburgh the BBC *Newsnight* programme abruptly changed the agreed terms of an interview. Their new proposal was to show him a Labour party political broadcast on the National Health Service and immediately to let Jeremy Paxman loose in questioning him. Although we did not know it at the time this was the notorious and inaccurate 'Jennifer's ear' film, which portrayed a small girl waiting and waiting for an NHS operation on her ears while another girl being treated privately was seen at once. Major, who was already exasperated by what he saw as the BBC's partial coverage of the election, was furious at the pro-gramme's change of tack. He threatened to cancel the interview and it became my job to persuade him to continue on the basis of the original agreement. We did not need a row, which doubtless would have been portrayed as Major running away from an interview with Paxman on the ever-sensitive subject of health.

At another point in the campaign Major was angered by the reports reaching him that Lamont was distancing himself from his desire to cut taxes. 'If he screws this one up I will get another chancellor,' the prime minister exploded angrily at one point. At the other end of the phone at No. 10 Sarah Hogg (ungallantly codenamed 'Piglet' for the campaign) had the ticklish task of translating this message to the Treasury. But such outbursts were short, and did not interrupt the whole campaign. There was never anything like Wobbly Thursday.

Of course there are some – mostly Labour politicians, as it happens – who say there was a third reason why Major won: Kinnock was unelectable. He certainly made a major mistake by marching thousands of supporters and the whole of the shadow Cabinet to Sheffield for what soon became known on our campaign bus as the 'Hitler Youth rally'. Quite what the aim of the rally was intended to be was unclear but what it achieved was to badly scare the middle class. At the weekend I found constituents lining up in my constituency not to ask me questions of policy but to be reassured that the Conservatives would win.

Against this it needs to be remembered that Kinnock was a skilled campaigner and considerable orator and that for most of the election campaign he was ahead in the polls. Viewed from Central Office the prospects looked anything but rosy. Quite apart from the gloomy national polls, some of the local opinion polls in the Midlands and north-west England showed massive swings to Labour. Inside the party there was much grumbling from senior figures such as Marcus Fox about what was seen as the lacklustre national campaign. Woodrow Wyatt in his *News of the World* column called for the sacking of Chris Patten while Thatcher was quoted in the *Sunday Times* as saying privately that the campaign 'did not have enough oomph, enough whizz, enough steam'.

Central Office itself dished up its own form of masochistic pessimism. Regular 'intelligence reports' from the regions were lovingly put together for the prime minister on the progress of the campaign together with what were considered useful suggestions. So on 22 March the report from the western region told of a 'shortage of workers' in Bristol, support slipping in Devon with 'much less eye contact in streets and markets', 'unhappy farmers and businessmen' in Falmouth and 'a marked swing against us' in Bridgwater. The one suggestion, succinctly put, concerned the chancellor: 'He *must* look cheerful or keep him off.'

My own view was that the potential killer for Major was that we were fighting the election in the middle of a world recession. Unemployment had risen remorselessly over the last eighteen months and manufacturing industry was in particular difficulty. The points were relentlessly put by the regional television

interviewers instructed by their producers to give the prime
minister a hard time. But the subject that was to dominate the
next five years – policy on Europe – was almost never mentioned,
either locally or by the established national stars such as Paxman,
the Dimblebys and Robin Day. It was the dog that did not growl
let alone bark.

In every other way though it was a rough campaign. One man
in south London covered the prime minister with printing ink. In
Bath and Southampton he was pelted with eggs. In Bolton he
faced one of the roughest demonstrations I had ever experienced,
even after six years being at the wrong end of the health unions.
At the same time the polls consistently showed him behind. If ever
a leader had reason to panic it was Major. Yet in the weeks of the
campaign I only once heard him contemplate defeat and then in
private. We had stopped for an hour or two at a country house
near Bath which was the venue of the evening rally. That morning, Wednesday 1 April, three opinion polls had shown Labour
with leads varying between 4 and 6 percentage points. It looked
as if they had at last decisively broken through. As we waited for
his speech to be typed Major tentatively pondered his future if he
was defeated. Predictably my advice was that he should 'stay on
and fight and win the next one'. He thought about that for a
moment and said, 'You know, I don't want to spend the next five
years in opposition working to get a job I don't particularly like.'
In his meteoric career Major had never gone backwards. The
same evening a different poll showed that the parties were running
neck and neck and the brief period of rural introspection was
brought to an end.

Nevertheless the polls remained a consistent puzzle. As we
neared the end of the campaign Major called me to one side after
the daily press conference to join a meeting with Chris Patten and
the Central Office polls expert, Keith Britto. There was a point,
he said, that he did not understand about this campaign. He went
out daily into the country. The longer the campaign had
continued the more enthusiastic the receptions had become – and
he was right. At Chester there must have been a crowd of 2,000
waiting in the centre of the city to hear him. At Yarm in North
Yorkshire he was almost mobbed as crowds crushed around him

in the market place. At York hospital he received the most welcoming health service reception I have ever seen accorded to a Conservative politician. And yet, Major said, when he returned in the evening it was to find another opinion poll showing the party behind. Could we explain? Of course we could not. We could say that the local telephone polls were often run by the politically inexperienced or that some polls were within the margin of error. I could rehearse yet again the tale of my first election in 1970, when, only days before Ted Heath's election victory, the polls showed Labour cruising to a decisive win. But we were in no position to assure him that the opinion polls had got it wrong.

On the Tuesday before polling day the headlines of the *Independent* said it all: 'Major warns against hung Parliament but regional polls suggest outright Labour victory. Labour surge in marginals.' A massive poll carried out by the Press Association showed an overall 7 point swing to Labour with bigger than average swings in south-east England and the Midlands. No poll put the Conservatives ahead and the very best had the party 1 point behind. Nor were the party's intelligence reports any more encouraging. On the same Tuesday the reports from the areas made the same grim reading, with massive losses being predicted throughout the country.

On polling day itself there were reports that the Conservatives could be closing the gap but even after most votes had been cast the exit polls still got it wrong. At ten o'clock that evening I was appearing on the BBC radio election night programme together with Labour's Bryan Gould and Alan Beith from the Liberal Democrats. As the chimes of Big Ben ended Brian Redhead rather portentously gave the result – a hung Parliament. Of course it was not. Against all the odds Major had won. Against all the arguments of 'time for a change'. And against all the critics in his own party.

In the election Major had actually polled more votes than Thatcher in 1987 and his share of the vote at 42 per cent was only a whisker behind. It was a victory spoilt only by the electoral system, which perversely left him with an overall majority in the Commons of twenty-one compared to Thatcher's lead of 100-plus. And there of course was the rub. The majority was perilously

slim. A handful of rebels at Westminster could derail any government legislation. The disgruntled (and at any stage in any party
there are some of them) could have disproportionate influence. It
would take substantial self-discipline to keep the party together
but literally in the hour of victory there was unmistakeable
evidence that not everybody was facing the same way.

On election night a party was held at the Westminster house of
the former party treasurer Lord McAlpine. Many of the guests
were drawn from the right of the party (they included Thatcher)
and like the host were no friends of Major. At one stage a cheer
went up as a result came through on the television screen. It was
the reaction not to a famous Conservative victory but to the defeat
in Bath of the party chairman, Chris Patten, who was blamed for
his part in Thatcher's fall. Thatcher herself did not join in the
applause and from all reports was irritated by it. But nothing
showed more clearly the internal tensions and the depths to which
enmity in the Conservative Party had sunk. When I later heard
the news of the reaction it was with disbelief. To cheer the defeat
of a Conservative Party chairman would have been utterly
unthinkable a few years before. The divisions inside the party had
been papered over for the duration of the campaign but beneath
the surface there was something approaching turmoil.

6

John and Margaret (1992)

'I don't accept the idea that all of a sudden Major is his own man.'
Margaret Thatcher, *Newsweek*, 21 April 1992.

Back in May 1989 the BBC organised a debate on Europe. It could easily have been staged in a television studio in Shepherd's Bush but the producers preferred the grander, and substantially more expensive, setting of the Hotel Crillon in Paris. Early on a Sunday morning I was flown to France to put the government case; against me I had, not a member of Labour's shadow Cabinet, but the former Conservative prime minister Ted Heath. His hostility to Margaret Thatcher was by now legendary. The producers hoped that all they needed to do was to light the touch-paper and retire to a safe distance. They were not disappointed.

Sunday 14 May 1989. For the opening shots of the programme all of us sit around the table. Ted confides to me that MT's view on Europe is disastrous and will split the party asunder. It is obviously going to be one of those programmes – and so it proves. Jonathan Dimbleby is only a few seconds into his interview when it becomes apparent that Ted is really going to have a go. It has obviously been boiling up within him and out it comes. MT was deliberately 'misleading' the country with her talk of Europe being a gigantic socialist state. Britain would just become a second-rate power if it did not respond to Europe enthusiastically. The time had come to speak out. Ted's message could not have been clearer or more hostile to Margaret.

It was just one of a long list of hostile actions by Heath to the woman who had deposed him from the party leadership. With the succession of John Major to the premiership there seemed one certainty: relations between him and Thatcher would be an immense advance on what had gone before.

Surely now it would all be different. Major after all was Thatcher's protégé. She had brought him into the Cabinet; she had promoted him to foreign secretary and then to chancellor; and she had put all her weight behind him in the leadership election after she herself had pulled out of the contest. The call I received from her parliamentary private secretary, Peter Morrison, asking me to support Major was repeated to other backbenchers. David Hunt, the then Welsh secretary, who had been absent from the fateful Cabinet meeting when she stood down, was telephoned personally by Thatcher and told not to back Michael Heseltine on the grounds that the Cabinet had decided that they could choose only from current Cabinet members, an instruction which with some character Hunt ignored. A member of Major's campaign team remembers her interrupting their first meeting in the small room behind the speaker's chair with the injunction 'make sure you win'. At a Downing Street lunch, as she waited for the new leader to be elected, any doubters were given the clear message that a vote for Major was the only course. Thatcher's aid may not have been as crucial as some think in Major's election – he had more natural support than was supposed – but what is beyond any reasonable doubt is that she did her utmost to assist his election.

Yet hopes that all this would lead to a happier relationship between the new leader and the old were quickly – very quickly – disappointed. Thatcher can certainly be acquitted of playing any part in the unpleasantness at Lord McAlpine's, which she probably regarded as little more than an undergraduate demonstration. Much more serious is the charge that over the years following her fall she helped undermine the successor she had all but anointed.

Relations started badly when in the aftermath of Major's election to the party leadership Thatcher told the press, 'I shan't be pulling the levers there, but I shall be a very good back-seat driver' It was a comment not made with malice but clearly implied that Major would not be his own man – and would simply be the 'son of Thatcher'. According to Major, 'the comment forced a wedge between us that was to grow wider as month succeeded month'.* The result was that consultations between the new and the old leader were few and far between. In the months that followed I began to read reports that relations between the two had deteriorated and that Thatcher was critical of the direction that the new prime minister was taking. On one occasion she was reported as criticising the government's economic policy when speaking at a private dinner. On another, in March 1991, she was entirely on the record when she told American television, 'I see a tendency to try to undermine what I achieved and to go back to more powers for government.'

As a backbencher some way from the action I did not take too much notice of these reports but when I was invited to Chequers in April 1991 there was no disguising the prime minister's irritation with his predecessor – at that time he was particularly irritated by her criticism of the way that Britain and the United States were handling the position in Bosnia. In my diary I wrote, 'It does not show up MT very well but I wonder even at Chequers John should be so free in his condemnation.'

The pre-election planning meetings also provided the occasional glimpse of the fractured relationship. Four months before the election, on 10 January 1992, Major was at Central Office to discuss his own personal programme, a meeting which was interrupted as we heard the thud of an unsuccessful attempt to bomb Downing Street. The difficulty in our discussion came on the role of Thatcher. My view was that we needed her to declare her support quite early otherwise it would become an issue. Chris Patten agreed and suggested that this should be done at the candidates' conference at the start of the campaign. The opposition came from Major himself. Thatcher, he said, had chosen to snipe at him and to hold dinners where her comments on the

* John Major, *John Major: The Autobiography* (London: HarperCollins, 1999), p. 200.

inadequacies of the government found their way into the press. 'It was not what I wanted,' he continued. 'I am inclined not to give her a role.' My counter-argument, as the only person at the meeting who was not in one way or another employed by Major, was that it was vital that the two should at least appear to be together for the duration of the campaign and after more discussion Major reluctantly agreed – 'I suppose you are right.' I noted in my diary, 'There is no doubt how deep and genuine is his resentment about the way she has behaved since leaving Downing Street.'

Major felt quite simply that Thatcher had consistently briefed against him. She may have supported him in the leadership contest but it became crystal clear within months if not weeks that this had been on the basis that he was the only candidate who could beat Heseltine. Soon afterwards she became one of Major's most influential critics, telling politicians and journalists who visited her at home about the defects of the new administration. She complained of the failure to control spending, she characterised the administration as a government without beliefs and, of course, she complained of the new more constructive stance towards Europe. Douglas Hurd, having listened with increasing impatience to this familiar series of complaints, once asked her why then she had supported Major for the leadership. 'He was the best of a *very* poor bunch,'[*] she replied, forgetting that the third candidate in the leadership contest had been Hurd himself – but also ignoring her own action in promoting Major to the two highest posts in the government outside No. 10.

After Major's 1992 victory she became even more outspoken and personally confrontational to her successor. In an important defining article she wrote for the American magazine *Newsweek* only two weeks after the election she used phrases that she must have realised would be picked up in the British press and would anger her successor. She said bluntly, 'I don't accept the idea that all of a sudden Major is his own man. He hasn't been prime minister for seventeen months and he has inherited all these great achievements of the past eleven and a half years.' She added the quotable sentence: 'There isn't such a thing as Majorism,' before qualifying it with the thought

[*] Douglas Hurd, *Memoirs* (London: Little, Brown, 2003), p. 404.

that it was too early for such descriptions. However, this did not prevent her from asserting a few paragraphs later that 'Thatcherism will live. It will live long after Thatcher has died.'

But perhaps the most directly damaging part of the article came when she observed, 'There is a line of analysis that says Mr Major synthesises the best of the "wet" with the best of the "dry" and forges a new consensus for Conservative Britain. But consensus is the absence of principle and the presence of expediency.'

A few weeks later, on Sunday 10 May, I travelled to Huntingdon for the announcement that I was to take over from Patten as party chairman. At lunch afterwards I raised the prospect of bridge building with the former prime minister. 'It would be a waste of time,' Major replied bleakly.

In October 1992 she published an article in the *European* attacking the Maastricht settlement but timing the attack for maximum damage in the middle of what by any standards was always going to be a difficult party conference. At the election the party manifesto had said that Maastricht had been 'a success both for Britain and for the rest of Europe'. Now the former leader explicitly raised the standard of rebellion against her successor. The Maastricht straitjacket 'would be ruinous', she said. 'I cannot support the ratification of the Maastricht treaty.'

When it comes to the lengthy and fraught passage of the Maastricht bill through Parliament, Major is in no doubt about Thatcher's role. He says that shortly after the Danish referendum vote, which narrowly rejected Maastricht and was a crucial stage in encouraging the Conservative rebellion, she began urging Tory backbenchers to oppose the government and defeat the treaty. Newly elected members were invited to see her so that she could persuade them to vote against. Major comments with feeling, 'It was a unique occurrence in our party's history: a former prime minister openly encouraging backbenchers in her own party, many of whom revered her, to overturn the policy of her successor – a policy that had been a manifesto commitment in an election held less than six months before.'*

* John Major, *John Major: The Autobiography* (London: HarperCollins, 1999), p. 350.

By the 1993 party conference all bridges were down. My view as party chairman was that even then, and in spite of all the difficulty she caused out of power, we should recognise that she had been a formidable leader. I wanted to change the process whereby she was almost smuggled into the conference like some discredited relative and then encouraged to leave again as quickly as possible. At Blackpool I planned to invite her to dinner together with Cabinet ministers such as John Wakeham and John Gummer, on the night before she was to appear at the conference. It led to one of the few rows I had with Major, who clearly thought that his party chairman should have nothing to do with hopeless peace missions of this kind. His suite was cleared so that he could personally give me his views on my tactics of reconciliation. My diary records something of the atmosphere:

> John's message is that it 'won't do'. He doesn't agree with how I am handling Margaret. He doesn't feel that she should have been made welcome. He doesn't feel that she should have been asked to fund-raise and he doesn't feel that she should have been asked to dinner.
>
> My reply to all this is that he does not seem to understand that the conference is going much better than we might have hoped, that the party is coming together and that part of the reason for this success is the silencing of the rebels because of the way we are handling Margaret. Well, he says, he is not going anywhere near her on the platform. My reply is that he should at least pat her on the shoulder as he goes past or shake hands. A friendly peck is quite obviously a bridge too far.

In fact, when it came to the conference the next day, he did kiss her on the cheek – much to the delight of the photographers. Fortunately his displays of ill temper were short lived.

As for the dinner itself, we were all reminded of the old style when Thatcher rounded on Gummer, who had rather unwisely led the discussion onto Bosnia. 'John,' she said, 'you are wrong. I am not going to continue arguing it. Just understand you are wrong.' I readily concede that the dinner did not restore relations – although I am told that when I was called away to be dressed down by Major, Fiona did wonders in the handling of the former prime minister, now in full flow.

This had not been my only effort to repair relations. A few weeks before the conference I had visited Thatcher at her then home in Chesham Place, Belgravia. As usual she was the model of courtesy about small things like ordering coffee – and outspoken on big things like the economy. My diary again takes up the story:

Friday 10 September 1993. She makes no attempt to disguise the fact that she believes the management of both the economy and the government to be shambolic. 'How have we reached this position?' she asks rhetorically. I let her speak on without interrupting and then ask, 'Have you put this to John? Do you see him?'

I think I detect – I cannot be sure – a flicker of sadness in her face. 'No, we don't meet at all these days.'

'Would you like me to get such meetings arranged?'

'No,' she says quickly. 'He doesn't want people peering over his shoulder.'

'What about Ken Clarke?' I persist.

'No, Norman. I am happy to see you but...' She leaves the sentence unfinished. 'I am not sure Ken wants advice. He doesn't lack self-confidence... I think you would have done better putting in Michael Howard as chancellor.'

On one point, however, she was more conciliatory. 'We cannot have a fresh leadership election, that would be ridiculous,' she said. My diary comment was: 'My guess would be that she believes there is only one proper heir and that is Michael Portillo. He needs time to challenge yet.' Major's own view, as set out in his autobiography, was that 'by the early autumn of 1993 she was telling friends that she hoped for a leadership contest a year before the next general election and for Michael Portillo to win it'.[*]

In truth the relations between Major and Thatcher were a nightmare. There was not the slightest prospect of them kissing and making up. She continued to hold forth on the inadequacies of the leader she had chosen; and as long as she did this he refused point blank to attempt to mend the rift.

[*] John Major, *John Major: The Autobiography* (London: HarperCollins, 1999), p. 351.

Of course there were other prominent Conservatives who also attacked Major. They included some who had fought hardest for the Thatcher revolution and by the same measure could see their achievement put at risk by a Labour government. The most prominent was Norman Tebbit, who, following Jim Prior, had been instrumental in reforming trade union law. His many public criticisms of Major included the one which begged every question in the book. He was fond of saying that Major took over with a majority of more than 100 and left with a majority against him of more than 170. It never appeared to occur to him that his own efforts just might have had some influence on that outcome. Another influential critic after 1992 was Ken Baker, who as party chairman a few years earlier had directed Henry V's rousing speech at Agincourt at any doubters in the ministerial ranks: 'He who has no stomach for the fight, let him depart now.' While Norman Lamont, once Major's campaign manager for the leadership, became seven years later one of John Redwood's most prominent supporters seeking to defeat him. As Virginia Bottomley once said to me, 'the people who ended up defending Major were often the people who had not voted for him'.

The irony was that in human terms Thatcher knew better than anyone how disruptive the opposition of a predecessor could be – particularly in the early years. She may not have been as strident a critic of Major as Ted Heath had been of her but she was infinitely more influential. Conservatives regarded her as a political giant so when she spoke other Tory politicians, editors and leader writers listened and many followed. She would provide the argument and often she would provide the backbone for Conservative backbenchers to continue the fight. She could have helped her successor immensely but instead she helped to make the years following his 1992 election victory some of the most tumultuous in the history of the Conservative Party. So why did she do it?

In part it went back to the leadership election. She had been removed from power in an abrupt, even savage, way. She did not accept that with different tactics she could have won the leadership election. In the aftermath of her fall she was obsessed with plots against her and perceived disloyalty. She never accepted that a significant number of MPs had suppressed their own doubts and through loyalty and admiration for her achievements had voted for her.

Chris Patten and Ken Clarke were suspected of supporting the overthrow even though both had voted for her in the first round. Lamont and Michael Howard were blamed for preparing Major's campaign too early, although as my experience shows a campaign manager had not been appointed even on the very eve of her fall. Most of the Cabinet were not forgiven because, when asked, they had advised her honestly that she might not win if she remained a candidate in the second round of voting. Those of us who had voted for Michael Heseltine on the second ballot when she was no longer a candidate were regarded by her, and some others in the party, as if we were partly responsible for her downfall.

There were even suspicions, fanned by one or two of her close friends, that Major had avoided defending her in her hour of need. The charge was that he had left the field of battle in the weekend before polling, so avoiding a television defence of the prime minister. (Thatcher herself, it might be remembered, was out of the country altogether.) Major's explanation that he was having a long-arranged wisdom tooth operation was rejected as inadequate. The charge was later made explicit by one of the leading members of her court in exile, Lord McAlpine. A bizarre addition to the charge was later made by one or two others. Doubts were voiced that Major had ever had the wisdom tooth operation. It is a suspicion still expressed over fifteen years later by some die-hard supporters.

I cannot claim to have been at the operation but by chance I was with Major in his room in the Commons when Bernard Ingham rang through to ask him to appear. He replied that the operation had been long planned and the diary cleared. There was no long discussion; no appeal for him to postpone the operation. The explanation was accepted. As for the leadership battle, I remember that we watched the results of an opinion poll on television which showed that although Heseltine was well in the lead with the public as Thatcher's successor, Major was ahead of the longer-established Douglas Hurd. When the discussion turned to the election itself I proffered the unasked-for advice that he should keep out of it. Major's only response mirrored the attitude of most of the Cabinet. 'I don't want Heseltine,' he said. Not once did he mention a campaign of his own or offer any invitation to be campaign manager. It would have been amazing if senior Cabinet members were not watching the evolving scene carefully – but to be frank the Cabinet behaved with a correctness not shown by all members of Heath's shadow Cabinet as they plotted in 1975 to depose the then leader.

But Thatcher's swift change of heart on Major was more than a personal reaction to her defeat. She was horrified when the new prime minister decided to restore Heseltine to the government; her horror turned to anger when it became clear what his chief task was to be. It was bad enough that the 'assassin' was being brought back into the Cabinet but to add to the provocation he was also being given the task of replacing the poll tax, which once had been her flagship policy. Yet from Major's perspective the recall of Heseltine was inevitable. He may have been defeated but even so he had been supported by 132 Tory MPs. Wounds now had to be healed. It was an obvious piece of politics to bring him back into the fold – just as Thatcher herself had given shadow Cabinet places to Willie Whitelaw, Geoffrey Howe, Jim Prior and John Peyton, who had stood against her in the 1975 leadership election. As for the poll tax it had been one of the main causes of the Conservative slump in the polls. It needed to be replaced and Heseltine, a leading critic of the tax, was better placed than most to come up with a replacement – although some saw his appointment to the Environment Department as more of a poisoned chalice than a spectacular comeback.

Another entirely different theory to explain the breakdown in relations is that Thatcher had believed that Major was an unqualified supporter of her policies and shared all her attitudes. She had been deceived, so the theory goes, and only discovered later that he was not quite 'one of us'. If they were her feelings then she was one of the few who thought that way. Major, after all, was the chancellor who took us into the Exchange Rate Mechanism. His manner was courteous, not confrontational. His liberal views on social policy, as she well knew, were never her own. When, surprisingly, he was appointed foreign secretary I wrote in my diary that night, 'It is a spectacular promotion for

John. I am delighted. He is one of the good men in politics. Sound in judgement and sound instincts. I suppose that means we agree on most things.' Politicians like me regarded him as a one-nation Conservative with mildly pro-European views. He was a loyal minister but few Tory MPs ever regarded him as the most obvious ideological successor to Thatcher.

Nor is there any evidence that Major wanted an early change of leadership. When Heseltine mounted his challenge he was forced to decide whether to enter the race or not, but in an ideal world Major would have had time to play himself in and prove himself at the Treasury. Then – and only then – would he have thought seriously of the next step. His assumption when he became chancellor was that he would be in the job until the general election and that Thatcher would lead the party into that election. He was entirely content with that scenario.

One of Thatcher's own defences of her later actions was that even former prime ministers were entitled to put their views. It is a rather more debatable proposition than it sounds. Harold Macmillan waited more than twenty years before publicly criticising the Thatcher policy of privatisation, which he characterised as 'selling the family silver'. Churchill, Eden, Douglas-Home never publicly attacked their successors. Major has notably avoided critical comment of any of the four party leaders who have followed him. Heath was the post-war exception to the rule and for the same reasons as Thatcher. Both were bitter about the manner of their departure; neither was ready to leave the public stage; and both felt that policy on Europe was of fundamental importance.

By choosing the European issue as his resignation cause Howe had at the same time handed Thatcher the perfect explanation for her defeat. She had not been defeated by the public: 'I never lost an election,' she was fond of telling uncritical American audiences years later. She had been defeated by politicians such as Heseltine and Howe, who were only marginally preferable to the favourite European hate figure of the time, Jacques Delors. She now intended to pick up the gauntlet. One way she could make sense of her new position was to fight back on that very European issue. The contest was not over.

In July 1991, eighteen months after her defeat, Thatcher announced that she was to leave the House of Commons. In the division lobby soon after the statement was made she was surrounded by Conservative MPs wanting to offer their regrets. Understandably enough she was on autopilot that afternoon, not responding directly to the MPs she was leaving. When I talked to her, however, she made one point with extreme clarity: she was determined 'to continue fighting' on the European issue. My diary comment was, 'This is bad news politically but even sadder in personal terms. Her belief appears to be in some kind of North Atlantic free trade area. But NAFTA is where we were twenty or thirty years ago. The caravan has moved on.' (*Tuesday 2 July 1991.*)

Nevertheless in the European fight, if not the NAFTA alternative, she was aided by a new generation of Conservative MPs who had arrived at Westminster following the 1992 election. Some of the old knights of the shires and suburbs – the men who had cheered Major on his return from Maastricht – had retired. The old and the bold were replaced by new and mainly young members such as Iain Duncan Smith, Bernard Jenkin and John Whittingdale, who not only agreed with Thatcher on Europe but were prepared to vote against the government in the division lobbies – or at least abstain.

If only it had been possible to put through the Maastricht legislation before the 1992 election then much of the later mayhem could have been avoided. As it was, Major's low majority made it a near-impossible hand to play as the Tory party plunged itself into a bitter and divisive civil war on Europe. Thatcher with her immense authority and reputation helped sustain the battle, which led inevitably to a further conflict of loyalties for the party's MPs. You could not support both the old and the new leader. They were on divergent paths. I had supported Thatcher in the 1970s and 1980s but turned away from her in the 1990s.

7

Smith Square (1992–4)

'We reveal from where we obtain almost every penny that we receive.'
Margaret Beckett, deputy Labour Party leader, House of Commons,
22 June 1993.

There had been a time when the Conservative Party organisation was without equal. In the 1950s it had been a formidable machine compared to what Harold Wilson had described as Labour's 'penny-farthing'.* Membership was strong, the Young Conservatives dwarfed the youth groups of the other parties and, above all, there were professional agents in virtually all the strong and marginal seats. My first serious party job was as a paid 'missioner' back in 1959, when during a university vacation three of us were drafted into the Labour marginal of Clapham, where we typically sought to persuade old ladies without cars to apply for postal votes. The exercise was so successful that come the election the slightly unlikely figure of Alan Glyn triumphed with a majority of more than 1,800 in what was then a run-down inner city constituency. By the time I became party chairman in May 1992 those days of smooth, well-financed organisation were long, long gone.

I needed only a few days at my office in the party headquarters to understand one central point: by normal commercial standards we were bust. Chris Patten, who after his defeat at Bath was now preparing to take up his post as governor of Hong Kong, estimated that we were in debt to the tune of £15 million. In fact when all the bills were collected and the numbers added up the true figure was nearer £20 million. Our only asset was the

* Philip Ziegler, *Wilson: The Authorised Life of Lord Wilson of Rievaulx* (London: Weidenfeld & Nicolson, 1993), p. 107.

headquarters building itself at 32 Smith Square, a short distance from Parliament. At this time the commercial property market was in the doldrums and an optimistic valuation was only £7 million.

As for income, I was shown graphs that dramatically illustrated how after every election since the Second World War it had dropped steeply away and did not recover until there was the prospect of a new contest. Sadly for us the post–election honeymoon in 1992 ended more quickly than any in living memory. Had we been a regular company we would have been in danger of being prosecuted for trading while insolvent. We were able to continue because of the forbearance of the banks, in particular the Royal Bank of Scotland, which was our major creditor. Even so, six months later as Christmas approached we faced the indignity of being pressed for an overdue national insurance bill. Maurice Saatchi, whose company was also owed money, commented, 'My God, they have left you a mess.'

A good organisation by itself cannot win elections but a bankrupt organisation is a party leader's worst nightmare. It means that you simply cannot afford to take all the actions that you know are needed. In the parliamentary boundary review then taking place, for example, I would have dearly liked to employ professional lawyers to argue our case at some of the inquiries. As it was, the exercise was conducted on a shoestring and was hampered by some strong local associations with big majorities refusing to cede territory to marginal neighbours, even though the result would have been extra Conservative seats. Even worse, in the 1994 European election we could not afford any serious national advertising – and yet the result of that election would determine the very continuance of John Major as prime minister.

So how had the Tory Party got into this incredible position? It was the oldest story in the book. While Conservative ministers toured the country preaching prudence and restraint we had consistently spent over our income. The usual excuse was that we would 'rather be a couple of million in debt than lose the election'. The truth was that none of the big pieces of spending which accounted substantially for our overdraft added one jot to the winning of elections. There was no relationship one with the other.

Like much else the rot started in 1987. It did not help that there were two campaigns being run. Norman Tebbit was the party chairman but he had to contend with an alternative campaign being run by Lord Young, who had never fought an election before but who answered directly to the prime minister. Matching Margaret Thatcher's panic at the way the opinion polls had turned down in the penultimate week of the election, Young ordered an extravagant £3 million newspaper advertising campaign. In truth the 1987 election was already won. The newspaper campaign was the equivalent of burning £50 notes.

The next extravagance was to build a conference hall inside Central Office at a cost of £4 million. This followed complaints from Thatcher about the cramped conditions in the 1987 election, but never at any stage was the money there to back the cost. It would have been substantially cheaper to hire a room at the Savoy Hotel when it was needed, not to mention the nearby Church House. Another error was to buy the next-door building, 34 Smith Square, from a grateful Thames Water Authority – and then, as my architectural advisers told me, to join it to No. 32 in such a way that it was both difficult and expensive to take them apart. The only place where there was no extravagance was in payments to the loyal permanent staff who had laboured in Smith Square for year after year.

So that was the black hole. You did not need much financial skill to see what had to be done. We tried to bring in money by a special appeal but that only established the truth of all past experience – that fund raising after an election was easier said than done. The only alternative was to cut costs. My first economy was Shaun Woodward, the director of communications, who at £70,000 a year was the highest-paid man at Central Office. He had been recruited by Chris Patten, who had a high opinion of him. It was not a view I altogether shared. When Woodward finally departed to join Labour some newspapers gave him the credit for the 1992 campaign. That was greeted with incredulity by all those who were in any way close to the campaign. His 'Meet John Major' events had been a failure and at Central Office there was a lack of direction and authority.

In insisting on cost reductions I was in a strong position. I was a voluntary unpaid chairman – albeit an MP with a number of outside interests. My only request was for a driver to take me to the constituencies but he also went in the economy cuts. Paul Judge, whom I recruited as the party's director general, was even less fortunate. He was offered a salary but, having seen the state of the finances, worked for nothing.

Changing Central Office was not just about getting the costs down; it was also about tackling its utterly extraordinary financial structure. Basically the position was that the treasurers of the party – Sir Hector Laing and Lord Beaverbrook – were responsible for raising income, while the chairman of the party – alone and unfettered by anything like a board of directors, which you would find in any half-decent company – was responsible for spending. No one, not even the chairman, was able to look at both sides of the accounts. The theory was that the treasurers answered directly to the party leader – in this case the prime minister himself. The other side of the coin was that it meant that anything that ever went wrong with fund raising could be placed smack at the door of John Major.

A prime example of the utter crassness of this divided system came a few months after I joined, in November 1992. It was a case that dated back to before the general election when the chancellor of the exchequer, Norman Lamont, had employed an expensive firm of solicitors to guard his interests after a newspaper article. The *News of the World* had reported that the Lamonts, having now moved to 11 Downing Street, had let the basement of their house to a woman who described herself as a sex therapist but was promptly christened by the press as 'Miss Whiplash'.

The case was a 24-hour wonder. Self-evidently no blame rested on Lamont. Nevertheless he believed, oddly but genuinely, that he was open to media criticism and even that he might be taunted with living on immoral earnings. The legal bill that eventually resulted from guarding his interests was for more than £20,000. The press discovered the bill and particularly that £4,000 of it had been picked up by the Treasury. Was this a proper use of taxpayers' money, they asked. To me the more important issue was the part that the party had played. Apparently at one stage the Treasury (on the basis that it affected Lamont as chancellor, not as a party MP) had agreed to pay the entire bill. Only later did they reduce their offer and it was at this stage that the party agreed to fund the difference. Personally I did not believe that it was up to Central Office to fund private spending of this kind but that was academic: the decision had been made months earlier. The issue now was how to counter the inevitable charge that the proceeds of constituency coffee mornings were being used to help out the chancellor.

Initially I was confident that we had a reply. Inside Central Office I was told that the bill had been paid by an individual donor. That seemed to settle the matter. But as no one oversaw both sides of the accounts no one could be totally certain. Further investigation revealed that the bill certainly had been paid by Central Office but there had been no individual donation to cover it. Ultimately I persuaded a party donor that a part of his donation should be earmarked retrospectively for the bill. No one could remotely pretend that it was a satisfactory position. We had become not only a lender of last resort but also a giver. I should emphasise that Lamont knew nothing of the financial arrangements other than that the bill was going to be covered by an individual donation. The criticism was not of Lamont. The criticism was of the fundamentally flawed financial organisation that we had at Central Office.

Reforming the organisation required changes in both structure and people. As far as structure was concerned, I was convinced that what we needed was the equivalent of a company board of directors. In that I was strongly backed by Basil Feldman, the chairman of the National Union, the body representing all the constituency associations, which quite rightly wanted a bigger input. The result was that we set up a board of directors – the first board in the history of the Conservative Party – which amongst other things checked spending. No longer would it be possible for major building works at Central Office to be approved by the chairman alone. Although one of my successors, Brian Mawhinney, was not a fan of this system I was glad to see that when Archie Norman, the former chairman of Asda, was asked to look at the structure of Central Office he also came to substantially the same conclusion and the board structure is now well established. Financial responsibility has become the responsibility of the chairman and the board, not the leader of the party and the treasurers. Given the perils of party funding I make no claim that the new system is utterly foolproof or, more to the point, totally crookproof. No party can ever totally guarantee that. I would claim, however, that it provides substantially more protection for the party and the public than what went before.

As for the people at Central Office, Laing was coming up to retirement, having valiantly tried to make the party's income equal its spending ambitions, and I persuaded Charles Hambro to take his place. At that stage to have a treasurer with the name of a bank was perhaps more than we deserved. The second treasurer, Beaverbrook, posed greater problems because of his own rocky financial position. In October 1992 he was banned from sitting in the House of Lords because he had declared himself bankrupt. To have a party treasurer going bankrupt was just about all we needed at the time but the damage was largely averted by Beaverbrook agreeing to resign several months before the announcement was made.

Eventually the party's debt began to come down but that was not remotely the end of the party's problems. With spectacular irony, given later developments, the Labour leadership started a virulent campaign attacking all Conservative Party donors. The justification for the campaign was the case of Asil Nadir. I had never met Nadir but there was no question that through his companies he had financially supported the Conservative Party in the Thatcher years of the middle and late 1980s. At the time his flagship company, Polly Peck, had been a darling of the stock exchange but that position changed dramatically when the company went bankrupt and Nadir fled to Northern Cyprus. The campaign then became more general. Who were the donors to the Conservative Party? How could we be sure they were not criminals? How could we be sure they were not buying influence? How could we be sure they were not buying honours? The questions became more and more frequent – as did the allegations.

In June 1993 there was a torrid debate in the Commons which plumbed new depths in hysteria.* A Labour backbencher, Clive

---

* House of Commons debate, 22 June 1993. See Hansard, HC Deb, vol. 227, cols 175ff.

Soley (now a Labour peer), used parliamentary privilege to intervene in another backbencher's speech. He said that he had received a letter from 'someone whom I know and in whom I have some confidence' alleging that Michael Heseltine had met with a member of the Saudi Arabian royal family to raise money for the Conservative Party. It was all utter nonsense and I said so on television. Soley's response was to threaten me with a defamation action together with a number of newspapers which had reported my response. Months later he withdrew his charge on the floor of the Commons in a personal statement, which by convenient tradition cannot be questioned. I heard no more about the libel action.

At the time Labour politicians lined up to condemn the Conservatives and make extravagant claims about their own party's position. Probably the most comprehensive was the claim of Labour's deputy leader, Margaret Beckett. In the same Commons debate she assured the House that in contrast to the secretive Tories 'we reveal from where we obtain almost every single penny that we receive'. Up to a point, Lord Copper. In the last few years a major donation was made to the Labour Party using the names of third parties rather than the donor; a Cabinet minister, Peter Hain, was forced into resignation after admitting that £103,000 of donations to his deputy leadership bid were not declared to the Electoral Commission; and the unfortunate party treasurer, Jack Dromey, confessed ignorance to loans totalling millions of pounds made to Labour in the run-up to the 2005 general election. Some of the questions that used to be directed at the Conservative Party have now been put firmly to Labour. How have they raised their money? Has influence been ceded? Have rewards been offered?

The cash-for-peerages allegations were a case in point. They showed the labyrinth that politicians and fund raisers can enter. Getting a peerage has always been something of a lottery. In practice the decision has rested with the prime minister, with the other political leaders having the right to put forward a limited number of nominations of their own. But government and opposition leaders are firmly based in the Commons and have been brought up in a place which does not take the House of

Lords particularly seriously. Periodically they visit the Lords to congratulate their team on its performance but it signifies very little. The only time they become fully engaged is when the Lords defeats a cherished piece of legislation. At that point all kinds of dire threats are uttered – publicly by Labour prime ministers and privately by Conservative ones.

The view from Downing Street is that power rests with the Commons and should not be challenged. My diary records a conversation at a Downing Street lunch in 1988 when Margaret Thatcher complained of the prospect of the Lords changing the community charge legislation. 'If this takes place then we will have to change the House of Lords. She particularly does not like the position where former Conservative ministers transfer to the House of Lords and then take on a new independence.' (*Monday 9 May 1988.*)

At a Cabinet meeting at the beginning of 1989 she responded angrily to another setback in the Lords:

> We have been defeated in the Lords on football identity cards, leading MT to ask more or less rhetorically, 'What's happened to all those peers I have made?' MT, who is no lover of the Lords, adds that we should consider making peers for one parliament. No one takes her up on this – indeed it is not intended for debate. It is intended to demonstrate to the unfortunate John Belstead (leader of the Lords) that she means to brook no nonsense from the peers on this subject. (*Thursday 23 February 1989.*)

As for MPs generally, most have not the faintest idea how the Lords works and are interested even less. It is against this background that decisions on peerages have been made.

There are some guiding rules such as the one I benefited from, which says that most former Cabinet ministers who want to will go to the red benches. 'It comes with the rations,' as Roy Hattersley once scathingly put it. But a place in the Cabinet is not the only way of securing political advancement – if that is what it is – to the Lords. Tony Blair specialised in moving long-serving MPs out of their elected constituency seats so that up-and-coming younger men and women could be given safe berths. The Liberal Democrats have promoted to the Lords former MPs who have crossed the floor to join them in front of more deserving long-standing party members. As for the party managers, they all want peers who will turn up, wait around, follow the party line and vote. They place reliability firmly ahead of any other quality including outside distinction.

It should be added that politicians are not the only group to have benefited over the years. The most notable have been the press barons, who have been rewarded because of their selfless service to the newspaper industry – although some cynics harbour the doubtless unjustified belief that the honours may have been given in hope of political support. Of course, not all proprietors are ennobled. Conrad Black was turned down by John Major – although later accepted by Tony Blair on the recommendation of William Hague – and the biggest newspaper proprietor of them all, Rupert Murdoch, as an American citizen does not qualify and probably would not accept in any event.

A hundred years ago another press baron, Lord Northcliffe, then Alfred Harmsworth, half-jested that 'when I want a peerage, I shall buy one, like an honest man'. At that time, especially under the Liberal prime minister David Lloyd George, the selling of honours was rife. In the 1993 debate on party funding the Liberal Democrat MP Archy Kirkwood described the situation as it was then: 'The last time the Liberal Party was in a position to deploy honours we were open about it. We had price lists. There were price tags on honours.'* That path was legally closed in 1925 when the Honours (Prevention of Abuses) Act made such transactions a criminal offence – and rightly so.

For the donor is not just getting a title which may or may not be useful in booking a good table in a restaurant – he is being enabled to take part in the legislative process itself. He can vote on any bill which comes before the house. He can defeat government legislation. He can hold up measures which the elected house has decided are important. Not even the Americans – who take fund raising to lengths so far unseen in this country – offer that kind of prize to the big donor.

In my time at Central Office we had many problems but this was

---

* Hansard, HC Deb, 22 June 1993, vol. 227, col. 212.

not one of them. As all who knew Major will confirm, he was deeply cautious about honours going to anyone who could be portrayed as just a contributor. If they were actually treasurers of the party – like Charles Hambro – and therefore working for the party they might just pass his scrutiny. Otherwise there was no chance of preferment. He wanted men and women who were rated high in the outside world or people who had unquestionably worked hard politically for the party, preferably women. In the first award of honours after I became chairman only one life peer was created, Shirley Williams, and consistently throughout his premiership Major appointed many fewer than Blair. Thatcher had created even fewer.

In defence of contributors it should be added that not all want honours and others believe that a political donation will harm not help them. I remember trying to recruit one man to help in our fund raising. He had a perfectly legitimate ambition to be a peer, not as repayment for any political gift but because of his generosity and work for voluntary bodies, which had been formidable. His concern was that being seen as a party contributor might entirely torpedo his ambitions.

In 1993 these subtleties were utterly ignored in the hysterical debate. I would be less than human if I did not take some wry amusement at the way that the very issue Labour exploited without conscience came back to bite them. Nor do the Liberal Democrats emerge entirely spotless, in spite of some of their more sancti-monious statements. Paddy Ashdown's diaries tell of a financial chaos which threatened the party with bankruptcy; while not all their contributors would pass muster before any self-respecting standards body. The biggest contributor to the party before the 2005 election was a businessman based in Spain, Michael Brown, who donated £2.4 million. In September 2006 Brown was jailed for two years after he admitted committing perjury and making a false declaration to obtain a passport. To date the Liberal Democrats have refused to repay the money – even though in the Asil Nadir case they were prominent in pressing the Conservatives to repay 'that money into court forthwith'.*

So perhaps rather than fighting old wars we should recognise

---

* Hansard, HC Deb, 22 June 1993, vol. 227, col. 212.

that all parties face very much the same problem of how to raise money without ceding influence or handing over unjustified rewards. The question is: what rules should be laid down to try to bring this about? Back in 1993 my case was that voluntary contributions should be allowed and that it would be strange in a free society to ban people's right to give whatever they liked to whatever cause they wanted. With the benefit of experience over the last few years I would change that evidence. I think there is everything to be said for voluntary contributions at the local level, everything to be said for having thriving autonomous local associations. One of the fundamental problems of the Conservative Party over the last thirty years is that they lost sight of this deeply obvious point. In government party leaders tend to take little interest in the party organisation until they reach election time. Then they ask for the whole machine to be cranked up in the expectation that it can be turned off again once the election is over and they can return to their proper business of running the country. Mirroring such attitudes, local associations hire agents for a few months before general elections and then swiftly make them redundant in the aftermath. So I would allow and encourage fund raising at the local level but with limits on what any one contributor could give, to prevent undue influence.

Fund raising at the national level poses bigger issues. For one thing the contributions can go into hundreds of thousands of pounds or even millions. Here the freedom to give can easily slip into buying influence. It is the case against massive trade union donations decided by union leaders as opposed to contributions decided on by individual union members. But concern should not just be centred on the unions. It is no healthier to have individual contributors signing cheques for several million pounds. There is an obvious risk that the donor wants some policy return for his money. The point was addressed by one of the Conservative Party's big donors, Stuart Wheeler, in a BBC interview in December 2007. Wheeler made it clear that he was neither seeking an honour nor any change in policy. He was, however, entitled to have his views listened to 'more than the man in the street'.* The difficulty with that argument is that the man in the street may be the councillor who has worked hard for the party for the last twenty-five years or the constituency chairman, who has the best of all views of the feeling in his local party.

In March 2007 the government published a review of party funding carried out by Sir Hayden Phillips.[†] When the review was announced I was suspicious. Phillips had been a senior civil servant and I had always thought that the first rule of being a civil servant was to have nothing to do with party politics. I imagined that his knowledge would be limited and unless he was careful he would end up producing the report that the government wanted. My suspicions were unjustified. The review was unquestionably independent, as could be judged by the party reactions. The Conservatives accepted the proposal for a £50,000 limit on any contribution from any individual or any organisation but were much less enthusiastic about a cap on total spending – although given my experience I cannot imagine why. Labour immediately accepted a limit on spending but rejected the proposed limit on contributions. Their fear is that if trade union members are given a real choice on whether or not they want to make a voluntary contribution to Labour then party income will fall badly.

In my view neither of these objections should hold up a settlement. There is little to be said for further escalation of the party spending war, which Conservatives might reflect does not always benefit them in any event. Equally, Labour objections to changing the union levy system are bogus. They might have had a strong case in 1908 – when, as Matthew Parris has pointed out, Labour was the political wing of the union movement[††] – but surely not a century later. As for reforming the appointments process to the House of Lords, it would be perfectly possible to take away the prime minister's power of patronage and to transfer all responsibility for nominations to an entirely independent

[*] Interview with Nick Robinson, *Cash for Politics*, BBC Radio 4, 22 December 2007.

[†] *Strengthening Democracy: Fair and Sustainable Funding of Political Parties* (HMSO, 2007).

[††] Matthew Parris, 'The union booby trap at the door of No. 10', *Times*, 8 December 2007.

committee. It would be an important step forward – provided it is recognised that it does not provide the answer to cash for honours. There are many honours and rewards that can be offered other than a place on the red benches.

Perhaps Phillips's report will prove to be the event which forces comprehensive reform. If it does I for one will applaud loudly. My fear is, however, that the government will come forward with proposals that are partial in both senses of the word. They will be incomplete and they will favour the government. If that is the case we will just wait for the next scandal.

Given all that I have described in the previous paragraphs, a reasonable question might be: what on earth persuaded me to come back to take on the chairmanship of a political party? It was a question that, ten years after his forced departure from Downing Street, John Major put to me over lunch at a West End restaurant. I told him of this book, which I had almost finished writing, and our conversation switched back to the 1990s. 'Tell me,' asked Major, 'why did you agree to go to Smith Square?' It was as if he felt a responsibility, even guilt, in drawing me into the bitterest period of political strife inside the Conservative Party since the 1930s struggle on appeasement.

I could have answered that it did not look like that when I accepted the job just after the 1992 election. None of us realised at the time quite how profoundly Conservative politics was about to change. Tim Collins, who I persuaded to become the party's new director of communications, was at first reluctant to accept on the grounds that the post-election period would be too serene and unexciting. He should not have worried. He spent the next years working round the clock heroically defending the party and the government in crisis after crisis.

In truth, even had I known the problems we were about to encounter I would still have accepted. As Fiona said with some resignation, once I was immersed again in national politics I would want to continue. For better or worse my first (occupational) love has been politics. I had always harboured an ambition to be party chairman and my time with Major during the election had served to strengthen that. He was a good man to work for. There is an obvious risk of tensions between party leader and party chairman but I thought that, whatever else might happen, this would not be a problem – and in the main I was right. We had our disagreements – it would have been amazing and unhealthy had we not – but our relations stayed good even in the worst hours.

For me, being party chairman also had one substantial personal advantage. It could be done outside government. I had absolutely no desire to return to government and race badly briefed from Cabinet committee to Cabinet committee. Outside government I could not only remain chairman of the Birmingham Post group of newspapers but devote myself to what I regarded as the most urgent task of clearing up the financial and organisational nightmare that Central Office had become. It seemed to me that what the party needed was a chairman who had the freedom and the time to devote to this task. For a few months it seemed that I would be allowed to work relatively undisturbed doing just that. But inside or outside government no chairman can divorce himself from day-to-day politics. Suddenly in the autumn of 1992 we were up to our necks in pure crisis politics.

The first years of the new Thatcher government were characterised by fierce public spending disputes between Cabinet ministers and the Treasury. Ministers who could not agree their budgets were taken to a 'star chamber' of other ministers (here, John Biffen *left* and Norman Tebbit) under Willie Whitelaw to decide.

After her third victory in 1987 Margaret Thatcher had unprecedented power over her Cabinet and such disputes became rare. In the carriage ride (*left to right*) Geoffrey Howe, Nigel Lawson, Douglas Hurd, Kenneth Baker, Nick Ridley, myself and Ken Clarke.

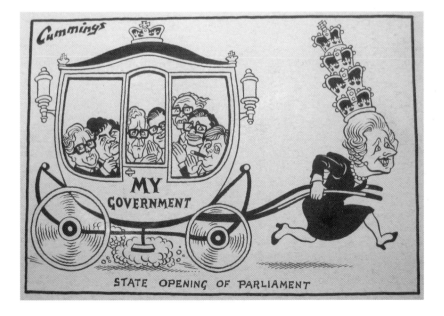

Margaret Thatcher in good times and bad. *Above* she greets well-wishers outside No. 10 following victory in the Falklands, June 1982. *Below* instead of campaigning at home in the last days of the 1990 leadership contest, she went with Douglas Hurd (*left*), the foreign secretary, to the Paris conference to mark the end of the Cold War. Here they are accompanied by President Mitterrand. (PA Photos; Peter Jordan/Time Life Pictures/Getty Images)

Demonstrations against the Thatcher government were common. Some were silent, as when the Princess of Wales came to be briefed on the work of the Department of Health and Social Security in 1984 *above*; some were violent, as in this poll tax rally in central London, March 1990 *below*. (PA Photos)

The beginning and end of John Major's administration. *Above* the newly elected leader stands with his wife Norma outside 10 Downing Street, November 1990. *Left* the prime minister campaigns on his infamous soapbox in Luton during the 1997 general election – but to no avail. (Tom Stoddart/Getty Images; David Thomson/AFP/Getty Images)

The ups and downs of 1992. *Above* With John and Norma Major, I visit a factory in the West Midlands in the last days of the general election campaign – which against all predictions the Conservatives won. *Right* the chancellor of the exchequer, Norman Lamont, leaves a Cabinet meeting in September following Britain's ejection from the ERM. Behind him are Virginia Bottomley (*left*) and Gillian Shephard. (Matthew Polak/Corbis Sygma)

The downward track. *Above* John Redwood (*front row, left*) introduces some of his supporters, including Norman Lamont (*front row, right*), in his unsuccessful attempt to depose John Major from the leadership, June 1995. *Left* Michael Portillo reacts to the news that he has lost Enfield Southgate in the 1997 general election. The victor, Stephen Twigg, stands behind him.
(*Daily Telegraph*; Kevin Lamarque/Reuters)

The aftermath. William Hague, Major's immediate successor, launches the Conservative campaign for the European elections, June 1999. Euroscepticism became a strong part of both the 2001 and the 2005 general election campaigns. (Sinead Lynch/AFP/Getty Images)

Starting the journey back from the wilderness. David Cameron celebrates victory with Edward Timpson, the Conservative candidate at the Crewe & Nantwich by-election, May 2008. (Stefan Rousseau/PA Photos)

1990. 'I have a young family': *left to right* Fiona, Isobel, Kate and myself at the time of my resignation from Margaret Thatcher's Cabinet. (PA Photos)

2008. More time with the grandchildren: *left to right* Isobel, Kate with her daughter Iris, and Fiona. (Guy Lucas)

8

'Black Autumn' (1992)

'I am very concerned about the position. I won't have any credibility with the other European leaders. I wonder if the negotiations should not be done by someone else.'

John Major, 22 September 1992.

The usual theory about the collapse of Conservative support after the 1992 election is that it was entirely the result of Britain being forced out of the Exchange Rate Mechanism and the destruction of the government's reputation for sound economic management. But from my viewpoint at Central Office that was only one part of the story. The Conservative Party could have recovered from the ERM debacle – just as the Labour government more than twenty years previously had substantially recovered from devaluing the pound – but government ministers, party grandees and a determined group of Tory backbenchers would have had to stop digging an ever-deeper political hole. This they resolutely refused to do. Crisis followed crisis, much of it self-induced, and by the end of the autumn the party's reputation was in tatters.

The government lost much more than a reputation for economic competence. The pit closure policy was seen as at best cavalier and at worst totally uncaring, while the divisions on the Maastricht settlement simply destroyed the Conservatives' reputation as a united party: at the general election only a few months earlier two thirds of the public had seen the party as a united force. The first Danish referendum, which rejected Maastricht, presented the government with a major dilemma on when the treaty should be considered by the Westminster Parliament. The promise of a fresh Danish referendum provided an easy argument for delay and the slender government majority meant that the Eurosceptics, their numbers now reinforced after the election, were in a position to defeat the government in the division lobbies if they combined with the Labour opposition. On Europe the danger was that John Major would head a minority government.

The position was further complicated by the exposed position of the prime minister himself. It had been Major who as chancellor of the exchequer in 1989 had persuaded Margaret Thatcher that Britain should enter the ERM. She had still been reluctant but she could hardly risk losing another chancellor. It had also been Major who as the new prime minister had negotiated Maastricht. On Black Wednesday Major saw one of his achievements come crashing to the ground. The question then became how to handle Maastricht. Had the French referendum rejected it then that would have settled the issue but instead, by the narrowest of margins, they voted in favour. Major was forced to defend the negotiation he had completed without the Conservative votes that were necessary to carry it through Parliament. At the time it was never fully realised just how close we came to a second Conservative prime minister being forced into resignation.

In early September 1992 the prime minister was conducting his business not from 10 Downing Street, which was having fresh security measures introduced following an earlier IRA mortar attack, but from Admiralty House, 400 yards down Whitehall. Sterling was coming under increasing pressure and was languishing at the bottom of the ERM table while the Germans were facing criticism for doing nothing to reduce that pressure. The reduction of German interest rates by a mere ¼ percentage point was seen as irrelevant and the remarks of the head of the German bank, who was arguing for a realignment of currencies (effectively devaluing sterling), had made matters worse. A further problem that autumn – a long way from the issue of the currency – was the clamour for the Cabinet minister David Mellor's head after a newspaper story that he had been having an affair.

The political handling of the government was partly the responsibility of a small committee which met on Mondays and Wednesdays (and later daily as the crises multiplied) at 12

Downing Street, the office of the chief whip, Richard Ryder. This No. 12 Committee was chaired by Ryder and its members were Tony Newton, the leader of the Commons; John Wakeham, the leader of the Lords; myself as party chairman; Sarah Hogg and Jonathan Hill from the No. 10 policy unit; and Gus O'Donnell (and later Christopher Meyer), the head of communications at No. 10. The committee had been established before the election and the idea was that we should look ahead for issues that could blow up, check on the announcements that were to be made, and provide a place of support and advice for ministers with particularly difficult situations to manage. Of us all the man who had the most difficult job was Ryder himself. He had always wanted to be chief whip. I did not always agree with every action that he took, as this chapter makes clear, but without his skill the government could have crumbled. As it was the team at 12 Downing Street had to handle an extraordinary three months of crises which almost brought down the prime minister and the foreign secretary and could very easily have led to another general election.

My diary now takes up the story. There is no better way of describing the drama, the overlapping political challenges, the pressure under which ministers were operating, and the periodic descent into shambles into which politics at times descended.

The ERM debacle

Wednesday 16 September 1992. An extraordinary day. Tim Collins and I sit down to work on my conference speeches, which are not getting the attention they deserve. We are interrupted by the news that interest rates have been increased by 2 per cent. That is bad but there is worse to come. It rapidly becomes clear that the interest rate increase is having no effect. It has not lifted sterling at all and it has hit the stock market like a sledgehammer. The news is now coming through that the chancellor in defence of the currency is to raise interest rates to 15 per cent from tomorrow morning. We are getting into catastrophe territory. A message comes through that John would like to see me at 5 p.m.

Tim Smith* drives me to Admiralty House through a vast swarm of photographers grouped around the gates. I meet Jonathan Hill in the hall and we walk into a big stateroom on the ground floor. Jonathan looks and sounds shell shocked. I soon see why. There is a special meeting of ministers going on but the prospect is that we will suspend membership of the ERM. The only briefing I have with me for my meeting goes into great detail on the benefits of the ERM and the folly of devaluation. Jonathan retreats back into the meeting saying that he hopes I will show suitable surprise when the PM tells me the decision.

About twenty minutes later I am called to the next room, which proves to be the Admiralty House dining room. The PM is in the middle of the table and facing him are Douglas Hurd, Kenneth Clarke and Michael Heseltine. Richard Ryder is on John's side of the table, as are the advisers such as Sarah Hogg. I take a place in the centre facing John which I imagine had been occupied by the chancellor. Douglas, Ken and Michael give a 'hear, hear' cheer of ironic approval when I appear. The reason soon becomes clear. I am to go on television and radio to explain the government's decision. The reason for this is that for our suspension to be official we have first to inform and meet the Monetary Committee. The Monetary Committee is not a body I have previously heard of but I gather, as the name suggests, it oversees European monetary policy. It is meeting in Brussels tonight. The theory is that until they have formally waved us goodbye no minister can really comment. Well, maybe. It does seem just a little curious to have the government's case presented by someone who has not heard the argument or been party to the decision.

John is very calm and for my benefit runs through the history of the day. There has been a 'tidal wave' of selling of sterling, he says. The pressure has come partly because of the uncertainty caused by the French referendum. But John blames most of all the Bundesbank and its president, Helmut Schlesinger. His comments last night to the effect that there should be a

---

* Party vice-chairman; stood down from Parliament after the cash-for-questions row.

realignment – that is, a devaluation of sterling – have been the immediate cause of the pressures. But these comments are obviously seen by John and the others there as just one item in a long list of complaints against the Germans.

Taking up the story again, John says that this morning interest rates were raised by 2 points but with no effect on the value of sterling. The promise of another 3-point rise had also done nothing to improve the position. A hefty whack of the reserves has already been committed. Faced with this situation, the government has four theoretical options: borrow, devalue alone, seek a general realignment of the ERM currencies or temporarily leave the ERM. Leaving the ERM and floating the pound is the only realistic option. Borrowing more is not an option; devaluing means a new battle to sustain the new value with the certainty that there will be very high interest rates; and general realignment is not in their power to deliver. So Cabinet will meet tomorrow at 9.30 to be told the decision – the decision has been taken only by those in the room. Parliament will be recalled next Thursday.

We discuss the possible presentation for a few minutes. Ken Clarke suggests that the best line on the inevitable challenge that the chancellor should resign is: 'If anyone should resign it is the president of the Bundesbank.' Ken regards the decision as totally inevitable in the circumstances and leaves us no option. Michael and Douglas also take this view, although Douglas is more subdued than the other two – doubtless because he sees his European policy badly holed.

The chancellor has left to prepare his statement. Apparently he intends to announce the decision very briefly on the steps of the Treasury but take no questions. I obviously can do nothing until the chancellor has made the announcement and John asks me to come up to the flat to see Marcus Fox, whom he has invited over. Marcus takes a gulp as John gives him the news but loyally offers to defend it on the media.

When the news comes through that the chancellor has made the announcement I prepare to leave. Up to now the PM has been remarkably cheerful. He tells Jonathan to ensure that there is a full note of the meeting that made the decision. Good or bad, it has been a 'historic day'. He thinks Margaret Thatcher should be informed and asks me whether he should do it personally. My emphatic advice is yes. With the prospect of that call coming through the reality of the outside world imposes itself. He basically now wants the room to himself so that he can talk to Margaret. She will find it very difficult to suppress her glee although it has to be remembered that she was the PM when we went into the ERM.

When I leave Admiralty House the cameramen have moved on to the Treasury to record Norman Lamont's brief statement. I return to Central Office and Tim rings both the BBC and ITN. The result is that live appearances are arranged on both the *Nine O'Clock News* and *News at Ten*. Curiously, although there has been no decision like this since Wilson and Callaghan devalued the pound back in 1967, I am not put under any real pressure. This is because the programme makers are still grappling with the implications of what has happened. It is a genuine shock. The well-prepared hostile questions have not yet been refined. Then there is the position of Labour. They urged our entry into the ERM and Gordon Brown is reduced to calling for a plan of national reconstruction with more emphasis on training. Very worthy but he is entirely silent as to what Labour would have done in the circumstances.

Thursday 17 September. The press is dire. It is a humiliating defeat for the government and the chancellor and leaves our economic policy in tatters. One or two commentators say that it is the best thing that has happened in years and will help recovery but their voices are drowned out in the general condemnation of the government.

Sunday 20 September. The French government wins the Maastricht referendum but only just. It could hardly be closer – a mere 2 per cent. It is certainly better that they have won than lost but in truth it does not really help our position. The sceptics will simply point to a divided Europe.

Tuesday 22 September. I am called to Admiralty House. I talk with Jonathan Hill as we wait for the PM. Jonathan says that the PM and everyone were very downcast on Sunday night after the French referendum but are much more chipper today.* When John arrives this is anything but my first impression. He seems tired and dispirited. He smiles but he is obviously still depressed about the position. We talk first about the Mellor affair. A libel case concerning a Palestinian lady whom he stayed with in Spain has just ended in 'farce', John tells me. For the first time I get the impression that time may be running out for David Mellor.

John says that he has had a long session with the whips. They say that (a) there is no majority support for ERM re-entry and (b) we will have the greatest difficulty in getting the Maastricht bill through. They also have reported (helpfully) that we will be in trouble if we go ahead with Maastricht – and in trouble from different quarters if we don't.

As I leave John comes with me to the lift. 'I am very concerned about the position,' he says. 'I won't have any credibility with the other European leaders. I wonder if the negotiations should not be done by someone else.'

'You mean a new leader?'

'Yes,' he says bleakly.

'That would be absurd,' I reply. 'There is no one else who could do remotely as well. The party in the country and at Westminster would think it extraordinary.'

'That's what the others say,' John says, unconvinced.

We go on talking at the lift head. His concern is that his two achievements – entry into the ERM and the Maastricht negotiation – have collapsed. He does not see how he can go back to his European colleagues, with whom a few months ago he made an agreement, and seek a new deal. I argue that he is the only man who can hold the party together on the European issue. He sees the issue as a matter of 'my integrity'.

Wednesday 23 September. A farce of a meeting at No. 12. Builders drill and hammer throughout. Gus bravely persists with his analysis of the morning's press. What this amounts to is that

---

* Had the French voted 'no' the Maastricht treaty would have fallen and the long Westminster debate would have been avoided.

yesterday's 1 per cent interest rate cut has been largely over-shadowed by the latest episode in the Mellor affair. Later Fiona and I arrive home in time to catch the last part of *Newsnight*, where David Mellor is putting up a stout defence against the irritating interruptions of Jeremy Paxman. David appears to be saying that he has no intention of resigning.

Thursday 24 September. Another dramatic day. I arrive early at Central Office. I am interrupted almost immediately by a call from Richard Ryder. He is concerned about the position of David Mellor but much more concerned about the voting position in the special economic debate this afternoon – for which Parliament has been recalled. He fears that we may have as many as eight voting against or abstaining. Added to this, the Cabinet is all over the place on policy towards the ERM and Maastricht. Richard believes that the capacity of the government to continue in its present form is now in question. He says that he is meeting with the whips at 9.45 and would like me and Marcus Fox to meet with him first and then come to the whips' meeting. We meet for ten minutes in his office in the Commons. It is a confused discussion, with two crises – Mellor and the vote – intermingling with each other. Our minds, however, are concentrated when David Mellor himself comes on the phone. Richard says that he would like both Marcus and me to speak to David and tell him how he stands. This is, to put it mildly, a bounce and I am certainly not prepared to have a talk over the phone with David which might result in his resignation.

Marcus speaks to him. He leaves David in no doubt that his support on the back benches is running out. I do talk to David but say I would like to see him. We arrange to meet at No. 12 after the morning Cabinet. 'Shall I go to Cabinet?' David asks. My view is that he should. Richard Ryder agrees. We then all go through to a meeting of the whips next door. It soon becomes abundantly clear that David's position is untenable. Only one whip (Nick Baker) thinks he should stay. There is a recognition that it has all slipped away. The reasons hardly matter any more. David has lost the support of the parliamentary party; at least that is the collective judgement of the whips.

I ask Marcus whether he feels the 1922 executive will come out against David. Marcus is cautious in his reply but fears that they may. I then give my own view, which is that there is not overwhelming pressure in the party and the country that he should resign. If, however, he is to go then he should go with as much honour and dignity as he can obtain. He should go under his own steam and he should not be forced out by the 1922 executive acting as judge and jury. That seems to be the consensus of the meeting.

Two hours back at Central Office and then to No. 12 again. Entering by Whitehall and avoiding the squads of photographers in Downing Street, I settle in Richard Ryder's office and a few minutes later David Mellor appears. He is in remarkably good shape for a man who has gone through so much. The only trace of the pressure he is under comes when he asks for some cigarettes. For the next twenty minutes David and I talk alone. He starts by saying that he has decided to go and that it is all rubbing off on the government. What do I feel, he asks.

I say that I believe the party in the country will go on supporting him as long as he wants that support. My concern is the meeting of the 1922 executive. I do not want to see him forced out.

David agrees and then says that he has been immensely grateful for my support. 'As it happens we have never come much into contact in our political careers nor got to know each other but no one could have done more.' For the first time in this whole sorry affair I am beginning to see some of the attractive side behind David's brash exterior. He is facing his fate with outward calm and good humour. The resignation is decided – the only issue now is the timing. David would ideally have liked to leave it until Friday but he does not want the 1922 executive to consider his position. We agree that there is no alternative but to announce today. It is not sensible to do it before the PM's speech. That means John should see him afterwards with an announcement in the early evening. I go out to find Richard Ryder, who returns and agrees with the arrangement.

All the whips' predictions that the start of the economy debate will be seriously delayed by Labour backbenchers prove false. I am

still at Smith Square as John starts his speech. I get to the chamber
after he has been speaking for about seven or eight minutes. The
chamber is packed. John's speech is workmanlike but not brilliant.
Given what has been happening over the last few days I am
amazed that he has had time to prepare anything. The damage is
done not by the speech but by the succession of interruptions
from our own side by people such as Taylor and Budgen.* As I
stand at the bar of the House it is abundantly clear that we have a
major problem of dissent on our benches. They may not all
interrupt but they are not convinced and are not prepared to be
convinced. Bad trouble ahead, I fear. Richard Ryder is definitely
right on that.

In contrast John Smith makes the most of his opportunity. He
gives a very polished Commons performance. I cannot help noticing
the saddest face in the chamber: Neil Kinnock is sitting squashed up
in the middle of the third row behind John Smith. A backbencher
with no particular role looking at what might have been.

When John Major comes out of the chamber I report to him
on my conversation with David Mellor. The announcement
makes the early evening news programmes. Once more I am busy
not so much defending David but defending John. The criticism
is that the PM should have acted earlier: in other words, thrown
David Mellor to the wolves without any attempt at defence.

Back in the Commons I catch the two wind-ups. Gordon
Brown is his usual mixture of humour and oratory. A great star
but without substance.† But the real surprise is Norman Lamont's
performance: fluent and forceful and on much better form than I
have ever heard him. Perhaps his possible imminent execution has
concentrated his mind – or perhaps, as some papers now suggest,
he is just happier with the policy outside the ERM. For whatever
reason it is a considerable Commons triumph and brings the
debate to a good end for us. In spite of all the chief whip's
misgivings we win the votes very comfortably.

---

* Teddy Taylor and Nick Budgen, two long-established Eurosceptic Tory
MPs.
† In those days on the opposition benches Brown was regarded as an
entertaining speaker but decidedly thin on policy.

Saturday 26 September. The government in general and John in particular have a universally bad press today. The general message is that we do not know where we are going, that there is a policy vacuum and that John should get a grip on events. When I speak to him on the phone he is very down about the press comment. He fears that he is 'damaged to the point of not being able to recover'. He adds, 'I am not going to take all this without answering back. The press all say they want action without having the first idea what the action should be.' Slowly he cools down. Two points really irritate him. The first is the poor reception his Thursday speech received, the second is that he does not know what the chancellor is up to. Norman is now basking in the praise of the Eurosceptics. Partly, I suggest, it is to preserve his position. It is after all only a few days ago that everyone was saying he should resign. John is in no mood to be cheered up. Did I know that William Hill were giving odds of 13 to 8 that he would not be prime minister by the time of the Budget? Fiona later tells me that the same bookmaker is giving 14 to 1 that I will be the next PM. It is all comic opera, but there is no chance of persuading John of that just now.

Sunday 27 September. I spend an hour on the phone with Richard Ryder. He is very pessimistic about the prospects of getting any Maastricht bill through. There are three options, he says. The first is to go ahead. The trouble is that a very significant proportion of the parliamentary party is now opposed to ratification – a hundred, he estimates. He tells me that John Major had two hours with the whips and they presented him with this bleak news – which explains why he was so down when I saw him last Tuesday. Richard says that the majority of the 1922 executive are against a Maastricht bill and probably twenty ministers. We will be introducing a bill against the background of the new council tax and public spending cuts. No other government has ever succeeded in such circumstances – but we could try.

The second option is to 'play it long' and wait for the Danes. The trouble is that the Danes will probably not decide until next summer. In my view this means that John's own personal position will be whittled away.

The third option is to say that circumstances have changed since we left the ERM. The argument would be: 'We can only govern with consent. We have not got that consent so we will abandon Maastricht.' The certain result of that course would be ministerial resignations. The most prominent pro-Maastricht Cabinet ministers are Heseltine, Clarke, Hunt, Waldegrave and Gummer. The sceptics are Howard, Lilley and Portillo.

Richard says that as a business manager he would prefer to play it long but, as he concedes, it is not his reputation on the line. The PM and the foreign secretary have given 'their word'. I say we need to do a number of things. We need to preserve the PM's position over the next week and we need to ensure that he does well at the party conference. He needs to restore his authority. 'How?' asks Richard. I reply that what is doing the damage is the different statements coming from ministers. Ministers should be told to toe the line or go. That order should be publicly related to the press. Richard's alternative or perhaps complementary strategy is that John should see the Cabinet one by one and see where they stand. 'That's fine,' I say. 'But on Thursday he should lay down the law at Cabinet.'

'But how can he do that?' asks Richard. 'They will all argue that they have kept inside the policy.'

'Do what Margaret did and take along the newspapers,' I suggest.

A few minutes later I hear the news that the cavalry have arrived to help us in our problems. At the start of the Labour Party conference Bryan Gould* has resigned over Labour's policy on Europe, which supports Maastricht and opposes a referendum. Tomorrow's headlines should be about Labour. Just what we wanted – in the nick of time.

The party conference

Sunday 4 October. To Brighton. All the press predictions are that this will be the most difficult Conservative conference for a very

---

* Bryan Gould was a prominent member of Labour's shadow Cabinet who subsequently left British politics entirely.

long time. Ken Clarke thinks it is potentially the most difficult for twenty years. Brighton itself is bathed in bright sunshine. I conduct a television press conference on the seafront, almost dazzled by the sun. From there I go to the Grand Hotel and am shown up to an enormous suite of two rooms, which I see to my alarm will cost £450 a day. I must check who is to pay this bill. I do not mind being an unpaid chairman but there is a limit to my generosity.

Monday 5 October. The dining room of the Grand is almost empty for breakfast. The representatives (we call them representatives in the Conservative Party, not delegates) will not arrive until this evening. For the time being I am the most senior politician in town. The result is that I give countless interviews to television reporters who appear to have an insatiable appetite for fresh comment. At midday I go out to a football pitch on the outskirts of Brighton to kick off a match between the Young Conservatives and the lobby and play for a few minutes in goal in a classic 'photo opportunity' arranged for the benefit of some fifty cameramen. The only trouble is when I throw the ball to one of the YCs he shows his prowess by kicking it into the far corner of the net.*

John and Norma arrive at six o'clock and John insists on opening the bottle of complimentary champagne which the hotel send up to him. He is in good form but irritated with the way Tory MPs are queuing up to present the anti-Maastricht case on television. He wonders aloud whether to be outspoken on this at the agents' dinner. My view is that there is no point in doing that at this stage. My speech the next day will have as its central message the unity of the party. John accepts the advice with some reluctance. He feels personally betrayed by some of the Eurosceptics. He regards the old-established sceptics such as Taylor, Cash, Budgen and Shepherd† as all irredeemable and

---

* Another player who trotted the length of the pitch with the sole aim of putting a ball past me was the political correspondent of the *Daily Mirror* – Alastair Campbell. He grimaced and returned to his end.

† Richard Shepherd is Tory MP for Aldridge-Brownhills and was my constituency neighbour.

sometimes plain batty. He is scornful of ex-ministers whose new position can be traced to the moment they were sacked from the government, while the biggest villain of all is Margaret Thatcher. Having selected John Major as her heir apparent she has done everything to undermine his authority. Having now met Margaret at home I can see the justice of John's resentment. She holds court on the inadequacies of the government in general and John Major in particular. I wholeheartedly share John's sentiments but I do not think much is to be gained by 'Major attacks Thatcher and Co' headlines on the first day of the conference. John agrees and gives a well-received and uncontroversial speech to the agents' dinner.

Tuesday 6 October. A day of high drama in the European debate. We begin at 7.45 with a meeting with Richard Ryder and the usual No. 12 cast and then Richard and I go on to the meeting with the National Union.* Basil Feldman's tactics are to call an amendment on the very general foreign affairs motion. The amendment sounds fairly ferocious in its opposition to a federal Europe but in fact is quite acceptable, having been drafted with Tristan Garel-Jones's help. As for speeches from the floor from MPs, peers and MEPs, Basil proposes a general exclusion – none are to be called. This all sounds acceptable and I go off to a room in the Grand Hotel to rehearse on autocue the speech which closes the morning. I then walk across with Fiona to the conference centre and have the ghastly period of waiting. This 30-minute speech has taken weeks to prepare and it is important to my position as party chairman that it goes reasonably well.

When I get to my feet my nervousness goes almost imme-diately. I know the words so well I actually enjoy delivering them. The conference like the jokes and applaud the attacking lines. The message is an undisguised plea for unity. 'We must all stand together and that includes our members of Parliament at Westminster.' John by my right side applauds enthusiastically throughout and at the end the conference rise to their feet in a standing ovation.

* The National Union was responsible for organising the party conference.

My joy is short lived. When I get back to the National Union room after lunch I find Basil in a great panic. He says that Norman Tebbit has put in a slip to speak. He and the conference chairman, John Mason, do not think they can refuse to call him. They fear he will cause a disturbance if he is refused. I say to Basil that this is a 'total reversal' of the policy that he was suggesting a few hours previously. He agrees somewhat sheepishly, saying that neither he nor John has the stomach for a fight with the conference on the calling of one of its all-time darlings. He suggests I ask Douglas Hurd whether he has any objections. Douglas is next door waiting to take his place on the platform. He thinks for a moment about the question and agrees that Tebbit should be called. So there it is. With minutes to go before we appear downstairs the decision is taken.

Right from the start it is clear that this debate is going to be unlike any other we have had at the party conference for the last ten or twenty years. Any criticism of things European is greeted with cheers and thunderous applause from a section of the audience. Any defence of Maastricht meets with catcalls. All the noise, which is substantial, is coming from a comparatively small part of the conference. As the debate goes on the noise increases and I try to identify the shouters. In the main they are young, in T-shirts, aggressively self-confident; their only reactions are moronic cheers or hisses. The kind of people who tried to interrupt my speech on AIDS at a Young Conservatives conference in 1986 – the lager louts of our party.

When Tebbit is called they erupt in joy. He receives a standing ovation as he makes his way to the rostrum. There then follows five minutes in which he knifes John Major and suggests in so many words that if the chancellor were to go on the issue of the ERM defeat, then the PM would have to go as well. He finishes with a number of rhetorical questions on the lines of 'Do you want a United States of Europe?'. Glancing maliciously back at the platform he returns towards his seat, to thunderous applause from the lager louts. Then Tebbit makes his real mistake. He pauses to stand, arms outstretched, accepting the plaudits of the crowd. The very nastiest display I have ever seen by a senior Conservative politician.

There are a few more speeches to the accompaniment of further catcalls, then Douglas is called. He begins as he told me he would: 'I could try to smooth my way to a standing ovation or give it to you straight.' He proceeds to give it to them straight and very good. There is some barracking but the conference rallies. Strong applause begins to punctuate Douglas's speech. He stands before them as an elder statesman. He appeals to their patriotism. He warns them not to split the party, for if they do we will be out of power for a decade. The conference rise spontaneously to their feet and at the end the vote sees the lager louts easily defeated. Douglas has won the day. We have survived.

Wednesday 7 October. This is a roller-coaster of a party conference. There are ups of great elation and downs of enormous gloom when you wonder whether the Conservative Party really wants to stay in power at all. The day starts with excitement. Michael Heseltine at the top of his form takes the Eurosceptics head on and wins triumphantly. Michael sets out the case for Europe without compromise and knocks down the hecklers with contempt. He is rewarded with a standing ovation in the middle of his speech which eclipses the reception for Tebbit yesterday. Michael's performance is much better than his usual conference triumph. All the conventional advice would be for him to keep out of the European debate and not to raise the temperature. Michael has ignored the safe course and taken a very substantial risk. It is an act of great courage.

I go to lunch feeling much better. However, we are soon brought back to the problems of conference. The news comes through that Margaret Thatcher has launched an attack on Maastricht in a newspaper article – in, of all newspapers, the *European*. It has been carefully timed and it has the intended effect. Michael's bravura performance is knocked off the top spot of the news. The new lead story is the attack on the government from Margaret Thatcher.

In the PM's suite I meet with John and Michael. Michael laments the fact that Thatcher now leads all the bulletins. I agree with his concern but add that although the press may regard it as good news for them it is anything but certain that the conference will take the same view. They are getting fed up to the back teeth with past leaders of the Tory Party attacking their successors.

After dinner I go to a party of Jeffrey Archer's which is inhabited by Cabinet ministers and editors. It is a tedious affair and Fiona and I leave after thirty minutes. We hear later that the party livens up when Ken Clarke accuses Tebbit of having declared war on the party. Apparently Tebbit is a bit put out by this accusation although why I cannot imagine. It is just what he has done. It is tragically ironic that the declaration of war should have been made official in Brighton. In 1984 he showed conspicuous courage and I was moved by his reaction to those cataclysmic events and admired him for it.

Thursday 8 October. The press is again horrendous, with Thatcher's attack dominating every front page. We should all be waiting for Lamont's speech. In fact we are most concerned about Thatcher. Margaret arrives on time and we give her coffee in the ministerial waiting room upstairs. I ask her twice whether she wants to say anything. She repeats twice that she does not: 'It would be quite inappropriate.' As we go into the conference hall it seems to me that Margaret is receiving a tremendous ovation but as I leave her and go to my chair it becomes apparent that this is not quite the case. It is not a repeat of 1991. There are quite a lot of people who are not standing at all – the *European* article has misfired. After a couple of seconds she appears to beckon me so I return. In fact I think the beckoning gesture was more of a nervous reaction to the applause. But being there I suggest she motions to the audience to sit, which she does; thirty seconds later they are all back in their chairs and the conference can commence.

The debate is on the environment and I listen with half an ear to a rather good speech by Michael Howard before going out to complete the rest of the Thatcher manoeuvre – getting her together with the prime minister. We join up in a crocodile with the chancellor and his team. John mutters about whether he should kiss her or not. Norma makes it quite clear that nothing is further from her mind. The crocodile then advances. The reaction to John's entrance is at least as good and arguably better than that of Margaret. He goes up to her and does kiss her, to the joy of the photographers. The audience then settle back and we start on what in all conscience is *the* political issue – the future of the economy. Norman makes a decent enough speech. It is not inspiring but he receives his standing ovation. Sadly I think the press will proclaim him overshadowed by the floor speakers. By some marvel the National Union has managed to call a long line of speakers opposed to the government's economic policy – which is bad enough – but they are also speakers of a very high quality. They lay into the chancellor's policies with gusto and the women are particularly outstanding.

The pit closure crisis

Tuesday 12 October. The pit closures announcement comes like a thunderbolt. It emerges that half the country's pits are to be closed down with thousands of miners declared instantly unemployed, albeit with generous redundancy. The immediate reaction is shock. No one has been prepared for the scale of this announcement. It has been utterly inept. At Central Office we are without briefing or explanation. No government or party can have entered a major political battle so unprepared. There is no doubt that we are now in a political crisis. We have survived the Conservative conference – even enjoyed something of a victory – only to fall flat on our face a couple of days later. For the first time the government is in really serious trouble. I will be amazed if we get the support of either the public or the party.

So what has gone wrong? The basic case for further closures is strong. We cannot go on stockpiling coal which we do not need. We are apparently paying out £100 million a month to produce coal we don't need but I only learn this from Michael Heseltine's announcement. Doubtless government ministers know this position. Doubtless energy experts realise it only too well but the general public know next to nothing of these arguments. We have failed lamentably to prepare the ground. When we abolished the dock labour scheme we took months to prepare our case.

Worst of all, we have not discussed it at the No. 12 committee, which is intended at the very least to prevent problems like this blowing up in our faces. Michael Heseltine must take the lion's share of the blame. His action has been politically culpable. Nevertheless what is also revealed is a gaping hole in the government's system for announcing its decisions. Presentation is not everything but it cannot just be disregarded in this cavalier way.

Wednesday 14 October. A horrendous press. We are condemned without exception. At the No. 12 meeting Richard Ryder asks me to lead the discussion. I say that this is the worst day's press ever and that the position for the government is serious. The public have not been prepared for this announcement. There has been no briefing. There has been no sensible explanation of why this closure programme could not be phased. More to the point, I say to Richard, I see no reason in having a No. 12 committee if we are not to have any part in an announcement of this kind. It is a complete waste of time.

There is an embarrassed silence when I finish. We all remember the guarded, almost secretive, way that the coal announcement was dealt with at our Monday meeting. When I raise it the impression given by Richard and in particular John Wakeham is that it was too sensitive to be talked about at our meeting. It is John who breaks the silence. 'Well, I agree with what Norman says,' he starts. 'I have to say that however it was announced it would not have been popular.' True – but if we took that view about political life we would not spend a penny on press officers, advertising or advice.

In the afternoon I go back to No. 12. We talk about the chancellor, who certainly I perceive as the real weak link in the government. Richard does not dispute this. The question is not whether we should have a new chancellor but when and who. Neither of us can be certain about the when. Christmas looks the earliest. As for the who, we have different views. Richard clearly favours John MacGregor. My view is that Ken Clarke is the only choice. We need someone who is genuinely tough and who will get out and present. Richard's fear is that the PM will quickly get irritated with the Clarke style. I say as someone who worked with Ken for five or six years that his fears are misplaced. We leave the issue in the air. The time may come for me to bang the table on this.

Thursday 15 October. To Solihull (for a board meeting) but frequent calls keep me in touch with the latest developments in what is now a full-scale crisis. The worst news comes from Tim Collins to the effect that the decision to close the pits went ahead without a full meeting of Cabinet. This news has apparently seeped out after today's meeting of Cabinet. It once again shows what a leaky vessel it is. I assume there are a number who are most concerned to preserve their own personal reputations. 'It wasn't me, guv. I knew nothing about it.' Nevertheless I have to admit it is an astonishing omission – quite astonishing.

One advantage of getting away from Central Office is that I can get some flavour of how industry views the developments of the last few days. Most members of the board are Tory voters. They think we have taken leave of our senses, and there is something else: a sense of shame. No one wants to be identified with a government which is perceived as having taken this draconian action against mining communities, including Nottinghamshire miners who supported us against Scargill.

Peter Tom, the chief executive, tells me a story that illustrates the general unhappiness. He is a member of a committee consisting of some of the best-known companies in the construction industry, Tarmac and the rest. He tells me that on Wednesday the committee seriously considered giving the industry a day off and marching on London. A march organised not by the unions but by the bosses. All the danger signals are flashing bright red.

Friday 16 October. The position continues to deteriorate. My interviews are dominated by questions on the mines and in particular on whether the Cabinet were consulted. I loyally defend the position and explain how Cabinet committees work but omit the self-evident point for any insider that an issue of real importance must go to Cabinet. The signs are that we are in serious trouble with the parliamentary party. Tory MP after Tory MP, including the chairman of the 1922 Committee, are coming out against us. I am coming to the conclusion that we cannot sustain our present position. The party and the country have not got their heart in it. The party at Westminster will not give us a majority in the debate that the opposition have put down for next

Wednesday. In my view we shall have to change. Awkward for Michael but necessary if we are to win the vote let alone have the acquiescence of public opinion.

Saturday 17 October. Steadily through the day I talk with some of the main players in the pits drama. First to ring is Richard Ryder. He confirms that it is the whips' view that the government cannot win on Wednesday without a change of policy. That change should include a new development board headed by a well-known figure like Peter Walker and the staging of closures. I say that it should also include the cancellation of some of the closures. We must ensure that what will inevitably be seen as a U-turn actually succeeds. Richard agrees and says that Michael Heseltine will have to agree to any new plan. At Cabinet on Thursday he appeared genuinely surprised that his proposals were causing such a reaction. He did recognise privately, however, that if the Wednesday vote were lost he would have to resign. And with Michael there was no doubt that he would resign. He would not cling onto office in the face of defeat for a policy for which he was responsible.

During the afternoon I speak to Michael and tell him about the reaction in the party and the country and that in my view we need a change of direction. He says that he understands but what change of direction is possible? He has no market for 25 million tons of coal and feels that he is being forced into this position by the pressure of the Treasury to have the savings made as quickly as possible. It is an unsatisfactory conversation. Michael is on autopilot addressing his audience, not talking with a colleague.

Half an hour later John Major comes on the line. I tell him my summing up: incompetent presentation, no support in the country and precious little in the party. The area agents say it is 'the worst reaction for twenty years'. John says that he has read the reports and believes that it would be a good idea if Norman Lamont also sees them. It becomes clear that John wants not only to announce a package on the mines but a bigger package for industrial recovery. The difficulty is the chancellor. Hence his desire that the chancellor should see the reports from our agents. John needs to persuade the chancellor. His concern is that if pushed too hard the chancellor will resign.

Sunday 18 October. The prime minister has approved a plan – which would involve phasing the closures – but so far this has not been put to Michael Heseltine. Everyone is nervous about the way he might react. There is a real risk that he could reject the advice to retreat and walk away from the whole problem. The issue will be put to him at 6.30 at No. 10. Earlier in the day Michael had looked tired and rather depressed as he fended off questions from Jonathan Dimbleby on the BBC. Dimbleby was uncharacteristically aggressive: 'the nation is up in arms', 'the party is in revolt', 'a spectacular misjudgement', 'public revulsion', 'Pontius Pilate'. The worst moment was when Michael tried to explain why the subject had not been put to Cabinet. His theory is that as it was agreed by ministers in the small group (unlike Westland) there was no need. That is frankly absurd. How do the other ministers know if they agree or not if they have not ever heard the arguments? Pure balderdash.

Monday 19 October. Richard Ryder rings early to say that the evening meeting with Michael went reasonably well. At first he wished to defend his existing position but was persuaded off this course. The question now is: how far is he prepared to go in the change of policy? At Central Office I receive a message that John wants to have a political Cabinet after the official business of Cabinet has ended. I return to Downing Street, past the cameramen and the shambles of building works in No. 10, to the bunker Cabinet Room in the Cabinet Office. What effect, I wonder, have the chaotic working conditions had on decisions made over the last two months?

To my surprise John really wants to talk about the position of the government rather than the specific coal dispute. He is concerned not only about the present position but about the impression the government has lost its way. Withdrawal from the ERM was a catastrophic blow. The decision on the pits another big blow. He wants to make a statement – with substance – which puts us back on course. John looks drawn but is obviously determined to take the fight to the enemy – including some of our own backbenchers.

Douglas strongly supports John's desire to make a statement which maps the way ahead. I say that the coal statement has been disastrous and we should learn the lesson. But what concerns me also is the alienation of industry. We have lost its support and it will require an effort from us all to get that support back. Lastly I say that it is important that ministers stand together. We cannot have ministers setting out their own position or standing a pace away from the government's policy.

In the discussion which follows Michael Howard argues for the postponement of the Maastricht bill but the really significant points are on the economy. It is not encouraging. There is a profound split on the way forward. John wants an industrial recovery package. He is backed as far as I can judge by the majority of the Cabinet. Ken Clarke in particular argues for no cuts in the capital programmes and observes, 'We have no economic policy.' John Gummer, Virginia Bottomley and Malcolm Rifkind also support this argument but the chancellor does not. He speaks like a Treasury mandarin, not a minister. He recognises that there may be some political difficulties but he suggests that we are ignoring the encouraging signs. There was a 20 per cent increase in car production, for example. His message is that we should persist and he 'must make his position clear'. I would judge his contribution as a clear warning against the government changing course with the additional threat that if the government ignores his advice then he will have to consider his own position. It is not a dramatic banging of the table but the threat is there for anyone who listens.

At 3.30 Michael makes his statement and lists the concessions he is now prepared to make. He avoids using the word 'review' but even without it it is clear that a number of Tory rebels are pacified. Not all, however. For example, Winston Churchill still says it is not enough but frankly I think we are at least out of the immediate parliamentary problems on coal.

Tuesday 20 October. It is Kate and Isobel's half-term and this morning I was to have stayed at home with them as neither Fiona nor the au pair are available. It ends up with the children plus a friend piling into the Rover and settling in my office at Central Office. Not that the girls object. They all get McDonald's brought in from Victoria and return to Hurlingham Road in the best of humour. Fiona and I go to a Foreign Office party. As we are entering I see Ken Clarke and we agree to meet in his room at 10.15. When we meet I tell Ken that my view is that we need a new chancellor. I have defended his position but the brutal fact is that we cannot restore his lost authority. I do not like saying all this but the priority is to preserve the position of the government and the position of the PM. Typically Ken does not beat about the bush. 'I agree,' he says. 'Norman is an old mate of mine. I have defended him. But I think he should go.' He adds that he believes that most other members of the Cabinet would agree with what we are saying. But who would take his place?

My reply to that is that he is the natural successor. I warn him, however, that the chief whip may be backing John MacGregor. 'The East Anglian mafia,' mutters Ken.* I say I would be against that. I like John but it would be seen as a safe compromise appointment and for that reason would get a bad press. Ken mentions Michael Heseltine and Michael Portillo as possible candidates but we both realise that John is unlikely to appoint either of them. Just as I am leaving Ken asks, 'You don't want to be chancellor yourself?'

'I do not,' I reply with total certainty. 'I am very happy as party chairman,' I add with equal certainty.

Wednesday 21 October. A No. 12 committee meeting. The most revealing part of the discussion takes place before the meeting begins. Richard has invited Michael Heseltine to attend, who arrives a few minutes early. Michael, John Wakeham and I go over the position while we wait for Richard. Suddenly John observes that in his judgement we were ill advised to press ahead with the plan to close thirty-one pits. 'How can you say that?' asks Michael indignantly. 'You were on the committee that agreed the policy. How can you say that?'

John begins to bluster. 'I can see why you say that,' he begins lamely but the sentence trails away into incoherence.

Richard joins the conversation and the meeting begins. A potential stand-up row is avoided. He cares passionately about his

---

* Richard Ryder and MacGregor both had Norfolk constituencies.

reputation as a good adviser and hence for sound judgement. He has no intention of standing by a policy which has become discredited and no intention of being associated with its failure.

After lunch to the chamber to hear the coal debate. It is pure farce. Labour MPs jump up to interrupt Michael Heseltine's speech. At first their tactics seem to be succeeding. There is continual uproar and Michael seems to be losing control of the debate. After more than thirty minutes of shouting points of order and cries to resign, Michael abandons his script and rounds on Labour, saying that they are not interested in debating the issues and invites the government benches to unite against such tactics. A brilliant piece of opportunism – he rescues his speech from disaster and unites all but the most hardline Tory critics. Five hours later we win the Commons vote with a majority of thirteen. Far too close for comfort but much better than looked possible a few days ago. The government has been damaged – Michael Heseltine has been damaged – but neither irretrievably. It is a vast pity to have resurrected Arthur Scargill and to make him something of a hero and it is an even greater pity to have torpedoed the Conservative Party in the way we have. But if we can develop a new economic policy we can recover. We are after all only six months into the new parliament. There is plenty of time to fight back.

The Maastricht vote

Thursday 22 October. To Weston-super-Mare to talk to a building industry lunch. I take the opportunity of talking to about a dozen local chairmen. They are shell shocked and dismayed about the events of the last week. They have all lost members through resignation although not as many as I might have feared. And they are pessimistic about raising money. But there is still life in the body. A lot of life. They grumble but in no way do they feel down and out.

At lunchtime a call comes through that the PM would like to see me at 6.30. I arrive a few minutes late straight from Paddington. John looks whacked. There was a story in the *Times* yesterday that he was 'cracking under the strain'. This is not true. The piece itself had so many factual inaccuracies that at times it was risible. Sarah Hogg for example was portrayed as hurrying home each night to her small children – who are in fact both aged around twenty and live independent lives. The magnificent flat where we meet tonight was described as small and pokey. Goodness knows what the *Times* reporters would regard as an acceptable standard of accommodation.

That John is tired cannot be denied. We are all tired. Not exhausted but battered. What the reporters from the *Times* failed to spot is the difference in the way that John responds to crisis and the way his predecessor did. Margaret Thatcher was capable of becoming hysterical. John remains calm under almost all circumstances. It is alleged by the *Times* that on Black Wednesday he had in effect some kind of nervous collapse. Yet the impression I retain was the calmness with which John was able to brief me at the end of the inner cabinet meeting. What we need now is a period when we can all recover and the party can bind its wounds. That is a point put to me with force by one of the chairmen I met at Weston-super-Mare – but John makes it clear that that prospect is not to be.

Cabinet this morning have backed his strategy almost unanimously that we should proceed with the Maastricht bill. The one exception to his advice is possibly the most important man of all, the chief whip. I bite back my view that we could do with a few weeks to put ourselves together. The decision has been made and announced. Any retreat from that would look like another U-turn; and that we really cannot handle.

There is no doubt that the PM hankers for a new chancellor. Norman simply does not carry conviction. I do not argue whether this is just or unjust, fair or unfair. It is simply a fact. He no longer has the authority to lay down economic policy. There is a gaping hole at the centre of government.

Friday 23 October. I go to No. 12 just before 9 a.m. Richard Ryder wants me to accompany him at a briefing he is giving to Trevor Kavanagh of the *Sun* and one of the paper's leader writers. Before they arrive we have a few words. Richard is cast down about the prospects on Maastricht and says that the Cabinet have decided on a course which is against the united view of the whips' office.

But this is not his only problem. Michael Heseltine is hopping mad about two pieces in the papers today, one in the *Times* and the other in the *Spectator*, which assert that he has presided over a disaster and that only the wise and steadying hands of John Wakeham can save the government.

The briefing with the *Sun* shows the quicksands we have entered. Trevor Kavanagh interprets John Major's position as being that if he is defeated over Maastricht he will call for an election. I say this is all inconceivable. There is no prospect of an election. I fear this has been started by John himself in a lobby briefing on Tuesday. At one stage he added words to the effect of 'back me or sack me'. He knew they were mistaken as soon as he uttered them but Trevor Kavanagh has interpreted them as being a carefully thought-out statement of his policy and a willingness to fight an election on Maastricht. Richard is out of the room taking another call from Michael Heseltine whilst most of this conversation is taking place and when he returns he maintains a silence on the future. Perhaps he thinks the prospect of an election may concentrate the minds of the rebels.

In the afternoon Fiona and I go to my Aunt Gwen's funeral in Wanstead. As we wait in the car park we listen to the *World at One* interview with Norman Tebbit. His attack goes far wider than Maastricht. John Major, he says, has changed his mind on David Mellor and on the pits. Why, he sneers, should he not change his mind on Maastricht? His view is that if we lose John as PM on Maastricht that is a minor misfortune which we can easily contemplate. This from a former chairman of the Conservative Party, someone who was scathing about disloyalty in others, someone who urged support for John Major in the leadership elections. I am reminded again of Virginia Bottomley's comment that the people who are fighting hardest for John are the people who were *not* members of his campaign team.

Saturday 24 October. John has taken off to Egypt for the fiftieth anniversary of El Alamein and the phone is remarkably still. I fear this is but the calm before the storm. Although the press have not yet quite realised it we are in very substantial difficulty. For the first time I think the prospect of the PM falling is more than evens. If Labour with the Lib Dems can find a reason to vote against us on the Maastricht bill then we will lose. The stakes are now enormously high. I only wish we had not decided to press on so precipitately. Even a couple of weeks would have allowed us to think out our strategy. I do not always back Richard's judgement but on this he was right. We should have proceeded with caution. Now our fate may well depend on what the Liberal Democrats decide. That is no position for a Conservative government to occupy.

Sunday 25 October. A disastrous development. The morning radio reports that John is threatening an election if we do not win the Maastricht vote. It is an unsustainable threat. We are not going to call an election on Maastricht and anyone who thinks about it for two seconds must realise that is the position. We are not about to commit suicide. After the pits fiasco we would be annihilated. The tactics of the threat are also absurd. It is threatening the nuclear deterrent before any serious skirmishing has begun.

At 8.45 Richard rings. The poor old chief whip sounds suicidal. He is deeply concerned about the course on which the government have now embarked. The truth is the whips cannot guarantee a victory on the vote.

The issue that now concerns us both is the election threat and in particular what to say on the mid-day television programmes, where Michael Howard and Tony Newton are appearing. I ring both and they agree that the election threat is nonsense. What to say, however, is the question. We don't know what the PM has said; he is in the desert for the El Alamein service and out of contact. The best lines we can come up with in the circumstances are (a) that the government will not lose and therefore the question does not arise and (b) that we do not intend to comment on rumours and unnamed sources etc.

As it happens Michael Howard gets away with this argument with Jonathan Dimbleby but Tony has a torrid time with Brian Walden. In fact the best arguments are produced by Ken Clarke on BBC radio. This is to attack Labour and to attack the rebels –

'do you want a government controlled by the likes of Budgen and Cash?' – and to make the obvious point that times have changed: now we have a majority of only twenty-one. The government is not to be run by the minority.

In the evening Gus O'Donnell rings, having just returned with the PM from Egypt. Wearily he tells me the tale of the briefing. On the trip over the PM settled down to an off the record briefing with three or four of the Sunday political correspondents. He had not thought what message he wanted to get over and as a result the agenda was set for him. The correspondents all knew of or had heard his 'back me or sack me' briefing on Tuesday. Did this mean he would resign if he were defeated? 'This is not a personal issue,' replied John. 'The Cabinet is unanimously behind me,' he added. Did a defeat mean there would be an election? 'You must draw your own conclusions,' John replied. John thus never used the word 'election' himself but had failed to guide them off the prospect. The result is that all the Sunday papers have run the election story.

Monday 26 October. The day starts with an interview for *Today*. The BBC has conducted interviews with Eurosceptics and unsurprisingly found them unmoved by the election threat. My interviewer, Peter Hobday, tries to get a definitive statement on the election threat which I am in no position to give. He gets a denunciation of Conservative rebels 'playing with fire' and the Labour Party's tactics: 'They never will be able to talk about U-turns again.'

In the meeting at No. 12 Richard advances an argument to the effect that our strategy should be to regard the Maastricht vote as a 'technical' issue concerned only with the restarting of the committee stage of the bill. If we lose he suggests we accept it rather than go for a vote of confidence. I am afraid that I bridle at this. 'Where does this leave the PM and his credibility?' I ask. 'We might, just might, have been able to regard it all as a technical issue a week or so ago but certainly cannot do so now since the election threat. It would look like the most extraordinary retreat.'

'What's the alternative?' Richard snaps, trying to force his way through.

'I don't know what the alternative is,' I reply. 'We need to talk it through. The trouble is that we are not giving enough consideration to these issues and we are making sudden decisions on the hoof.'

Richard sees my irritation and Tony, bless him, comes in to support me. We do not decide what course we should take but at least we do not decide to execute what would be perceived as a particularly craven retreat.

At 9.45 we proceed to No. 10 and the Cabinet Room, which is back in use. John looks gaunt and there is no doubt how he views the Maastricht vote. He says he is 'not prepared to hide behind the Danes', and neither is he prepared to see our position in Europe undermined and Britain sidelined. There have been three historic mistakes in British policy towards Europe when we have missed the opportunity of joining in European development. He does not propose to miss a fourth. As for the 'election threat' story, he says that it is all ridiculously overdone. We all know, he says, what he would do if he lost the vote. The word 'resignation' was not used but the meaning was clear to every one of us there. More or less collectively we all tried to move him off that line of thinking and onto a consideration of the motion for Wednesday.

Tuesday 27 October. Another crisis day. The press still have not moved off the unsustainable election threat story. At ten o'clock we assemble in the Cabinet Room. It becomes clear that John has reached the end of his tether with the Tory rebels. The officials and advisers are asked to leave and he talks privately with his parliamentary colleagues 'not just as colleagues but as friends'.

John says his belief is that with the help of industry and the centre of the party we can win. He favours a straightforward substantive motion. 'If we lose, well, we lose with honour.' He will resign but we should understand that he is fed up with being 'pushed around' by a small minority of rebels. (What was it Nixon once said about the press not having him to kick about any more?) We all start to argue with him. Richard Ryder says the parliamentary party would regard his resignation as a disaster. I say the party in the country would regard the prospect as unthinkable. They would think we had taken leave of our senses in having this discussion. I try to get the discussion back onto the road – 'trying to avoid defeat is not a dishonourable course to take'.

But John is not convinced by this. We leave the decision on the motion to one side. It will have to be decided on Thursday in Cabinet and we agree in outline some positions for Prime Minister's Questions in getting off the election threat.

In the loo by the Cabinet waiting room Douglas Hurd and I are alone. We both use the same phrase: 'John seems to have a death wish'. But Douglas then spells out his own position. If we lose the vote on Maastricht he will have to resign. I reply that I will spend all night persuading him not to take that course. He also is not convinced. The stakes in this debate get higher and higher.

In Prime Minister's Questions, incredibly, no one asks John about the election threat. Perhaps even now we can count on some Labour incompetence to help us. I look in to see John straight afterwards to see if he wishes Gus to guide the lobby, but his prepared answer is so convoluted that it is an impossible message for Gus to relay at a lobby briefing. Of course the trouble is that the PM does regard the Maastricht vote as of paramount importance to his continuance.

Thursday 29 October. The comparative calm is broken. Richard Ryder tells me that one prospect for the motion in the House is that we put Maastricht and the vote on confidence into the same motion. My reaction is that such a prospect is crazy. If we lose then we are forced into an election. But Richard Ryder says that if we lose a straightforward Maastricht vote then both the PM and the foreign secretary will resign. Combining the votes could be the best way of retaining them. My reply is that it is a colossal gamble. The only course must be to persuade the PM and Douglas out of these resignation threats. I warn that we are in no position to fight an election. 'We are bust – and furthermore we would lose.' As I put down the phone I cannot but feel we are bent on suicide and the collapse of the government.

Jonathan Hill does not cheer me up when I ring him. He does not believe that the PM will agree to us making the Maastricht vote a confidence motion but that John personally will regard it in those terms. If we lose he will resign and he believes that the

PM is 'immoveable'. At No. 10 they have been living with this threat for six months.

Sunday 1 November. I am now seriously tired and could do with a day off. It has been solid pounding since Black Wednesday but there is no respite even on Sunday. The alarm goes at 6.30 and the 7 a.m. news reports quite wrongly that Central Office is ringing up the constituency chairmen of all the European rebels asking them to apply pressure. I ring up the news editor to complain – a complaint which is accepted – and bolt down breakfast and get in a taxi to TV-am. Next I go on to do a long interview with ITN. Back home the phone starts to ring almost immediately. The most important message is from David Davis, asking for help on a couple of possible rebels. I get through to one, Robert Jones,[*] but without success. Although a member of John Major's campaign team he is deaf to pleas that the vote may mean John's resignation. He believes that we have pushed the pace too hard and is concerned about a possible return to the ERM. The best we can hope for here is an abstention. If the whips are having similar reactions from the apparently persuadable then we are in very real difficulty. David says that as long as the Liberals vote with us then we can afford twenty-six or twenty-seven votes against. It is all going to be desperately close.

Monday 2 November. The worst day so far. The No. 12 meeting is particularly grim and ends up with Richard Ryder and myself very obviously falling out. What caused my explosion was the chief whip's views on the weekend's programmes. David Hunt is taken to task for having suggested that Tory MPs should show their 'confidence' in the PM. This was wrong and so too was any suggestion that the 'rebels' were playing with fire. We need to keep the temperature down. Ministers who ignore that are being 'self-indulgent'.

This is too much. 'It is ludicrous to talk about ministers being self-indulgent,' I break in. 'The fact is that David was the only

---

[*] Conservative MP for West Hertfordshire and later a junior minister at the Department of the Environment.

member of the Cabinet prepared to appear. The self-indulgent ones stayed in bed.'

At 9 a.m. I move upstairs to John's flat at No. 10. He is in very sombre mood. By his side he has a notebook. He looks at it from time to time as he speaks. It contains what is in effect a statement of his position, which is that he intends to resign if he loses the vote.

There are, says John, a number of resignations that he has refused over the last few months which he should have accepted. He should have accepted David Mellor's resignation earlier.

'That was perfectly understandable and defensible,' I murmur.

'Understandable but not right,' replies John. 'Politics is a rough game and part of it entails dealing with those kinds of situations.' As for Norman Lamont, he thinks he was wrong not to make him stand down. The reason was because of his own responsibility for entry into the ERM − he himself had a resignation broadcast written. He then reveals that Michael Heseltine and Tim Eggar also offered their resignations for the pits debacle. He does not suggest that he should have accepted that − as indeed he should not − but he feels that it all adds up to a picture. A picture of a government where ministers cling to office irrespective of mistake. He feels that if he stays on after losing the vote his credibility will have gone.

John believes that a successor would be able to start anew, unencumbered by past mistakes. He would be strengthened by what had happened to him. It would bring the rebels up with a jolt. It would enable Maastricht to get through.

There is a pause. John does not really ask my view but I volunteer it nonetheless. I say that I believe that his resignation would be wrong. It is simply not true that anyone else would find it easier to get Maastricht through. Resignation is not remotely necessary. We should go for a vote of confidence and get back to government. John says simply, 'I don't agree.' He says he is quite aware that history will say if he goes that he went too early in a fit of pique. On the other hand if he stays he will be pilloried for clinging on to office. My reply to this is that his course should be to stay and fight back step by step. The next months will not be fun but he can get through them. Ultimately he will get a lot of credit for so doing. He remains unconvinced. 'I don't know how much more of this I can force on my family,' he replies.

Tuesday 3 November. I go over to the House of Commons in search of Euro rebels who may be persuaded to change their mind. Peter Fry* is my best hope for conversion. I helped him at a point in his past career when he missed a vital vote and he rather owes me a favour. Like several others Peter is torn. He opposes Maastricht but he does not want to bring about John's resignation. My efforts have not been helped by a whip's gauche attempt to bring pressure to bear through his constituency. Nevertheless we can win him over. Trevor Skeet, the ancient and rather eccentric member for North Bedfordshire, is entirely unpersuadable. There is nothing we can do with him and I assume even pressure from the constituency would be unavailing as I cannot believe that he will do another parliament in any event. The voting position is getting a little better but the whips still believe we are heading for defeat.

I go to the Commons for a ten o'clock vote and take the opportunity to have a word with Ken Clarke in his rather bleak and bare office behind the speaker's chair. I tell him I may need his help with John tomorrow night after the vote. The PM must not be allowed to resign. Ken agrees. He volunteers his position – in typically open fashion – which is that if John stands down in several years' time he would like to be a candidate for the succession, but he does not believe any more than I that John could resign simply because he loses the vote. I warn him that we may have an uphill struggle in persuading the PM.

Wednesday 4 November. The crisis is over – for the present. The House is packed. Labour MPs spill onto the floor of the chamber as the tellers push their way through to give the result. There is a great roar from our side when the government whip takes up the winning position. We have won by six votes. Labour are furious. They turn on Paddy Ashdown and his colleagues and shout at them. They would have done worse were they not in the

---

* Long-serving Conservative MP for Wellingborough.

chamber itself. They don't give a damn about the issue of Europe. All they care about is that had the Lib Dems voted with Labour then the government would have been defeated. What they don't know is that we would have lost a prime minister and a foreign secretary. In the lobby I say this is a personal triumph for the prime minister and that it has been a terrible mistake for Labour to try to exploit a position they did not believe in. In reality it is a triumph for Richard Ryder and the whips but it is not remotely the end of the story. Twenty-six Tories voted against us on the blackest of black three-line whips and six others abstained.

9
Back to basics (1993)

'We must go back to basics. We want our children to be taught the best; our public services to give the best; our British industry to be the best. The Conservative Party will lead the country back to these basics right across the board.'

John Major, Conservative Party conference, October 1993.

Even today the 'back to basics' speech made by John Major in Blackpool on the last day of the 1993 party conference is reported as a moral campaign mounted by the prime minister which swiftly and disastrously blew up in his face. This always was nonsense and following the revelation of Major's affair with Edwina Currie it can now be seen to be so. Major was never a fool. He was not likely to start a campaign that could leave him as the chief victim. He guarded his privacy. He detested press intrusion into private lives. He was never likely to have started a moral witch hunt. It is much more likely that his own experience made him more tolerant of the personal affairs of others. Indeed the evidence of those preparing the speech is quite specific – Major wanted no part in a campaign based on personal morality.

The truth about the ill-fated 'back to basics' speech was very different. Like Margaret Thatcher, Major was concerned to say something new at the end of four days of ministerial conference speeches and like her he cursed inwardly when some of his prepared best lines were used by others. The leader's speech was a well-guarded secret and although Major did not follow the Thatcher example of working virtually through the preceding night to find the right words, the completed text was ready late. There was no time for collective examination of the words before they were spoken. Questions and answers could not be prepared; press officers could not be properly briefed.

For Major the 1993 party conference speech was very important. In the months following 'Black Autumn' Conservative fortunes had not improved. In the Commons rebellion followed rebellion on the Maastricht bill and inevitably spread to other areas, with Tory MPs realising that they too could take advantage of the government's low majority. The parliamentary party seemed strangely apathetic to what was happening in the real world outside Westminster. At the beginning of May the Newbury by-election had been lost to the Liberal Democrats with a massive 28 per cent swing and in the county council elections at the same time the party had been routed.

Three weeks later Norman Lamont was moved at long last from the Treasury and replaced by Ken Clarke with Michael Howard taking Clarke's place at the Home Office. We had done Lamont no favours in rallying to his defence in the aftermath of leaving the ERM. The public and the press wanted someone to take responsibility and the obvious action should have been a swap with Clarke – just as Jim Callaghan had switched with Roy Jenkins after the devaluation of 1967. Such a change would also have been in Lamont's interests. It would have been seen as the honourable act of a man who had not taken us into the ERM but who had been in charge when the ship went down. As it was, Lamont's personal position deteriorated week by week and his authority simply melted away. All he was offered in the end was the job of environment secretary, which, predictably, he refused. I had suggested defence secretary, but I doubt if he was in any mood to accept that either.

Almost no one challenged the move itself but that did not prevent Lamont leaving the government a bitter man. In his resignation speech Major's former campaign manager attacked the prime minister on his weakest flank – he was 'in office but not in power'. Of course there was some truth in the charge. With such a low majority power was an elusive concept: the government necessarily lived from hand to mouth with too many of the Commons votes being votes for survival. Not that I acknowledged this point at the time. Instead I countered with an ill-tempered attack on the former chancellor on breakfast television, which succeeded beyond all my expectations in making me the lightning conductor for the prime minister but it did not repair the damage. We urgently needed a new political start.

Part of Major's recovery plan was to announce at the conference a new emphasis upon areas such as education and the public services. The phrase itself was provided by his policy unit but the ideas were very much his own. 'We must go back to basics,' he told the party conference.

> We want our children to be taught the best, our public services to give the best, our British industry to be the best. And the Conservative Party will lead the country back to these basics right across the board: sound money, free trade, traditional teaching, respect for the family and the law. And above all, lead a new campaign to defeat the cancer that is crime.

Reading those words today it seems incredible that the speech should have been interpreted as some kind of crusade for personal morality. Major consistently protested that this interpretation was wrong and that he had no intention of trying to tell people how they should lead their private lives. The justification for such an interpretation is claimed to be a press briefing given by the Conservative Party's director of communications, Tim Collins. According to one or two accounts of those who were there, Collins proffered the view that the basics that Major had in mind included moral basics. But if this is the defence then it is extraordinary that the point was not pursued at the twice-daily lobby briefings at Downing Street during the following weeks when the action returned to Westminster. Had this been done then journalists would have received the authentic reply that Major sets out in his memoirs: 'I had, of course, no plan for a puritanical moral crusade.'*

A much more likely explanation is that the speech gave the media a bogus justification to do what they wanted to do in any

---

* John Major, *John Major: The Autobiography* (London: HarperCollins, 1999), p. 55.

event. The David Mellor affair had been pursued relentlessly way before the 'back to basics' speech, with pure invention on occasion taking over from telephone-tapped conversations. Major's speech was useful fuel for a fresh foray into the private lives of Conservative politicians. And let no one think that the reporters who donned their dirty mackintoshes belonged exclusively to the so-called 'red top' newspapers.

Just before Christmas 1993, after the last meeting that year of the No. 12 committee, Richard Ryder asked me to come next door, where I found John Gummer already settled. The point of the meeting was that Tim Yeo, who had been having an affair, was now the father of a child. Ryder thought that the birth of a child outside marriage made the government's position on the family look ridiculous and that Yeo – a minister of state at the Department of Environment – should go. Gummer, on the other hand, a deeply religious man himself, disagreed. The mother was able to look after the child; she was a professional woman who was not suddenly having to rely on social security. The crisis was that the *News of the World* was about to run the story. I was asked my view. This was that it was a private matter and did not remotely affect Yeo's job in the Environment department. If we were to go in for moral judgements on all our colleagues then it seemed to me that we might be harder on Steve Norris, minister of state for transport, who appeared to be running a whole string of girlfriends.

The Yeo story duly appeared but with very little impact. We were not deluged with requests to comment, or calls for his immediate sacking. It was not until Thursday 30 December that the story was really given legs. I was giving the traditional New Year's message to the party: a mixture of the usual defence of the government and attack on Labour. In questions the Yeo case was not raised and at the end the reporters, including those from the much-abused tabloids, withdrew – with one exception. A BBC reporter, Nicholas Jones, had asked for a separate interview which he would prefer to have in private to preserve the sound quality. He asked me one question on my political statement and then followed up with a whole series on the position of Tim Yeo. I had heard that Labour had been quietly suggesting to journalists that they might raise the issue along the lines of 'Do you think that

Yeo's action is compatible with a government pledged to family values?'. They had generally been met with the response 'If you think that why don't you raise it?'. I was therefore genuinely surprised to find that a reporter from the BBC should be doing Labour's work. First time round I gave a not very effective reply to Jones's questions. I then asked for it to be recorded again and this time the result was crystal clear.

The next day the press in a traditionally non-news period attacked with gusto. 'How dare I suggest that this was a private matter for Yeo and his family. It was clearly a matter of public interest.' Later both I and Michael Howard were asked on the *Today* programme to define the government's attitude to adultery. My reply was to the effect that it depended on the case but if it did not compromise the minister in some way or impact upon his job then it was a private matter for the minister and his family. This was reported by the press under headlines of the kind: 'Forgive the Tory Sex Scandals'.

From beginning to end of the Yeo case, no one was able to say how it affected his job at the Department of the Environment. Nevertheless by the first days of the New Year unnamed government sources were being quoted as saying that Yeo would be out 'in days'. I noted that even though he was still a government minister I appeared to be about the only person to have publicly defended him. What seemed to be happening was the familiar and depressing process of politicians putting some distance between themselves and the unfortunate colleague in trouble. In the end Yeo was forced to resign. In a self-congratulatory book he later wrote Jones said that he had no 'particular sympathy for Yeo' and added that the Conservatives had prepared their own bed of nails by encouraging unparalleled competition between newspapers, television and radio, which has had an impact on editorial standards. Even if one accepts Jones's premise, the great advantage of the BBC is that it does not need to reduce standards for commercial pressures – and if it does then it loses its reason for being.

The truth about this period is that the media suddenly became hysterical and balanced judgement simply went out of the window. A prime example of hysteria taking hold were the comments of my old editor at the *Times*, William Rees-Mogg, who, in an article disobligingly headed 'Fowler should go next', attacked my 'eager support' for Yeo and quoted with approval the view that 'a man who is known to have fathered a child outside marriage and with no expectation of marriage' is no more fitted to public office than 'a man convicted of drunken driving'.

One of the *Times*'s political staff did say to me the same day that he was not quite sure that it was my job as chairman of the Conservative Party, outside the government, to start sacking ministers. But far more important than my personal position – I was by this time becoming the lightning conductor for the government generally – was the issue itself. The Yeo affair in effect destroyed the 'back to basics' message of John Major. More than that, it encouraged further investigation into any Tory MP who could be tolerably described as being up to some moral mischief.

A scurrying around the undergrowth produced evidence that a Conservative backbencher had shared a bed with another man in a French hotel and that Margaret Thatcher's successor in the Finchley constituency, Hartley Booth, on one weekend had travelled to New York with his female research assistant. The Booth story was a classic of its kind. Booth had the unpaid and lowly job of parliamentary private secretary to Douglas Hogg, then a middle-ranking minister at the Foreign Office. He was nevertheless transformed into a 'senior Conservative' and forced into resignation – even though to his credit Hogg strongly opposed his enforced departure.

In amongst this trivia were two cases of undoubted personal tragedy. In January the news came through that the wife of a Conservative minister, Lord Caithness, had shot herself. The media suspicion was that he was involved with another woman. The result was that the press besieged the home of the Tory minister Michael Ancram, whose wife's maiden name was similar to that of the alleged 'other woman'. In fact the media had entirely the wrong person and at Central Office we issued a statement from Ancram that said, 'My wife Jane Ancram has met Lord Caithness only once or twice in the mid-1980s at public functions and otherwise does not know him. I would be grateful if you would now leave our premises. We do not intend to answer

further questions or issue further statements.' A day or so later
Ancram told me that he counted no fewer than thirty-five
journalists and cameramen, some from the BBC, outside his
home. Surely there must be editors who are uneasy at the way
such things can get so out of hand?

An even darker tragedy was the case of Stephen Milligan at the
beginning of February 1994. Milligan was one of the brightest
Conservative backbenchers and, although an undoubted loner,
could have looked forward to a successful political career. He was
found dead at his house by his secretary, who, having been taken
to Hammersmith police station, rang my office. I went down to
Hammersmith to see her while back at Westminster the garish
details of the death leaked out: a naked body; women's black
stockings; a plastic bag over the head; an orange in the mouth.
The next day most of my colleagues in the Commons considered
the Milligan case above all a personal tragedy – but not everyone.
One Tory MP came up to me to say that I should stop praising
Milligan's political skills; and another offered the view that 'we
should keep people like him off the candidates list'. The more
typical response was again for politicians to keep their distance in
case they might be contaminated by association. I had noticed
before that when for example Nicholas Fairbairn was about to
perish as a Conservative minister gaps developed on both sides of
him as he sat for the last time on the government front bench. In
the case of Milligan I thought that we might have done better
in the turnout of Cabinet ministers at his later memorial service in
nearby St Margaret's Church, although some, such as William
Waldegrave and Peter Brooke, did attend, as too did Ted Heath.

Ironically – and utterly extraordinarily – it was in the aftermath
of these cases that the government gave its most serious
consideration to introducing privacy legislation. The timing could
hardly have been worse. I had obviously known Major's views on
the need to 'do something' in this area. I knew nothing of his affair
with Edwina Currie; had that affair been revealed in the feverish
atmosphere of 1993, who knows what the consequences would
have been? Perhaps this fuelled Major's views but it was not
remotely a complete explanation. I remember how much he
disliked the film made as a party political broadcast for the 1992

election which charted his rise from Lambeth to Downing Street. It was not that he was in any way ashamed of his background but he did not want to see it exploited. I remember also his outrage that his teenage son and his young girlfriend had been pursued by photographers.

From my position outside the government I did not know just how far the process had gone in framing new privacy laws. The revelation came in a meeting of the No. 12 committee on Monday 7 March 1994. It was announced that Peter Brooke, the national heritage secretary, intended to make a statement in the House of Commons the following week and introduce a white paper on privacy. I was horrified. This was after the most prolonged attack that any government had been under on the issue of morals and politics for thirty years. It would be seen as clearly self-serving – to say nothing of alienating the press in the run-up to the local and the European elections. The other members of the committee knew my professional interest as an ex-journalist and chairman of a regional newspaper group. But even so there was a remarkable agreement with my view. Although three of the ministers had allowed the preparations to get to this stage none of them actually supported legislation in this area. Richard Ryder said he had always been against it and obviously welcomed my intervention. Tony Newton conceded he had his doubts and believed that ministers were split on the subject. And most significantly of all, John Wakeham, who was the chairman of the committee that decided which legislation should go forward, said that it was always dangerous to bring in legislation when ministers were split. 'This has been driven by the prime minister,' he explained. Doubtless it had but one of our functions as advisers was to tell the prime minister when we thought he had got it wrong. We were after all politicians not courtiers.

Only Sarah Hogg from the policy unit had a good word to say for the plans, and her suggestion was that rather than a white paper it should be 'greener', or more tentative. I replied that that still did not meet the point. We would still be launching a debate. It was precisely what the party did not want at this stage. Apart from Hogg no one raised a single argument in favour of going ahead.

Quite the contrary, in fact. The deputy chief whip, Greg Knight, argued passionately that the plans should be abandoned on the grounds that we were in serious risk of not getting them through Parliament.

The meeting then moved to No. 10. Normally I (a government outsider) was careful to avoid meetings where civil servants were present. On this occasion civil servants such as Robin Butler were there. For the first time I argued openly with the prime minister. I repeated the arguments that I had put at No. 12 including the one on the ministerial split. Major smiled and looked around the table. 'Well, if we had not gone ahead with proposals when ministers were split, then we would not have introduced very much.' My sour reply to that was, 'Some might say that we would have been better advised not to have done so in those circumstances.'

At the meeting there was no doubt that Major was isolated. John Wakeham had now become an almost passionate advocate of abandoning the white paper; Ryder and Tony Newton agreed. The prime minister did not explicitly surrender. He asked for advice on how long the white paper could be delayed and the reasons that could be given. Nevertheless the conclusion was clear – the white paper would not be published before June and there was a substantial chance that the plans would be abandoned altogether. I noted in my diary, 'My interest as a party manager ends after the European elections. But if the government have the slightest sense they will abandon their plans altogether.' In fact no white paper ever appeared.

Of course it is one thing to oppose legislation on privacy, but does this mean that the media should hound politicians out of office for no other reason than that they have had an isolated affair? My answer to that is that politicians themselves have to decide what is important if a minister is to continue in office and what is not. They need to distinguish between fundamental issues that go to the heart of public trust in the politician's ability to carry out his job and personal matters which are best left to the individual and those closest to him to reconcile.

Instant dismissal should follow evidence of dishonesty or financial wrong-doing. Instant resignation should follow the collapse of a minister's policy or where a minister has left himself or herself compromised. After I left the chairmanship we had more than our fair share of the indefensible. Cash for questions, where backbenchers took payment for putting a commercial case while pretending it was a matter of public concern. Jonathan Aitken's suicidal libel action against the *Guardian*. Alan Clark's change of evidence in the arms-to-Iraq affair. The media is entirely entitled to pursue such issues – indeed if they do not then it is difficult to see who will act as the public guardian.

But the 'back to basics' cases were of a different kind altogether. They were essentially private affairs. They had no security implications. They might well have caused harm and distress to the individuals concerned and their families but the question was whether they had any wider political significance. Rather than running for cover or leaving their colleagues undefended politicians should be ready to say that such affairs are politically irrelevant.

That means changes in attitude, not just of individual MPs but also of all the party organisations. For in relying on the sturdiness of politicians there is one substantial road block. The political parties have consistently shown a willingness to exploit the personal difficulties and embarrassments of their opponents if they feel they can make capital.

Labour – New Labour – exploited 'back to basics', with – ironically – John Prescott helping to lead the attack. An ex-Labour MP tells a story of defending David Mellor and being roundly criticised by Alastair Campbell for his action. The Liberal Democrats on the ground have the reputation with both the other political parties for using any information which comes to hand for smearing their opponents. In the 1983 Bermondsey by-election a leaflet put out by the Liberals presented Simon Hughes as the 'straight choice' in contrast to the gay Labour candidate, Peter Tatchell. In 2006 Hughes admitted himself to having had gay relationships. The broadcast comments of several Liberal Democrat MPs at the start of 2006 about the plight of Charles Kennedy as he confronted his alcohol problems had already destroyed any lingering impression that they were 'the nice party'.

Nor, I suspect, can my own party claim to have clean hands. On 21 July 1992, very soon after I became chairman of the Conservative Party, an article appeared in the *Sun* by its editor,

Kelvin Mackenzie. Mackenzie was the most successful popular journalist of his generation. Like most newspaper people he was passionately opposed to a law on privacy. He had therefore been very alarmed to read a report that Major even then intended to introduce such a law. Mackenzie's case was that when it suited them political parties were quite prepared to intrude into the private lives of their political opponents if they thought there would be any electoral advantage.

To back up his argument Mackenzie claimed that he had been approached by a Cabinet minister during the 1992 election and given information which alleged, entirely wrongly, that Paddy Ashdown had had a number of affairs beyond the highly publicised one with his secretary, Tricia Howard. That was the charge and at Central Office we were asked whether such an approach had been made. Personally I had not heard a whisper of any such approach to the *Sun* during the time that I was with the Major campaign – although I spent virtually all of my time with him out on the road. Richard Ryder felt that the allegation was serious enough for me to ring up all the members of the Cabinet and ask them one by one if they had been involved.

This I duly did. I talked to Cabinet ministers in Westminster; I found John Gummer on an agricultural showground in East Anglia; and I reached Chris Patten in Hong Kong, where he was now governor. My report back was that no one admitted to knowledge of the affair. Grumbling gently to Ryder on why the chairman of the party should do this job, the chief whip replied succinctly, 'Welcome to the Gestapo.'

Some Gestapo. It certainly allowed a confession like Lord Jellicoe's honourable admission of indiscretion following the more lurid Lambton affair in the early 1970s – but that was all. What I did could not be dignified with the description of an inquiry: ministers were put under no cross-examination. That certainly was not the job of a party chairman outside the government. In due course Tim Collins rang Mackenzie to tell him the news that every Cabinet minister had denied making such an approach. He was greeted at the other end of the phone by gales of laughter and the next day the *Sun* gave odds on which Cabinet minister had been in touch.

I have never been happy with the outcome of this case and, as the person who was charged to inquire into the *Sun*'s allegation, I think I am entitled to state my belief. I do not believe that Mackenzie simply made up the story: he never recanted his account in the conversations I had with him long after we had both moved on. My belief is that the journalistic rule that newspapers do not reveal their sources prevented the exposure of the minister who approached him, although the more important questions were where the information came from and who plotted the course. Few issues in the 1992 parliament did the Conservative Party more harm than the allegations of personal sleaze – and yet in the preceding election it seems that one or two in the party were prepared to try to exploit the very same issue for political advantage.

10
Living on the edge
(1994-6)

'I see your problems, Norman, and I don't envy you your job.'

Margaret Thatcher, 25 May 1994.

At a meeting at Downing Street in June 1993 John Major had raised with me the prospect of his standing down if that was the only way the government could regain its strength. His concern was that if the government could not recover then the economy would not recover either. If his resignation was in the national interest then that was what he was prepared to do. 'Your job', he had told me, 'is to advise me if the position becomes irrecoverable. It's not just a question of defending me. If I went we would be able to turn over a new page. Even the blood lust of the press would be satisfied.' (*Monday 14 June 1993.*)

In essence my reply had been that we had twelve months to put things right, the crucial test being the mid-term 1994 elections. It was these elections that had now come. As well as the local elections in May there were the European elections at the beginning of June and, on the same day, a by-election at Eastleigh following Stephen Milligan's death. The European elections would be the first since the 'diet of Brussels' fiasco five years earlier, when only thirty-two of the eighty-one possible seats had been won, and we would be fighting on our weakest ground.

The prognosis was not good. In the opinion polls Conservative support now stood at a meagre 25 per cent with Labour a massive 20 points ahead. The 'back to basics' stories had filled the newspapers relentlessly, week by week since the beginning of the year. At the end of March the government's 'compromise' settlement on qualified voting in the European Council was widely seen as a humiliating defeat, provoking the maverick Tory MP Tony Marlow to call for the prime minister's resignation on the floor of the House of Commons. Polls to mark the second anniversary of Major's successful 1992 election campaign showed that two thirds of the public thought he should stand down. The mood inside the party – at least that part which was not in constant rebellion – was also changing. When once they had wanted moderation, they now hankered for a 'strong' leader who with one jump would restore them to electoral success. Among MPs Michael Heseltine still had many supporters – although my guess is that Major himself would have nominated Ken Clarke as his successor.

First into battle were the Conservative councils. Something of the mood at the time was provided by the leaders of Wandsworth Council, one of the party's undoubted flagship authorities. At Central Office we received the blunt message that in the local election they would be fighting on their local record and wanted nothing to do with any national campaign, a fact which fortunately received no publicity. They were embarrassed by the government's disarray but even more by the activities of those Conservative MPs at Westminster who, with elections looming, were still fighting very public battles on European policy. The point was put to me in the West Midlands a few days before the elections themselves. As I was talking to a group of Conservative council leaders in Wolverhampton, one of the councillors looked over my shoulder to where Nick Budgen, the fiercely Eurosceptic MP for Wolverhampton South West, was standing. 'Just keep the MPs off the air,' he said. I had known Budgen since Cambridge and just as I was leaving he came up and smilingly said, 'I am keeping a low profile so you can't blame me if things go wrong.'

Even this limited objective was not followed by all. As I drove away from Wolverhampton to my constituency *The World at One* carried an outspoken interview with the Tory MP David Evans, who had acquired a Commons reputation for the loudness of his voice and his right-wing views. His 'authority' came from the fact that he had been elected to the executive of the backbench 1922

Committee. With four days to go before vital elections he delivered a blistering attack on the government and called for the sacking of half the Cabinet. The political lunatics were threatening the asylum. No fewer than 84 per cent of the public now thought of the Conservative Party as disunited – the traditional reputation for unity had been entirely demolished. Major was once again fighting to survive.

The council results were bad. We held Wandsworth and Trafford but that was about the limit of our success. All told, the party lost more than 400 seats and control of eighteen councils, including Wolverhampton. The Conservative share of the vote was a meagre 27 per cent. The biggest advance came from the Liberal Democrats, who matched us at 27 per cent, while Labour at 41 per cent were well ahead but below their opinion poll rating. All eyes were now on the European elections. If the voting deteriorated further then Major's position would be untenable.

In fighting this election we faced one potentially fatal problem: we had no money. Slowly the party was recovering from its bankrupt state but there was next to nothing to spend on advertising. It is true that with the help of a bright young man called Steve Hilton (who now is a senior adviser to David Cameron) we devised challenging posters, which we launched with great gusto on advertising vans in front of the cameras in Smith Square. But, as one or two of the more sharp eyed complained, they never seemed to appear on any hoarding outside in the country. The truth was exactly that. They did not and we went through the whole campaign virtually without national advertising. What little money we did scrape together was devoted to party political broadcasts, which we could not avoid. Fortunately for us we were rescued by Labour, who certainly had more money to spend than the 'rich' Conservatives but mounted such a lacklustre campaign that it could scarcely have influenced anyone.

And there is the rub. My abiding memory of my two years at Central Office was that Labour campaigns did us little harm. I never felt we were up against political giants. Leaving John Smith and Tony Blair to one side, it was difficult to spot the stars. Robin Cook was one – a politician who was more effective in opposition than in government – but Gordon Brown was never a feared opponent. Most of the others on the Labour front bench were worthy enough but decidedly supporting actors. The truth was that the political damage to the government was predominantly self-inflicted. That was certainly the view of the party in the country. At party conferences attacks on Conservative MPs were greeted with strong applause. At a meeting in the West Midlands one MP, Ivan Lawrence, was virtually shouted down as he sought to defend his colleagues in the aftermath of the council elections. The agents were particularly critical.

Not that any of this criticism had the effect of abating the European debate inside the parliamentary party. By now it was well known that the doubters were not confined to the back benches but included several Cabinet ministers, dubbed the 'bastards' by Major in a careless comment transmitted from a television studio to the outside world. For such ministers the European elections provided an acutely difficult test. They had not supported the Maastricht settlement; they were followers of Thatcher, not Major, on Europe; but even so they could not campaign against Conservative candidates. Such action would have been regarded as treason. In elections you support Conservative candidates or you leave the party. Accordingly a new tactic was followed by the doubters. Rather than campaign for Conservative candidates they would quietly absent themselves. Although the prime minister's fate self-evidently depended upon the outcome and although they were ministers in his government, they did not intend to take an active part in the battle.

At a crucial stage in the campaign the issue became, of all things, aggressive beggars on the streets of Bristol. Major had condemned such intimidation in an interview for the local evening paper and had been promptly condemned by the other parties as 'uncaring'. Their case was that it was a lack of proper social security support which forced young people to take this step. So where was Peter Lilley, the social security secretary, when we needed him? In France.

Another non-combatant was Margaret Thatcher. With two weeks to go before polling I asked her to issue a warning against voting Liberal Democrat. There was nothing doing. The former leader was perfectly friendly but conceded that she was keeping 'a low profile' in the European election. Her view was that most Conservative MEPs were the worst kind of federalists. 'I see your problems, Norman, and I don't envy you your job,' she said cheerfully, before adding comfortingly, 'I shall be voting, dear, and so will Denis.'

To add to Major's dangerous vulnerability the vast majority of the British press, including all the papers of Rupert Murdoch and Conrad Black, had now turned against him. Major, of course, has been much mocked for his legendary sensitivity to the press and there is no denying that at every opportunity he would pick up newspapers. Any newspaper would do, from the midday *Evening Standard* outside the Cabinet Room to whatever local newspaper happened to be around. Equally there is no doubt that it had a debilitating effect upon the man himself. There is no joy in reading day after day of criticism and personal abuse.

So why persist? Certainly he did not lack advice to stop reading but he ignored it all. Personally I had found that six years handling both health and social security had taught me the days to skip the press. Perhaps Major's ascent to No. 10 had been too rapid for him to develop the defensive reflexes of a minister under fire. It was only after he became prime minister that the journalistic bombs started landing. He had never before had to deal with the hostile profile or the scathing editorial. But having said that, there is one point which should not be forgotten – not least by some of the smug and self-satisfied journalists who rather relished the power that they had been given. If anyone ever had reason to feel badly treated by the press it was John Major.

In the autumn of 1993 I was sent on a peace mission to Wapping to try to improve relations with the *Sun* and its editor, Kelvin Mackenzie. My diary set out a note of Mackenzie's advice:

1. We will support the Conservative cause.
2. Rupert Murdoch will support the Conservative cause.
3. We may not have been helpful since the last election but we will be there on the day, i.e. at the next election.
4. We report what we hear. We are a newspaper. It is not personal.
5. Provided John Major survives, we will back him.

6. Tell the PM to relax. Tell him not to read the newspapers in the way he does.
7. Don't punish us with VAT on newspapers.
8. Meetings between me and the PM are not a good idea. We are never likely to have a meeting of minds.
9. Tell the PM not to be rude to my staff. Following some article or other John Major turned his back on Trevor Kavanagh.

Of course there are glaring misstatements in this advice. The *Sun* did not back the Conservatives and by the time of the 1995 leadership contest was urging MPs to dump their leader. But as a statement of how politicians and journalists should handle their relations it was not altogether bad advice. They should be apart. Politicians make themselves weak by wooing the proprietors, the editors and the correspondents. It also has little long-term effect. Blair may have courted Rupert Murdoch but that did not prevent Murdoch's papers turning on him as his unpopularity rose. Newspapers do not like being out of step with their readers.

In 1994 there was much more to it than that. Most of the press was owned by confirmed Eurosceptics and unsurprisingly many of their editors and columnists were in the same mould. Murdoch owned the *Sun*, the *News of the World*, the *Sunday Times* and my old paper, the *Times*, which was edited by the sceptical Peter Stothard, supported by columnists such as William Rees-Mogg, who patronisingly wrote off Major as a chief whip who had missed his vocation. For Murdoch Europe was non-negotiable. This was made clear to Major at a private dinner that the two men and their wives had at Downing Street in the mid-1990s. From that conversation Major is convinced that had he changed the government's stance on Europe to one of scepticism then the Murdoch press would have thrown its support behind him. To his credit he refused – you only had to observe the caution on Europe by Blair to understand that not all leaders are so brave.

At the *Daily Mail* there was Paul Dacre – and Simon Heffer, who shared most of the views of Enoch Powell (including his antagonism to any move in the direction of European union) and was implacably opposed to Major. Most interesting of all was the position on the two Telegraph papers, which had traditionally supported Conservative governments. For most of Major's premiership the *Sunday Telegraph* was edited by Charles Moore. He left to edit the daily in 1995. Moore was close to Margaret Thatcher in her exile and later was appointed her official biographer. He shared most of her views and even today divides the Conservative world into true Thatcherites and the rest. On Europe he was a dedicated enemy of Major. His counterpart on the *Daily Telegraph* for most of the Major years was Max Hastings, whose closest political friends were Michael Heseltine, Douglas Hurd and Ken Clarke. He was neither an ideologue nor a confirmed sceptic. However, he was content to take his line on Europe from his proprietor and defended his position to me by saying that any complaint about his paper's hostile position should go to Conrad Black. He was just a 'journo' – or more accurately the hired hand.

To be fair, not all the government's problems could be blamed on the sceptics and the press. Clearly the single currency would be an issue in the 1994 European campaign and Major saw the advantage of promising a referendum on whether we should join – an initiative I strongly supported. So would I ring the Cabinet to find their views? This was beginning to become a habit but I did so and discovered that ministers were all over the place. There were strong supporters such as Michael Howard, who believed that we would be 'mad' not to keep the referendum option open, and Virginia Bottomley, who saw it as the only way of 'lancing the boil', while the leading opponents were the Europhiles in the Cabinet. Heseltine thought a referendum would be 'bananas' and Clarke was not much less outspoken. In the middle was a group of ministers such as David Hunt and Ian Lang,* who would go along with a referendum if the prime minister thought it would take the trick. In a vote around the Cabinet table Major would have certainly won but a vote would have ignored the fact that some of the prime minister's most senior colleagues and his strongest personal supporters were implacably opposed. In the end it was the Liberal Democrats, not exactly Eurosceptics, who first

---

* Scottish secretary, later trade and industry secretary.

grasped the opportunity of promising a referendum. Major was prevented from (or at least persuaded against) doing what he wanted to do by his friends.

Just as the European elections were getting under way there came a day which fundamentally changed the political picture. On Thursday 12 May the leader of the Labour Party, John Smith, died. Smith had been a popular figure on both sides of the Commons. He could be a devastating debater but there was also an appealing sense of mischief about him. After an attack on the government front bench he would look around the Commons' chamber with a satisfied glint in his eyes as if expecting his opponents also to share in his success. Serious campaigning ended and it was not until ten days later that it properly resumed – although even then Labour were as concerned about the leadership succession as the European elections. From the Conservative benches Tony Blair always seemed the obvious successor: he epitomised a new, fresh Labour Party far more convincingly than Gordon Brown.

At Central Office there were some optimists who thought that Major – once himself the new young man on the block – might be now seen by the public as the leader of experience, the great survivor. In fact in the aftermath of Smith's death the Conservative position worsened. On Thursday 2 June – a week before the vote – the news came through that Gallup in next day's *Daily Telegraph* would show the party running third. In findings which were extraordinarily bad, even by the dire standards of that time, Labour were at 54 per cent, the Liberal Democrats at 21.5 per cent and the Conservatives at a pathetic 20 per cent. Even on election day itself the opinion poll in the *Times* showed support at 23 per cent and predicted that the number of Conservative seats won would be less than ten.

By now no one expected the Conservatives to improve on their 1989 result. The question was: just how bad would defeat be and, above all, how many seats did Major have to hold without his position becoming untenable? Expectations were revealingly low. Major's view was that the 'acceptability level' was ten to fifteen; mine was that we could live with anything in double figures. We both agreed that if we went into single figures then there would be a personal crisis for the prime minister.

Major was determined to continue whatever the result. I was not so certain that that was a realistic prospect and remembered his earlier injunction that my job was not just to defend but to advise.

The first indication from polling day on 9 June was anything but encouraging. In the Eastleigh by-election the party not only ran third but failed to win even 20 per cent of the vote. If that kind of result was replicated in the European elections then the party faced wipe-out. But there was a delay of a few days, as all the results from the different nations were to be announced on the same day to avoid the risk of one country influencing another.* When eventually they were announced it was clear that the worst crisis had been avoided.

The Liberal Democrats' challenge had faded and they achieved just 16.7 per cent of the poll. Labour had won 44 per cent – well below their opinion poll rating – and the Conservatives had ended with almost 28 per cent of the vote and eighteen seats in the new European Parliament. In most times this would have been seen as an unquestionably bad result: a 5 per cent swing from the much criticised campaign of 1989. But this was 1994. Expectations were so low that it appeared a modest success. The *Times* reported that there had been 'no melt-down' and judged that Major had won himself 'a breathing space'. That was also the view of most other commentators, although one or two did note that if only a few thousand votes had switched then the Conservatives would have been left with four or five seats – virtual wipe-out. For once luck was with the prime minister. A day later, when I went to see him in the garden of Downing Street to present my own resignation, he moved his hand across his neck in mock relief. He had escaped the executioner but, as he recognised, only 'just'.

My two-year stint at Central Office had now ended. The party's debt was continuing to reduce and, extraordinarily given all the government's problems, the organisation was in better shape than when I arrived. The Research Department, thanks entirely to the then director, Andrew Lansley, and some star staff, maintained a very high standard in both research and briefing. The

---

* Britain traditionally holds its national elections, including the European election, on a Thursday, while France, for example, votes on Sunday.

next stage was to prepare for the general election. What was now needed was not only a new face – I had taken more flak in two years at Central Office than in eleven in government – but also a chairman who would be part of government with a seat at the Cabinet table.

Jeremy Hanley succeeded me as chairman – being preferred to other well-backed candidates such as David Hunt, Gillian Shephard and Jonathan Aitken – and I returned once more to the back benches. It was not until June 1995 that I was brought back seriously into the fray. In my absence the position had not improved, which on the surface was curious. For although Major's ministerial team of the mid-1990s may not have been a government of all the talents, neither was it one of second-raters and no-hopers. Michael Heseltine was a pivotal figure in the Cabinet and in July 1995 became deputy prime minister, only a tantalising step away from what had always been his ultimate ambition. At the Treasury Ken Clarke presided over an ever-strengthening economy and added to his reputation as the government's most robust communicator. Michael Howard pursued initiative after initiative at the Home Office in an effort to bring down crime, while the Foreign Office was in the safe hands of first Douglas Hurd and then Malcolm Rifkind. Beneath them there were Cabinet ministers of undoubted worth such as Michael Portillo, John Gummer, Ian Lang and Virginia Bottomley. It was a team more than able to hold its own against the Labour front bench and as the months went by there were occasional flashes of light which gave hope that the government might even now recover support. In particular there was the prospect that Major might succeed in bringing the bloody conflict in Northern Ireland to an end.

But movement consisted of a faltering step forward followed by several decisive paces back. By far the most serious development was a series of political scandals which went far beyond the issues of personal morals raised by back to basics. In July 1994 the *Sunday Times* revealed that two Conservative MPs had agreed to put down questions to ministers in the Commons for the payment of cash. A newspaper reporter had posed as a businessman to get the story but the MPs could hardly complain of that.

A few months later in October allegations were made that two further MPs – Tim Smith and Neil Hamilton – had accepted money from the owner of Harrods, Mohammed Al Fayed, without declaring the payments. Most of the allegations referred back to the 1980s, when Margaret Thatcher was in power, but it was not considered a defence, any more than Gordon Brown is able to defend his party's funding scandals by pointing to Tony Blair. The public were not interested in the exact timings. When all was said and done they were Tory MPs who became Tory ministers. It gave credence to Blair's often-repeated charge that the government appeared 'tainted'. It all seemed to be ending in the same way as Harold Macmillan's government in the 1960s after thirteen years of power.

The issue of Europe continued to divide the party. At the end of November 1994 the sceptics mounted a new challenge on the European Communities Finance Bill, which they saw not as an 'international treaty obligation' (Douglas Hurd) but a measure 'to increase the taxes we pay to Brussels' (Norman Lamont). Major quite explicitly treated it as a vote of confidence and when, even in those circumstances, eight Conservative MPs abstained the whip was withdrawn. The eight included Nick Budgen, Theresa Gorman and Teddy Taylor, and a slightly farcical addition was made to that number by the long-serving Richard Body, who insisted on joining them in exile. Nothing on this scale had happened in living memory. But it was a tactic which misfired. The Whipless Nine, as they had now become, received more attention than before and if anything were treated as martyrs punished for their beliefs. They were later readmitted to the parliamentary party on an assurance of 'good behaviour'. But that was soon forgotten and they strutted their success. The attempt at firm discipline had been defeated. The government with its wafer-thin majority showed itself dangerously powerless.

Against such a background election success was impossible. There were still several years before there needed to be a general election but in the meantime the public took every opportunity to give the government a good kick. In the Scottish council elections in April 1995 Conservative representation was reduced to a mere eighty-one councillors and in the English council elections the next month the Conservatives lost more than 2,000 seats. During the parliament every Conservative-held seat falling vacant in a by-election was lost.

By June 1995 the position had never looked more desperate, a leadership challenge never more likely. In my diary, I commented:

> The latest opinion poll shows us down to 20 per cent and Labour with a virtual 40 per cent lead. John has escaped so many crises that perhaps he will escape this too. Perhaps Northern Ireland will emerge as the success we all want. As a party we are reduced to hoping that something will turn up. No one is very confident that it will. If nothing does then a leadership challenge in the autumn must be a possibility. I wouldn't entirely rule out John standing down. (*Friday 9 June 1995.*)

I was not far out. Having been barracked at a 'private' meeting of sixty Eurosceptic backbenchers Major was at the end of his tether. He felt he had two options. He could stand down voluntarily – and he certainly seriously considered this step – or he could call a 'back me or sack me' election. He decided to confront the party well before it or any likely contender was expecting. Personally I doubted the tactic. It all had an uncanny resemblance to Thatcher's unsuccessful leadership campaign in 1990 but I had to concede that there was one crucial difference. Major had no intention of absenting himself from the field of battle. He intended to fight for every vote.

Even so, no one predicted the opponent. Norman Lamont had seemed the likeliest man to stand against the prime minister from the back benches, while supporters of Michael Portillo hoped that he would raise the Thatcherite standard. The prospect that the Welsh secretary, John Redwood, would resign from the Cabinet to take on the prime minister was largely unconsidered. I had first known Redwood when he was part of Thatcher's policy unit, a position which suited him down to the ground. He was bright and challenging but, like most other Tory MPs at the time, I had never in my wildest dreams contemplated him as party leader. Given his stance on Europe he was lucky to be in the Cabinet at all and my abiding memory of him in office as Welsh secretary was him standing on a platform attempting to sing the Welsh national anthem. An even more bizarre sight came at the start of his campaign, when he was photographed with his leading supporters: on one side political eccentrics such as Gorman and Tony Marlow, the latter resplendent in an old school cricket blazer rescued from the recesses of some wardrobe for the occasion; on the other Lamont, wondering quite what he was doing in this company. But for all that it was a serious challenge from a member of the Cabinet and it held the prospect that a vote for Redwood would not necessarily make him prime minister but it would certainly depose Major.

The election was set for Tuesday 4 July and the electorate of Conservative MPs did not lack advice from Major's enemies in the right-wing press. Conrad Black's two papers spoke as one. The *Sunday Telegraph* said that Redwood offered 'a bold readiness to lead and a clear sense of direction' and should be backed, not as a stalking horse, but on his own merits, while the *Daily Telegraph*, having invited Major to set out his case, published an entirely hostile leader next to it, written by Max Hastings himself, which strongly argued that it was 'time for a change of leadership'. The Murdoch press was equally united. The *Times* accused Major of setting out 'deliberately to antagonise the right' and said that a vote for him was a vote 'for disunity and defeat'. The *Sunday Times* wanted to depose Major so that 'the Cabinet's frustrated heavyweights' (Heseltine and Portillo) could enter the lists. The *News of the World* took a similar line, while the *Sun* published a front-page leader headlined 'Vote Major – and vote in Labour', which followed an article by Norman Tebbit two days before entitled 'If the PM won't change the policies we'll have to change the PM'. As for the *Daily Mail*, it devoted the entire front page on polling day to a leader proclaiming 'Time to ditch the captain'.

Major, then, was fighting on two fronts. A minority wanted to see Redwood win for his own sake (they included Tebbit and Iain Duncan Smith) but many more wanted to use the vote to displace Major and have a second round of voting with new candidates – as in the Thatcher leadership contest. For Major the test was how many votes he needed to stay on as leader. Technically the answer was 165, a majority of the parliamentary party, while also gaining a 15 per cent margin over the other candidate. David Davis, who was operating as Major's chief whip in the campaign, provided background briefing to justify even that figure but in truth everyone knew that the majority had to be greater. Major certainly had to poll 200 votes and his own test was 215. In the event he won 218 votes, with Redwood on 89 and 20 abstentions. It was not a bad result but it could not disguise the fact that one third of the parliamentary party had either voted against the prime minister or abstained. Not that his campaign team allowed any such doubts to surface as, on script, we claimed a decisive victory in our instant responses before the television cameras and the radio microphones. Compared to the Thatcher leadership contest five years previously, the Major campaign was a model of how it should be done.

We were, of course, far too tactful to crow about another victory – our victory over the media. Who knew when we would need their support again? But it is at least an interesting piece of political history that Major won against the overwhelming pressure of the British press. Leader writer after leader writer had condemned our man but most of the parliamentary party had ignored their splutter. The man who had been freely attacked as too weak, too sensitive, too indecisive had taken a brave stand and come out victorious. Not of course that the victory was a knockout. Even now in the internet age you can never entirely defeat the people who control the printing presses. The proprietors, the editors, the leader writers will always have the last word. Their view would be that if the party had taken their advice then the catastrophe of 1997 might have been avoided.

11
The rout (1997)

'We have secured a mandate to bring the nation together – to unite
us – one Britain, one nation.'

Tony Blair, outside 10 Downing Street, Friday 2 May 1997.

There was no new chapter. John Major had won the battle with
his parliamentary rebels but nothing changed. The arguments
were not stilled. In the twelve months leading up to the 1997
election campaign the same issues divided the party. There was
the same open dissent. The same kind of side issues tripped up the
government. The economy might have strengthened beyond
recognition, so that after the election Ken Clarke could boast of
the golden legacy he had passed to his Labour successor, Gordon
Brown; unemployment might have fallen; and compared with
much of the European Union Britain was basking in prosperity.
But Major's government received precious little credit for this
improvement and was just about to disprove the conventional
wisdom that the only thing that matters in elections is 'the
economy, stupid'.

The government was portrayed as 'immersed in sleaze' and
utterly disunited, but the most extraordinary feature of the whole
period was how so many Conservative MPs ignored the
undoubted signs of impending catastrophe. They refused to mend
their ways. They continued to batter the government as if it were
run by Labour or the Liberal Democrats. They walked blindly to
a disaster where sceptics and non-sceptics perished together. They
did nothing to avoid their fate – and by their actions some helped
bring it about.

One of the most damaging examples was the action of a
government minister, the diarist Alan Clark, in advising British

firms how to evade a trade embargo on the supply of arms to Saddam Hussein. The case had first become public at the beginning of December 1990 with a report from the *Sunday Times* Insight team, who had an enviable record in exposing scandal. In essence the charge was that in 1988, when Clark had been minister of state for trade in the Thatcher government, he had an important meeting with a number of representatives from the British machine tool industry. At the meeting Clark had advised that any applications for licences to export machine tools to Iraq should emphasise the 'peaceful aspect to which they will be put' and stress the 'general engineering' usage of machine tools.

One passage from the report quoted a managing director present at the meeting:

> The minister left those at the meeting in no doubt that the government was prepared to allow the export of machine tools, even if they did end up producing shells for the Iraqi army. 'Everybody knew the machines could make shells,' he [the managing director] said. 'The minister was giving us a nod and a wink.'

The day after the *Sunday Times* articles appeared, Clark was interviewed personally by Major, accompanied by Robin Butler, the head of the civil service. Clark flatly denied the 'nod and a wink' charge and maintained that any guilt lay with the firms involved. He maintained that position in a witness statement given to Customs & Excise and the result was that in October 1992 three men were put on trial at the Old Bailey. It was at this point that Clark, who had now left Parliament, changed his evidence. In cross-examination he said that he thought the government's guidelines 'tiresome and intrusive' and agreed he had been 'economical with the *actualité*'. The prosecution case collapsed in total disarray.

This was not remotely the end of the story. Major had no alternative but to set up an independent inquiry, under Lord Justice Scott. Extraordinarily, Scott's process of investigation was so prolonged that his final report was not published until 1996. During that time allegation followed allegation about government dishonesty and, although when the final report was at last

published most of the allegations were knocked down, the
political damage had been done. Four years of hostile headlines
were not forgotten. Much worse, three men had been put on trial
at the Old Bailey on the evidence of a government minister who
had had countless opportunities to tell the truth. The proper end
would have been for Clark himself to be put in the dock.

In the immediate prelude to the election the divisions and the
squabbles continued. In February 1997 almost 100 Conservative
MPs voted against the government's gun control legislation; Ted
Heath attacked the government's policy on Europe and on the
constitution; Norman Tebbit attacked Michael Heseltine as
'tacky' and accused him of killing off our greatest peace-time
leader; and, unsurprisingly, a by-election at Wirral South was lost
with a 17 per cent swing against the government. 'Why do we
think this is all going to change by the time of the general
election?' I asked in my diary. 'Why do we assume that the
conventional political wisdom, that it will be "much closer than
you think", is right?'

In the first weeks of March the former treasurer of the
Conservative Party Lord McAlpine attacked Major as completely
inept; Margaret Thatcher was reported as praising the abilities of
the man most likely to be the next prime minister, Tony Blair;
while Stephen Grabiner, the executive director of the *Daily
Express*, told me that all the leading Tories who came to lunch at
the *Express* were much more interested in the leadership contest
which they believed would follow the party's defeat at the
election rather than escaping the defeat itself. It was as if they
could not conceive of life seriously changing. Certainly they
would be in opposition but they would bounce back, just as the
party had bounced back after Heath's defeat in 1974. The
Conservatives, after all, were the natural party of government.

On Monday 17 March the election was finally called. The
government had served a full term and had run out of
parliamentary road. It was to be a six-week campaign with polling
on Thursday 1 May. The expressed reason for the campaign's
unusual length was to allow Labour policies to be put under
scrutiny: the sub-text was that it might allow the government to
recover in the opinion polls. These showed the Conservatives at

only 31 per cent and Labour 22 percentage points ahead. The Liberal Democrats were trailing with a mere 12 per cent. Straightaway the *Sun*, which claimed (wrongly) that it had won the 1992 election for Major, declared for Labour, while the campaign itself opened to the worst possible start. Almost immediately the public were reminded of the two issues that had scarred the last five years – sleaze and Europe.

In the Cheshire constituency of Tatton Neil Hamilton found himself opposed by an independent candidate, the well-known BBC correspondent Martin Bell; Labour and the Liberal Democrats did not put up candidates. The Scottish Conservative Association – in any event a shadow of its former self – seemed to be embroiled in feuding which became ever more personal, leading to its chairman, Michael Hirst, giving up public life. While at the end of March the *Sun* led with a story, together with photographs, of an affair between Piers Merchant, the Conservative MP for Beckenham, and a young night-club hostess.

There was not much that any uninvolved Tory candidate could do about such goings on – except curse – but on Europe there certainly was. The question was whether Britain should join the single currency. By now the government was pursuing a policy that amounted to keeping options open *plus* the assurance that no decision would be taken without the approval of the public in a referendum. But even this was not enough for many Tory candidates. They wanted to say that they were irrevocably opposed under any circumstances to such a change. Some said it explicitly; some kept to the official line in their published material but left it to their campaign offices to make it clear that they were opposed; some signed up to a *Daily Mail* declaration under a 'Battle for Britain' banner and were rewarded by inclusion in a roll of honour.

Once again the party was all over the place and on 16 April Major had to use a party political broadcast to make a direct appeal to his own party not to wreck his European policy. It was one of the most effective broadcasts he ever made – but who has ever heard of a party leader having to appeal to his own party for loyalty in the middle of an election campaign? Even worse, it did not work in providing unity. Two days later Central Office produced a poster which showed Blair as a ventriloquist's dummy on the knees of the German chancellor, Helmut Kohl. This time it was the turn of the pro-Europeans to react. Ken Clarke described it as 'puerile', Geoffrey Howe said it was 'damaging' and Ted Heath denounced it as 'abhorrent'.

Not surprisingly, during the campaign the media concentrated on Europe and sleaze. A later survey which measured the relative importance of the issues reported by BBC 1, ITV, Channel 4 and Radio 4 found that the most important issue covered was, of course, Europe. This was followed by the partly connected issue of the constitution, with 'sleaze' at number three. In the 1992 election neither Europe nor sleaze had featured in the top eleven news subjects and numbers one and two were the economy and tax. It all defined an election which the Conservatives were never going to win.

And so it seemed from the ground throughout the long campaign. With the exception of periodic forays into other constituencies, optimistically rated marginal, I spent the general election of 1997 solidly knocking on the doors of Sutton Coldfield. This was not an election to take your constituency for granted. It was crystal clear how it was proceeding. 'Tell me privately,' said a genuinely puzzled voter, 'are you really trying to lose this election so that Labour can inherit all the problems there are?' As far as I could judge he was a Conservative voter, absolutely serious, convinced that there was some rational explanation for our behaviour. If only that had been true.

Summing up my own views in my diary the weekend before polling, I wrote bleakly of my experience in the constituency and elsewhere in the Midlands. 'I have yet to meet any voter who voted Labour or Liberal Democrat in 1992 who is now going to switch to us. Not one. On the other hand I have met plenty who voted Conservative in 1992 and are now moving away.'

The final results were just as dismal as I feared and the opinion polls predicted. The swing of 10 per cent from Conservative to Labour was greater than anything since 1945. Labour won 418 seats and an overall majority of 179. The Conservatives were reduced to 165. Seven Cabinet ministers were defeated, including possible leadership candidates such as Michael Portillo, Malcolm

Rifkind and Ian Lang. The Liberal Democrats won forty-six seats and gained traditional Tory strongholds such as Harrogate, Lewes and Wimbledon. Bell beat Hamilton in Tatton. Major announced his resignation and on the doorstep of No. 10 Blair stole some more traditional Conservative clothes when he declared: 'We have secured a mandate to bring the nation together – to unite us – one Britain, one nation, in which our ambition for ourselves is matched by our sense of compassion and decency and duty towards others.'

Could the defeat have been avoided? Almost certainly not. The result established again the political truth that the public will not back an utterly divided party to govern the country. They are not fools.

The Conservative government had been in power for eighteen years and had won four elections in a row. Even without the five years of suicidal madness leading up to the 1997 election it would have been a brave person who would have bet on a fifth victory. But had the Conservative Party changed its leader, as most of the press wanted, would at least some part of the rout have been avoided?

I am doubtful. There were undoubted drawbacks to Major's consensual style of government: holding the balance risked becoming a way of life. It prevented Major from doing some of the things he wanted to do, which might have made a difference if done at the right time. An earlier promise of a referendum on the single currency was a case in point. Another issue, far away from the politics of Europe, was railway privatisation. Major was in favour of privatising the railways into regional companies so that the operating company was also responsible for the track. The Treasury and the Department of Transport supported separation. Major's solution would have avoided the later quarrels of whether it was the operating company or the track company which was responsible for failures in service. Major was right – his gut instincts often were – but he deferred to his ministers and their advisers. Neither Michael Heseltine nor Ken Clarke would have been so accommodating – so collegiate – on an issue where their view clashed with the departmental advice.

But the truth is that the government's perilously low majority often determined what could be attempted. It became in effect a minority government – and not just with regard to Europe. Take the possible privatisation of Royal Mail. The case for allowing Royal Mail to develop and expand in the private sector was overwhelming. In Germany Deutsche Post did just that to its enormous advantage. In Britain the plain fact was that Major's government would never have succeeded in taking such a privatisation measure through Parliament. It could have been done in the 1980s but not in the 1990s. The government would have been opposed outright by Labour and the Liberal Democrats and joined by Tory rebels claiming to guard their rural interests. Any prospect of privately financed development was prevented.

Simon Jenkins suggests we were just too 'kind' and that a really gritty party would have removed Major. But who would have replaced him? The two most senior members of the government were Heseltine and Clarke, but both were massively out of sympathy with the rising tide of Euroscepticism inside the party. Portillo was certainly one of the leading Eurosceptics but even then they were not in the majority in the party or the government. And here is one of the difficulties in contemplating even in retrospect any alternative to Major. If this quintessentially reasonable man could seriously think of himself as personally divisive, what kind of impact would Heseltine or Clarke or Portillo have had?

It is just possible that had Major voluntarily stood down in favour of Heseltine with, say, a year to go before the election, then the bounce might have worked – provided that the initial period of inevitable turmoil was surmounted. He would have taken on the sceptics in Parliament and appealed over their heads to the party outside. It would certainly have been an exciting ride and the style of the new man might have avoided the very worst of the defeat – although not the defeat itself. After all in 1963, when Harold Macmillan gave way to Alec Douglas-Home (not, I concede, exactly in the same mould as Heseltine) he almost pulled off a fourth election victory. But to swap Major for Heseltine would have been a colossal gamble and success would have depended entirely upon the parliamentary party supporting or at least following. To hope for that in 1997 would have been a substantial triumph of desperate hope over bitter experience.

Would Margaret Thatcher or Norman Tebbit have welcomed the change? Would the fervently Eurosceptic press have rallied to Heseltine's cause? I very much doubt it.

The party had not yet become accustomed to changing its leader every few years. Forcibly dropping Major would have split further an already fractured party. The wreakers of havoc were never the majority. Most MPs and ministers, myself included, admired Major for his grit in a near-impossible position, resented the attempts to hijack the party onto another course, and were certainly not persuaded that a change of leader meant that with one bound the government would be free. What is certain is that we would have given in to some of the worst elements inside the party. Decency would have been defeated. Politics might be a rough game but thank goodness that even in the context of the mid-1990s such considerations still mattered.

At the end of a long strike the public only remember who won and who lost. The same is broadly true of prime ministers when their periods in office are assessed. Among recent Conservative premiers Churchill and Thatcher will be counted as undoubted winners and Eden and Heath just as certain losers. Douglas-Home was a stop-gap who did rather better than was thought, and views still differ on the record of Macmillan – although I for one give the great showman credit for having rescued the government after the debacle of Suez. By this bleak and generalised measure Major, in power for a lengthy seven years, undoubtedly lost. The public will remember the scale of the 1997 defeat, the party divisions and the sleaze. They will remember the 'nasty party', as Theresa May, a chairman of the Conservative Party, so memorably described it. Inevitably Major will carry the can for all that. But if there is any political justice (a rather doubtful proposition) future historians will also recount his impossible inheritance. How he was substantially brought down by his own side. How his predecessor was prepared to fight back against her dismissal on the one issue that was capable of breaking the Tory Party asunder. How he was undermined by a determined group within his own parliamentary party. And how many of the same people who brought him to power turned their back on him after he had served their purpose of defeating Heseltine.

They might also reflect on some of the government's undoubted successes. Major left behind an unquestionably strong and growing economy. He had inherited an inflation rate of 9.7 per cent and brought it down to 2.6 per cent; he had inherited interest rates at 14 per cent and brought them down to 6 per cent. But was this not all a result of leaving the ERM? Major's reply to that would be that the inflationary psychology had been broken precisely because of Britain's membership of the ERM. By the time Britain left inflation was established on a firm downwards direction. Its job had been done and it is even suggested that by the autumn of 1992 some inside No. 10 were contemplating a voluntary departure.

Away from the economy Major laid the necessary foundations for peace in Northern Ireland, a contribution that Tony Blair very fairly acknowledged. Meanwhile in political terms, although he did not keep the Conservative Party together, he at least kept it as one party. Most important of all, by winning the 1992 election and persisting, often in the direst political weather, Major achieved a sea change in British politics.

A popular theory inside the party has always been that in 1992 the Conservatives would have done much better to have narrowly lost the election and then bounced back next time. But it is a theory that overlooks the central political point. By the time of the election the Conservative government had been in power for thirteen years but that did not mean that all the changes so painfully made would stick. Defeat would have put it all at risk. The then leader of the Labour Party was Neil Kinnock, not Blair. His political career had been built from the socialist left of the Labour Party. To his credit he had taken on the Militant Tendency. Nevertheless he was pledged to restore some of the damaging labour laws which after titanic struggles had been abolished by the Thatcher government. Had Kinnock been elected there would have been no pledge to keep to the public spending plans of the last Conservative chancellor; no partnership agreements between public and private sector; and no 'one nation' plan to promote home ownership for all.

The 1992 result and Major's dogged retention of power in the years that followed had a profound effect upon British politics. It forced Labour finally to change. The message was driven home that change had to go further than a red rose in the buttonhole of a few smart suits. A change of substance was required. The Labour Party was forced to recognise that if it went back to the kind of old socialist policies so many of its activists hankered for it would simply lose. The election marked the final defeat of old Labour. In party political terms it certainly meant that Labour would be more difficult to defeat but for the country the change was undoubtedly for the better.

By the same measure Major's 1992 victory and his determination to continue in spite of all the attacks also had vast importance for the Conservatives. He saw to it that the changes so painfully won in the 1980s were made permanent. The privatised companies remained privatised; the labour laws remained reformed; and the economy remained strong. Major ensured that the Thatcher revolution was consolidated. The irony – some would say tragedy – is that it is doubtful whether either Margaret Thatcher or the man himself would be altogether happy with this verdict on the Major years.

As for the Conservative rebels who had done so much to bring about the 1997 rout, they might like to recall the scene in the first parliament after the defeat. The chamber in the Commons was crowded to overflowing as the new Labour prime minister delivered the first speech after his victory. In his prepared script Blair turned to Europe. Immediately two of the leading Tory sceptics, Bill Cash and Michael Spicer, rose to their feet to intervene. In the previous parliament there would have been expectant cries and the house would have listened intently for the anticipated broadside. But this was a new parliament, with a Labour majority bigger than anything they had achieved in their history. The appearance of the two was greeted with hilarity and sustained laughter. The final *coup de grâce* was delivered by the new prime minister, who to renewed laughter congratulated them and their friends 'on the magnificent part that they played in our victory'.

12

The aftermath (1997–2008)

'It is only our first exchange and already the prime minister is asking me the questions. This approach is stuck in the past and I want to talk about the future. He was the future once.'

David Cameron to Tony Blair at Prime Minister's Questions, 7 December 2006.

None of us quite realised at the time just how totally irrelevant we had become after the 1997 rout. It was not remotely like our defeats in 1974. We were not seen as the alternative government in waiting. The public just wanted us to go away. We could have been led by Churchill or Disraeli but it would have made no difference to our position. We were down and out. The charges of sleaze had discredited us. Years of infighting on Europe had left us with no way of influencing the European or any other debate. We had been eighteen years in power and we had had our chance.

In the immediate aftermath of the election I was at home, waiting for the Commons to return to business. My own majority had been reduced but at just under 15,000 it was beyond the dreams of most of my colleagues and put me in the top five Tory-held seats in the country. Just after midday the phone went. It was William Hague, who wanted my support in his leadership bid to succeed John Major. I rated Hague very highly. My reservation was not his ability but rather that he should have more experience in a serious opposition job before taking on the leadership. Hague listened to my advice and typically, rather than arguing the point, honestly conceded that a number of others had said the same.

My next caller shortly afterwards presented an easier decision. It was John Redwood, also in search of votes for his new bid for the leadership of the party. He reminded me (unnecessarily) that he had left the Major government and therefore could not be associated with its failure. Why he should have thought that this line of argument would go down well with someone who had spent month after month defending Major was slightly beyond me. Perhaps he had just written 'Norman' on his blotter and had simply contacted the wrong one. There was always something eccentrically distinctive about Redwood leadership bids – not least when he ended his hustings speech to the 1922 Committee with the rousing words, 'My colleagues, let me be your leader.'

Unsurprisingly my candidate was Ken Clarke, but not before I had put to him that he needed to make some concession to the European doubters in the parliamentary party. Had he done so he would have almost certainly won. But Clarke's view was that it was one thing winning a leadership election but quite another living with the consequences. A Euro-enthusiast pretending to have hitherto unsuspected doubts would have offended his own personal code of blunt honesty. Another leadership candidate from my Cambridge past, and at one stage the favourite, was the former home secretary Michael Howard. But although an undoubted sceptic on Europe he was publicly assassinated by Ann Widdecombe, who generously described her old boss as having 'something of the night' about him. With Howard shot, where could the 'anyone but Clarke' voters turn? Redwood was not considered a credible candidate and the only option became Hague.

With only a few days to go it was clear to those of us in the Clarke camp that unless something dramatic was done our man would be going down to defeat. Tactics were considered early one morning at a meeting in Clarke's room, across the road from the Commons. The first idea certainly did not lack drama. It was that Clarke should stand down as standard bearer and hand over to Michael Heseltine, who it was thought might poll better. The problem was that it was by no means certain that Heseltine would be willing to stand. Having consulted his doctor and his wife he came back with a sad but firm 'no'. Then a new idea was floated. Why should Clarke and Redwood not stand on a joint ticket?

In truth there were a thousand reasons why they should not have done so. Politically the two men did not occupy the same planet but this was an election and every vote counted. The plan went ahead and was announced to an astonished press at Church House to the accompaniment of much muttering about the Ribbentrop–Molotov pact of 1939. It was a desperate step which even in practical terms was ineffective: Redwood may have voted for Clarke but he brought precious few of his supporters with him. Margaret Thatcher immediately emerged to be photographed with Hague and in the final vote he won by a comfortable 22-vote majority. We had skipped a generation and elected a leader before his time.

Once Hague was elected, the pressure of the outside world began to assert itself. He had to build a shadow Cabinet and preferably a balanced one. He offered Clarke the job of shadowing the deputy prime minister, John Prescott, whom Tony Blair had put in charge of a vast department covering the environment, transport and the regions. But again Europe intervened, as it continued to do in the years that followed the party's electoral rout. Hague's formula for dealing with the single currency question was not to close the option for ever but to rule it out for the foreseeable future. For someone such as Clarke this was unacceptable and he declined. The new leader next contacted me to offer the same job.

My reservations were rather different. I had already resigned twice. I was already the subject of jokes about comebacks and Frank Sinatra. Much worse, I remembered the trials of the shadow Cabinet in the 1970s, when, as one commentator unkindly pointed out, I sat with Angus Maude, the father of the new shadow chancellor, Francis. But then at least I was a young politician with the ambition of going into government. There was only one reason why I should now agree to be called up: our defeat had been so devastating that it was a case of 'all hands to the pumps'. On this basis I agreed – as did Cecil Parkinson, who returned to become party chairman.

For Hague the leadership proved to be an unenviable inheritance. Not only was the party seen as irrelevant but it continued in its old bad ways. Grumbling about the leadership soon resurfaced and the single currency continued to divide. Outright opponents thought the Hague formula too weak;

supporters publicly counter-attacked, proclaiming, just as the sceptics had done earlier in the decade, that Europe was an issue which 'transcended' party politics. It was service as usual.

As it happened, the most dramatic falling-out came not on Europe but on a very different subject: the future of the House of Lords. At the end of 1998 the leader of the Conservatives in the Lords, Viscount Cranborne, came to an agreement with the prime minister to retain ninety-two hereditary peers in the second house without the small formality of consulting his own leader or the shadow Cabinet committee which believed that it was deciding the party's policy. Blair, not believing his luck, crowed at Hague's ignorance of the deal on the floor of the Commons and a furious Hague summarily sacked Cranborne. Cranborne later described his action as that of an 'ill-trained spaniel'. But that was to substantially understate his political crime. It was an almost incredible rejection of any idea of collective responsibility which damaged both Hague's authority and his standing.

In my diary I commented:

> William is now under more fire today than at any stage since his election as leader. Cranborne has hurt him at a point where he was already vulnerable. The senior politician treating the newcomer with disdain. To my mind Hague has made a really good fist of his first eighteen months, particularly in the Commons and on public platforms. But as the opinion polls show, the public is anything but persuaded. William needs time to establish himself. He needs support from the party's toffs and elder statesmen. (*Thursday 3 December 1998.*)

Ultimately Cranborne's action did the party in the Lords no favours either. The shadow Cabinet was outraged and its view of the Lords visibly hardened. The seeds of the party's advocacy of an 80 per cent elected house were sown in the Cranborne deal.

Hague himself proceeded through his four years as leader with quiet determination. His style in shadow Cabinet was very different to that of the man he had defeated, as I wrote after our first meeting.

Ken is expansive, rumbustious, generally funny and indiscreet about his head-banging opponents. William is scrupulously polite and listens to any point made and never interrupts. Equally he does not hesitate to give his immediate view. There is no chewing on the pipe or a 'how interesting' response. If he disagrees he says so – albeit in the same scrupulously polite manner. (*Monday 23 June 1997.*)

Of course where Hague shone was as a speaker, both at party conferences and pre-eminently in his performances in the Commons. The most difficult test for any opposition leader is in responding to the Budget, which he hears for the first time as it is being delivered – as in March 1998.

Gordon Brown sits down to a great Labour cheer and waving of order papers. A very difficult wicket for William. 'I don't see how he follows that,' says Brian Mawhinney, sitting next to me on the front bench. But he does and with considerable effect. It is one of the best speeches I have heard an opposition leader make in response to a Budget. William does it better than either Kinnock or indeed Thatcher. He is the strongest debater we have had as party leader for a very long time. (*Tuesday 17 March 1998.*)

Without such efforts Tory backbench morale in the 1997 parliament would have been markedly lower but sadly the impact never seemed to go wider.

As for myself, I settled down to my job as John Prescott's shadow. Today Prescott is largely written off but that is to underrate him. We entered the Commons on the same day in 1970 and for a brief period Ken Clarke and I shared an office with him, another Labour MP, Tom Pendry, and the Liberal Cyril Smith. Such were the office arrangements in those far-off days. I remember his baleful gaze as I dictated down the phone some defence of the Heath government. It is fair to say that Prescott would not give the time of day to a Tory politician like myself. There would not be the slightest chance of having a drink in the smoking room after a debate in the Commons. For Prescott the Tories were quite simply the enemy.

In one way, however, Prescott was an object lesson to all

politicians. At the start he was not a great speaker but he learnt from his mistakes. Over the years his debating style, although remaining highly idiosyncratic and a gift to the sketch writers, improved out of recognition. He became an effective conference orator. Above all he persisted. It is comparatively easy to persist for ten years in government but eighteen years on the opposition benches is very different and infinitely more frustrating. You have no power. You have a back-up which can never compare with the civil service machine. You are a bit player in a performance dominated by government ministers, advisers and spin doctors. Labour politicians such as Prescott and Margaret Beckett, whom I had also known in the 1970s, deserve credit for lasting this frustrating course.

After a year with Prescott I was 'promoted' to shadow home secretary to face another Labour survivor, Jack Straw, whom I had first come across when he was Barbara Castle's special adviser at the Department of Health. At one stage in my career the Home Office had been my political goal but after six years at the double department of Health and Social Security the ambition had become less than burning. I mused that now I had no political ambition job offers were coming in fast and furious. There was even a suggestion before I finally left the front bench that I might like to shadow the Foreign Office with the attractive prospect of keeping the party together on Europe.

In reality opposition is a miserable time and particularly miserable when you face an overwhelming majority. It was not just the public who saw us as irrelevant; the media took the same view. We were in a one-party state and they knew there was nothing we could do to come near to defeating the government. Even when Straw placed an indefensible injunction on the whole of the British media barring them from reporting an internal leak of some of the findings of the Stephen Lawrence inquiry, their protests were relatively muted.* Just imagine the collective

---

* This was not the only action that Straw took against unauthorised publication that he found inconvenient. Later, when foreign secretary, he helped ban a book on Iraq by Sir Jeremy Greenstock, Britain's permanent representative at the United Nations between 1998 and 2003, because it was

outrage if the gag had been applied by John Major's government. But this was 1999. Labour ministers were the masters now and Labour's new backbenchers voted for anything that was put in front of them. Straw's proposal for a list system for the European elections was as unpopular with Labour as it was with Conservatives but that did not prevent the measure going through with massive Commons majorities.

I left the Commons at the 2001 election after thirty-one years and walked the 200 yards down the corridor to the Lords. Back in the Commons Hague resigned after the party's second overwhelming general election defeat and we progressed to another election which only a Conservative could win. There were three leading candidates: Ken Clarke, Iain Duncan Smith and Michael Portillo. Clarke had been both chancellor of the exchequer and home secretary. He was well known and liked by the media and the public generally – but he was an enthusiast on Europe. Duncan Smith had voted consistently against Major's government on Maastricht, had never been in government and had no particular mastery of the Commons chamber. But with him there would be no nonsense about keeping options open on the euro: he was flatly opposed to it on any terms. The third candidate, Portillo, was the most interesting. Once regarded as the natural heir to Margaret Thatcher he had been influenced by his stay outside Westminster following his 1997 defeat. His message was that if the party wanted to regain power it had to change and become more inclusive, reaching out to minority communities; a diagnosis that was correct but immediately alienated him from some of his former supporters.

Under the new system of voting party members would have the final say but only after the MPs had thinned out the field to two finalists. On Tuesday 17 July 2001 the parliamentary party made its choice and on College Green, over the road from the Lords,

critical of parts of the government's Iraq policy. Later still he called for the sacking of Sir Christopher Meyer, the chairman of the Press Complaints Commission and previously ambassador to the United States, after Meyer's book *DC Confidential* had, amongst other comments, made critical remarks about Straw.

Cecil Parkinson and I awaited the result in front of a BBC television crew:

> And what a result. Ken comes out top. Second is Duncan Smith and then – by one vote – Michael Portillo. Portillo is now out of the race, which is ridiculous. There are two serious candidates – Clarke and Portillo. Now Portillo is eliminated the only Eurosceptic standard bearer is Duncan Smith. It is a bad, bad result. Worse news comes as the evening progresses. Portillo announces he is quitting front-line politics. His political career has been ended by one vote. One of our very few stars has been eliminated.

With Portillo gone my prediction for the eventual result was bleak:

> IDS has kept his head down and could well win the leadership on the depressing basis that he has fewest enemies. No one seems to worry whether he has the ability or experience to win a general election. Another leader elected before his time. Another leap into the dark – each one bigger than the one that has gone before.

The leadership campaign now went out into the country and the Clarke team set out his case in constituency visits and weekend interviews. 'Already used by Thatcher, Major and Hague,' I wrote of my own effort. 'Now in the service of my old pal Clarke. A media Jeeves for the politically oppressed.' (*Tuesday 21 August 2001.*) And Clarke was oppressed. In spite of everything that had happened in the suicide years of the 1990s the party's self-destructive obsession with Europe continued. They preferred the candidate who on one subject represented the views of the comparatively small band of elderly party members. A total of 250,000 party members voted in the leadership election compared with the 9,600,000 electors who voted Conservative even in the devastation of the 1997 election.

A few days before the closure of the election there was an event whose repercussions still dominate our lives. The devastating attack on the twin towers in New York on September 11 made the world a more dangerous place overnight. If ever there was a need for experienced leadership it was now. But by the time of the attack the vast majority of the votes had been cast and Duncan Smith had won with 60 per cent of the poll. The election had been all about Europe and the euro but ironically the result was announced on a day when no one was talking about either.

The significance of the contest is that the party not only rejected experience; it also turned away from any idea that a new start was needed, in spite of two devastating election defeats. For some the lesson was quite the contrary. As the Duncan Smith victory was announced at Central Office I waited with Bill Cash in front of another television camera. Cash in the flush of success gave it as his view that 'the trouble with the 2001 election is that we did not give enough emphasis to the European issue'.

Duncan Smith's most important decision as leader was to commit the party to support the invasion of Iraq. In fairness to him oppositions can only rely on the good faith of governments in a war situation and, however many private briefings their leaders receive, they can never have the same access to advice. Perhaps Duncan Smith could have questioned the government more deeply but it should be remembered that most of the Tory Party (myself included) relied on what the government said and supported the invasion. A few Tories in the Commons were opposed – notably Clarke and the former foreign secretary Malcolm Rifkind – although in the Lords the opponents were more numerous and included Geoffrey Howe and Douglas Hurd.

In the event it was not Iraq that brought Duncan Smith down. It was his lack of public impact. The opinion polls showed no signs of recovery; the Liberal Democrats were challenging; and in the cruel weekly contest of Prime Minister's Questions he was consistently trounced by Tony Blair. Within months the grumbling started anew with some of his old supporters making for the lifeboats of the heavily listing ship. Given his own voting record in the 1990s, Duncan Smith's appeals for party unity appeared conspicuously hollow and in the autumn of 2003 he joined Austen Chamberlain as the only other Tory leader to be deposed before he had even fought an election.

The prospect of yet another lengthy leadership election loomed but both the party and the public were tiring of the process. Clarke, having lost two leadership elections, made it clear that he would not be standing; Michael Howard, now restored to the shadow Cabinet, made it equally clear that he would. The only question was whether another contender, David Davis for example, would enter the fray. When he announced that he would not be standing the way was clear for Howard's unopposed election. It was a decision that gave Howard unquestioned authority and at long last it seemed that a Conservative recovery might begin.

At Westminster the change was marked. Howard was a long-standing Eurosceptic so could not be faulted by the party's ideologues. More important, he was a vastly experienced politician well able to take on Blair, whose star was now in the descendant. The invasion of Iraq had been completed; the ill-prepared occupation and bloody aftermath had begun. Worse for Blair, it was becoming clear that the main justification for the war – Iraq's possession of weapons of mass destruction – was bogus and the intelligence information had been grossly exaggerated. A later report by Lord Butler's committee of inquiry found that the intelligence authorities had warned that they had had no reliable information from inside Iraq on chemical and biological weapons since 1998.* The indications were that the decision to go to war had been pushed through on a false prospectus and with scant regard to the collective views of ministers.

Although the Conservatives had supported Blair's policy some hoped that it would be the government who would pay the price. 'Oppositions do not win elections; governments lose them.' The media began to take the Conservatives seriously again, not least because Howard started to restore discipline to a party that had been seen for over a decade as fractious and unwilling to be led. Sometimes he over-reacted – as with his unnecessarily cruel decision to deselect Howard Flight as an MP for some careless remark he had made at a meeting in the City – but at long last the leader exercised power.

Outside Westminster, however, the impact of Howard's leadership was less certain. The party made all too little progress

* Lord Butler of Brockwell, *Review of Intelligence on Weapons of Mass Destruction: Report of a Committee of Privy Counsellors*, HC 898, 14 July 2004.

in winning back support in the cities and towns of the Midlands and the north. Labour lost support but the Tories were not seen as the alternative. In by-elections in July 2004 in Birmingham and Leicester the Liberal Democrats were the beneficiaries of dissatisfaction with Labour, and the Tories were pushed into third place: in the Hartlepool by-election a few months later in October the party was pushed into fourth place behind the UK Independence Party. The opinion polls seemed obstinately stuck with Conservative support at around 30 per cent. 'The public may grumble about Blair but they feel relatively prosperous,' I wrote in my diary. 'Frustratingly we cannot convert public dissatisfaction into support for us.' (*Saturday 26 February 2005.*)

At the general election in May the party took what was perceived as hard lines on Europe and on immigration but the campaign did little to change the public mood. It seemed the same mixture as before and as a third defeat began to look probable the public criticism from inside the party began again:

> More polls going the wrong way and the inevitable has happened. The newspapers report criticism of the campaign from unnamed 'senior Conservatives'. Just like 1997. Just like 2001. We are unable to present a united front even for three weeks – and even given what has happened to us over the last ten years. (*Tuesday 19 April 2005*)

In spite of all Howard's efforts Tony Blair won again in 2005 with a reduced but substantial majority of almost seventy. Another Conservative leader swiftly resigned. Howard had been tough and utterly professional but perhaps the trouble was that he was associated with a political age that had passed. Whether we liked it or not, all of us of that vintage were associated not just with the glory days of the Thatcher government but also the long decline from 1987.

The election of David Cameron to succeed was an undoubted surprise. The assumption had been that David Davis was the man most likely to take his place, with some of us still hankering for a Clarke leadership. In the event Clarke was eliminated early on in the process; Davis made a lacklustre party conference speech; and Cameron, the young outsider, swept everything in front of him.

The party began to recognise that Cameron was by any measure an outstanding communicator with something of a young Bill Clinton about him. For the first time there seemed to be the prospect of a leader who was in tune with the younger electorate and might appeal to them in the way Blair once had.

Cameron won comfortably and took the sensible step of explicitly moving to the centre ground, a case in point being his endorsement of the National Health Service. No longer was the party seeking some private insurance solution but became so credibly committed to the NHS that it started challenging Labour in the opinion polls on the handling of this sensitive policy area.

The vindication of his tactics seemed to come in the local government elections of May 2007. The Conservatives took 40 per cent of the poll against Labour's 27 per cent and gained councils and councillors from both the other parties. It almost approached the scale of the defeats that Labour were inflicting in the mid-1990s – but the real test was still to come. Blair had been in the very last stage of his premiership. Like Margaret Thatcher he had stayed on too long and was paying the price. The public were tired of the man they had once welcomed as a fresh face. The cash-for-peerages investigation dogged his last days and seemed to make a mockery of his claims that he would clean up British politics. He had overplayed his hand in opposition, as he now seems to recognise, and sleaze had come back to haunt him. The extra money pumped into health and education did not seem to be buying the promised improvement in those services, while public and party alike now saw the Iraq invasion as an almost unmitigated disaster. Blair had become a lame duck prime minister and the new Tory leader successfully exploited his position.

In July 2007 the position changed when a visibly impatient Gordon Brown finally took over after a delay which compared with Eden's long wait to take over from Churchill. At first Labour's fortunes recovered. At the end of July there were two by-elections in safe Labour seats: Ealing Southall and Blair's old seat of Sedgefield. It was the first time that Brown had come up against Cameron face to face in an election. In both seats there were distinct swings away from Labour but not enough to lose them the constituencies. However, the beneficiaries of the swings were not the Conservatives but the Liberal Democrats. The Tories ended up third in both constituencies and the pressure now moved onto Cameron.

The veteran election watcher Professor Anthony King was in no doubt about the reason for the setback. It all went back to the suicide years. In the *Daily Telegraph* he wrote:

> The two by-election results reinforce the point made by the opinion polls: that, just as it took the Labour Party a generation to slough off the reputation it acquired for governmental incompetence during the 1970s, so it is likely to take the Conservatives many years to restore public confidence following the chaotic displays they put on during the early and mid-1990s. If a party flounders under five successive leaders, as the Tories have done since 1994, the problem lies in how voters have come to see that party rather than in the inadequacies of any one of its leaders.*

But that was not how some others inside the party saw the position. The right had never been altogether happy with Cameron's election. Privately they characterised the new leader as a man without beliefs – really meaning that they did not share his beliefs. They wanted the mixture as before: instant pledges to tax cutting and, of course, fierce Euroscepticism. They viewed with deep suspicion Cameron's attempt to broaden the appeal of the party by highlighting policies on the environment, child care and the NHS. With the by-election setbacks they were now able to attack publicly. It was a crucial moment in the battle to modernise the party.

Almost inevitably it was Norman Tebbit who led the attack. In an interview with the *Times* published just before the Conservative Party conference he compared Cameron unfavourably with the new prime minister. Cameron, he said, had 'no experience of the world whatsoever'; but Brown was 'a clever man and I have a very considerable regard for him'. The picture of internal disharmony

---

* Anthony King, 'By-elections show Tories still lack voters' confidence', *Daily Telegraph*, 21 July 2007.

was perfectly caught by the extraordinary photograph of Margaret Thatcher outside 10 Downing Street, side by side with the Labour prime minister.

The Conservatives looked as though they were back to their oh-so-familiar old ways. During August and September public opinion and the views of many of the commentators moved strongly in favour of the new man at No. 10. It was at this point that Brown made what history may well see as his decisive mistake. The new prime minister moved to the verge of calling a snap election. The polls were with him; the Conservatives appeared to be imploding and some even questioned whether the party had any future. An election would give Brown his own mandate. The likely announcement would be when Parliament resumed, straight after the Conservative Party conference – but Brown, the experienced politician, reckoned without that conference.

The party was being explicitly threatened with another electoral drubbing. Now, the easiest speech to make at a party conference is the fighting speech when you are under attack. I should know: when I was in charge of health and social security I was constantly under attack come the party conference season. At your own party conference you are among friends and they are willing you on. The Blackpool setting is ideal. If you cannot make a rousing political speech in the old theatre atmosphere of the Winter Gardens then you cannot make a rousing political speech at all. William Hague and George Osborne set the scene – Osborne's pledge to reduce inheritance tax almost took the roof off – but the star of the conference was Cameron himself.

Speaking without notes – deliberately, in contrast to Brown's scripted autocue offering at his own conference – he set out both policies and beliefs. But he also went back to the party conference of 1987, when democratically elected leaders from Eastern bloc countries praised Margaret Thatcher and her government for the inspiration they had given. 'I felt proud that day – proud of our values, proud of our party, proud of the part we played in helping them forge the movement that brought freedom across our continent,' he said. 'But the triumphs of the past aren't enough. Every generation of Conservatives has to make the argument all over again for free enterprise, freedom, responsibility and limited government.' The reception was thunderous. For the first time in fifteen years the Tory Party stood truly together.

So was that the turning point for the Labour government? The Conservatives went 3 points ahead in the polls and suddenly the pressure was on Brown. He could have gone ahead regardless – and there were many Tories who believed that, even given the party's good conference, had he done so he would have won. Instead he backed down and memories went back to 1978 when Jim Callaghan fatally delayed an election he probably would have won. It was true that there was nothing as dramatic as the winter of discontent but the months that followed were cumulatively the worst in Labour's entire period of government. Northern Rock was rescued from bankruptcy but only at massive potential cost to the exchequer. Computer disks containing the personal details of more than twenty million people were lost in the post. A property developer in north-east England was found to have donated substantial amounts of money to Labour using third parties, which was specifically in breach of the legislation that the government had introduced only a few years previously. Cabinet ministers were forced to defend their own financial accounting methods in raising money for the deputy leadership contest which accompanied Brown's accession to power.

Most serious of all was the government's loss of reputation for economic competence. The new chancellor, Alistair Darling, was already under pressure. His autumn Budget had seemed lazy and unimaginative and was noted mostly for adopting the Tories' policy on reducing inheritance tax. That might have been acceptable as a counter-blow just before an election but there was to be no election. The final nationalisation of Northern Rock in February 2008 followed months of delay – and the suspicion was that Darling had not acted earlier because he did not want to cast a shadow over the election that never was. The next month he presented a Budget which did nothing to lift the gloom that had descended following the credit crunch and all the problems of the banks with sub-prime mortgages. The government seemed to be reduced to crossing its fingers and hoping it would all go away.

At Westminster Brown was characterised as a 'ditherer' in contrast to Cameron who, faced with as big a crisis as any leader is likely to face, kept his nerve. The public mood was caught by the stand-in Liberal Democrat leader, Vince Cable, who wondered at 'the prime minister's remarkable transformation in the last few weeks from Stalin to Mr Bean'. In a remarkably short time Brown had managed to lose the reputation that his advisers wished to cultivate for him of cool wisdom based on experience. The government was floundering. What was it that Norman Lamont had once said about the Major administration? In office but not in power.

It is possible that something fundamental happened in British politics in the last months of 2007. Rather than a government of the experienced and skilled, Labour suddenly looked old and tired. The sight of Brown and Jack Straw sitting next to each other at the Cabinet table only underlined the point. It was Brown as chancellor and, even more, Straw as foreign secretary (together with Geoff Hoon, still at the table as chief whip) who helped lead the country into the Iraq conflict. But it was not just the familiar faces – a lethargy seemed to have overtaken the government. It seemed to be doing what Thatcher had feared most as she reached the ten-year point – running out of steam. There might be a new leader but this did not look like a new government.

In his first Prime Minister's Questions after his election as leader Cameron scathingly told Blair that his 'approach was stuck in the past and I want to talk about the future'. He paused and pointed at Blair: 'He was the future once.' The same charge can be made against Brown. When Major took over from Thatcher almost no one held him responsible for what had happened in the previous years. His ascent to the Cabinet had been too quick and his promotion to the topmost jobs too recent. Brown on the other hand was party to each and every one of the decisions of the Blair government. He might not have enjoyed the position but he was the undoubted number two in the government from the beginning. 'Time for a change' is a powerful slogan against any long-serving government – as it proved in the local elections of May 2008.

Labour's performance was disastrous. Their share of the poll was a meagre 24 per cent – even less than the Liberal Democrats and a massive 20 points behind the Conservatives. The comparison with the Conservative result in 1995, when Labour raced into a decisive lead they never lost up to and beyond the next general election, was direct. The story of the two declines had become strikingly similar.

When local Labour leaders distanced themselves from the performance of the national government, you could be straight back in the mid-1990s. When Labour backbenchers attempted to vote down government measures in the division lobbies, the echoes of the Maastricht rebels were unmistakeable. And when sacked ministers combined with those still in office to offer guidance on the errors of the prime minister, the picture was complete. Even the official Labour explanations for the defeat and pleas for support bore an uncanny resemblance to the calls made by me and my successors as party chairman: 'mid-term unpopularity', 'need to listen more', 'we must explain our policies more clearly'.

Perhaps the truth is that after a long period in power a public reaction is inevitable. There is no one else who can reasonably be blamed if things go wrong. The wonder is not that it is now happening to Labour but that Major managed to buck the trend in 1992 after thirteen years of Tory government. The next election will come at the same stage in Labour's long period of office. Can Brown do the same as Major?

I doubt it. No government has recovered after the kind of drubbing Labour received in May 2008, but there is more to it than that. Major was a fresh face; he presented a more sympathetic image than the leader he succeeded; the public liked him. Brown is no one's idea of a natural communicator, and he has the misfortune to follow one of the acknowledged masters of that art and find himself up against another. He was too long at the Treasury: ten years as chancellor following five years as shadow chancellor. In this time he was accustomed to having his way rather than arguing his case. The abolition of the 10p tax rate was a prime example of his style. It is inconceivable that his officials did not show him in detail the breakdown of losers from the policy change. He chose to ignore them and reaped the electoral whirlwind.

Time will tell whether the autumn of 2007 was the turning

point for the government. What can be said is that it certainly
represented that for the Conservatives. It was the point at which
the public and the media started to reappraise not just the
government but also the opposition. Commentators began to
note that shadow ministers were now more than a match for their
government counterparts. George Osborne had more life than the
chancellor; David Davis more conviction than the home
secretary; Andrew Lansley more ideas than the health secretary.
Old wounds had been healed and some of the party's former
leaders were now being used to advantage. William Hague,
restored to the shadow Cabinet, could outshine anyone on the
government front bench; and Iain Duncan Smith, to his credit,
worked in the unfashionable but desperately important area of
social policy. While in the background there were a range of up-
and-coming younger men such as Michael Gove, Andrew
Mitchell, Jeremy Hunt and Chris Grayling, well able to look after
themselves and develop policy.

For the first time for a decade the Conservatives were now an
entirely credible alternative government. Wisely Cameron had
resisted the siren calls to promise immediate tax cuts and promised
first to repair the public finances. He had underlined his
commitment to the public services such as health and education
and had sought new paths in family policy. Crucially, both at
Westminster and in the country he had brought the party together
for the first time since the days of Margaret Thatcher. The ancient
and not so ancient internal grumblers had been seen off. They
might come again but never with the force they once had. Their
day has passed.

The stage is now set for Cameron to bring a decisive end to the
party's suicide years – although before going on he and, most of
all, the party would do well to consider some of the lessons from
those years. For, as William Hague said in a Commons debate on
Iraq, 'we cannot proceed blithely into the future without
understanding what has happened in the past'.[*]

[*] Hansard, HC Deb, 25 March 2008, vol. 474, col. 47

Nine lessons

When I started this book I had expected the lessons of the suicide years to be for Conservatives only. With Labour facing many of the same problems that dogged John Major's government, my view now is that many of these lessons have a wider and more general application. I start with two which should be obvious but, evidently, are not.

The first lesson

A party which appears disunited, quarrelsome and frankly unpleasant will never win an election. This applies not just to backbenchers openly rebelling in votes and speeches but also to the grandees of the party. It applies to former leaders attacking their successors; and it certainly applies to Cabinet and shadow Cabinet members quietly dissociating themselves from decisions which have been taken. 'Another great triumph' was the sardonic comment of one of Major's ministers when a policy hit the buffers. It was a pound to a penny that this minister would repeat those words when lunching on the restaurant circuit, sponsored by the political correspondents and commentators. Politicians should remember that the good food and wine is provided not for the pleasure of their company but for what they will reveal: secrets, hopefully, but if not then certainly their own attitudes to government policies and their colleagues. All the pressure is on ministers not to disappoint but even so they might reflect that 'it was nothing to do with me' is a fairly demeaning excuse.

The second lesson

Politicians must tell the truth. I do not subscribe to the theory that political standards are at an all-time low. You only have to read accounts of how at the beginning of the 1950s the Labour government exiled Seretse Khama from his native Bechuanaland (now Botswana), once he had taken a white bride, in order to appease the South African government, which was just starting its immoral policy of apartheid – and government ministers lied in the Commons to avoid criticism. Or take the Suez crisis a few years later, when Conservative ministers sought to cover up the direct collusion between Britain, France and Israel to justify the disastrous attempt to prevent Egypt's President Nasser from nationalising the Suez Canal. Nevertheless when I look back on the 1990s I cringe when I remember that it was a Conservative, Alan Clark, who admitted that he had been 'economical with the *actualité*', an economy which just happened to have the effect of putting three men on trial at the Old Bailey. I wonder how such a talented man as Jonathan Aitken could talk of taking up 'the sword of truth' in his libel case against the *Guardian* – or for that matter what possessed Jeffrey Archer to pursue his own libel case. I suspect the answer is that they both put their political careers before anything else – which in itself is a warning. I do not understand how two MPs thought it right to accept money for putting down parliamentary questions or how anyone thought it was right to accept cash in brown envelopes for undeclared influence. These cases are now matters of history and the individuals concerned deserve to be able to put their lives back together. But no politician should forget their example.

The next lessons have been underlined by the experience of all the parties over the last thirty years.

The third lesson

A wise party does not become financially obligated to any individual or group. Such an arrangement may get the party out of an immediate financial hole but it will end in tears. Most big contributors want something. It may be influence over the direction the party is taking; it may be a particular policy; it may be an honour. All have clear dangers for a political party. Raising money at the local level should be encouraged but the big contributors – the contributors whose donations run into hundreds of thousand pounds – should be stood down. It gives them disproportionate power.

The big sticking point is replacing them with limited state funding. All the opinion polls show that the public are sceptical about taxpayers' money being used to finance political parties. Virtually all the leader writers combine in a great puffball of indignation. Why should the taxpayer be forced to make a contribution to a party he or she hates? Why can the political parties not put their own houses in order?

These are powerful arguments. I know because in the past I have used them. But before they are accepted hook, line and sinker, the public need to decide a number of questions which have become clearer in the last ten years. They need to decide whether they are happy to see one or two big contributors financing a political party and in so doing potentially gaining a measure of control over that party. 'I want to check that my money is being put to best use' would be the excuse. They need to decide whether they are happy to see one or two big organisations demanding support for their policies in return for financial support. 'No say – no pay', as one trade union leader once inelegantly but frankly put it. And they need to decide whether there is any other way of preventing corruption in the process.

More state funding will not by itself guarantee absolute probity. For one thing there has been unmistakeable evidence in recent years that party fund raisers have been prepared to seek new ways around new rules. So there are no guarantees but, provided that further state funding goes hand in hand with controls on spending, there are undoubted advantages. The system would be better regulated and more open. It would take some of the pressure off the party fund raisers and would prevent the spending war escalating out of control. It would end the cash-for-influence payments of both the unions and the big individual contributors.

And it would justify a new warning to all the political parties that they should proceed with caution or face the consequences.

The fourth lesson

The importance of Parliament and Cabinet government must be re-established. The public interest would be better served if governments were better held to account. It is a scandal that major parts of bills which will become the law of the country can be guillotined through the House of Commons without any consideration whatsoever. Inside government the power of the small group and of the advisers needs to be reduced. Proper consideration by Cabinet and properly constituted Cabinet committees should take the place of informal 'sofa' government or diktat from No. 10. It may take longer but error and harm are most likely to result when the full issues are not exposed for collective discussion. Power should be restored not just to backbenchers but also to ministers.

My next two lessons are counter-intuitive and will be opposed by the men and women who are more at home in the murky rooms of political fixing than in the debating chamber.

The fifth lesson

Do not slavishly woo the media. Surely, you might say, that must be wrong? Well, consider the evidence. Special relationships do not last. The *Sun* backed Margaret Thatcher but advised its readers to vote Labour in the last three general elections. In the end it also turned against Tony Blair in spite of his trips across the world to keep in with its proprietor and his other media mates. Everybody is much more comfortable at arm's length. More than that, the public are looking for a leader who puts some distance between himself and the media. The public interest is not served by cosy relationships between politicians and the media – the private dinners for proprietors at Chequers or No. 10; the attempts to gain political or commercial influence. Nor is it served by the tactics of spin, designed to avoid proper questioning – the 'exclusive' stories offered by ministers in exchange for support of their policies; the government statement of policy not made in Parliament but deliberately leaked in advance to gain a more favourable press.

The sixth lesson

Never exploit the personal. It may be tempting for a politician to do so. There is a constant appetite for personal scandal. So you may win some headlines but, as several politicians have discovered to their cost, it could be your turn next. And even if it is not, it leaves a nasty taste in the mouth. It is not what politics should be about. Reveal the corrupt but leave the personal affairs to the media.

The last lessons drawn from the suicide years are directed at the Conservatives.

The seventh lesson

The party must have the courage to raise issues which are important but will not bring automatic headlines of praise. In the political debate of the last five years there is one issue that dwarfs all else: Iraq. Even if the Iraq conflict ends tomorrow the damage done will have been immense and appalling. In the aftermath of the invasion at least 150,000 Iraqis have been murdered, torture has become commonplace and more than two million Iraqis have been forced to flee their country and live as refugees. Attempting to keep a peace has led to dead and seriously wounded British casualties, while Britain's name in the Middle East has become mud and will take many years to recover. An enormous price has been paid for the invasion and at the very least we deserve to know if the actions taken were in good faith and on the best available advice.

'But wait a moment,' you might say. 'Weren't you and your party in favour of the invasion?' My reply is that we were and that is the reason why we have even more reason to be appalled. Personally I wrote to both the prime minister and the foreign secretary supporting their action. We supported the government on the information we were provided with. The other side of the coin is that we have the right to know whether we were misled.

We know now that there were no weapons of mass destruction. What we do not know is whether ministers were really justified in believing there were. Had we waited only a short time, would the United Nations weapons inspectors have been able to make the position clearer? Politically, what was the advice of the Foreign Office, given all its expertise in the region? Did it support the invasion and, if it did not, did the other Cabinet ministers around the table know of their reservations? Was the Cabinet consulted as Margaret Thatcher consulted each Cabinet minister before authorising the sending of the task force to the Falklands? When did George W. Bush and the Americans decide that Iraq was to be attacked?

I pose some of the questions; others would be more assertive. But the point is that five years have now passed since the invasion. The British commitment has been dramatically reduced. The time has surely come to seek answers to the many questions that surround the invasion of Iraq by setting up an independent inquiry, as was done after the Falklands – and was done at the height of the First World War after the Dardanelles disaster. If the government has not conceded an inquiry by the next election it should be a manifesto pledge. Discovering the truth is never a worthless thing – discovering the truth is the very least we can do for the thousands who have been killed, injured and displaced.

The eighth lesson

The party must find a way of working together on Europe. Many, perhaps most, in the party today would call themselves Eurosceptics. But what does that mean? For some it means opposing literally anything that emanates from Brussels. It means the rejection of any form of shared sovereignty and any joint measures – even on issues such as terrorism where the public interest demands such cooperation. It means trying to move the nation to a point where the final step of withdrawal from the European Union can be contemplated. I do not believe that withdrawal is the majority view among Conservative voters. Much of business would be appalled and many of the public would think such a policy suicidal.

If hard-line Eurosceptic policies were election winners then the party would already be back in power. William Hague, Iain Duncan Smith and Michael Howard hardly pursued middle-road policies. For those who wish to leave the European Union there is already UKIP – and for those who want a more centralised Europe there are the Liberal Democrats.

So how do Conservatives meet the genuine fears of middle England about a Europe which too often seems determined to interfere in national life? I return to what was my personal feeling when I was first elected to the Commons in 1970 – the important decisions should be put to a referendum. But, as this book shows, some of the fiercest opposition to the referendum path comes from those most enthusiastic for the European ideal. They need to reconsider their position. They are never going to convince the public by apparently doing everything by the back door. They must have the confidence to go out and persuade. At present their reluctance to do this plays into the hands of the enemies of European cooperation.

The opportunity for the Conservative Party is to set out a new approach. The aim should be to become the reforming party of Europe. We need to continue the fight on the indefensible Common Agricultural Policy and make the single market truly one without protective competition barriers. Our options remain open on the single currency and we remain in favour of a Europe of nation states, not some centralised superstate.

But we should go one step further. We should press for the European Union to have more influence in world affairs – and more influence than Britain can have alone. This last point is probably anathema to many sceptics but consider the present position. The self-evident policy of the Blair and Brown governments has been to follow the United States. It is a policy that has taken us into Iraq and prevented us from even condemning the loss of civilian life in Lebanon. And yet the Middle East is a region where Britain and a number of other European nations have a long history. Are we content to see policy in this most inflammable area utterly controlled from Washington? Is the only role for a British prime minister that of being some subservient cheerleader for the American president?

The public may not want a European state but they certainly do not want a foreign policy laid down in Washington or one-sided agreements which place obligations on Britain but leave the United States unencumbered. Of course friendship and cooperation with the United States remains a cornerstone – but on a more independent basis than we have seen over the last few years. No one pretends that there will be a European influence overnight. And of course some of the developments in the last few years, where different nations have refused to cooperate fully, have taken us backwards. There will always be European leaders who go their own way. But difficult as the path of greater cooperation may be, it does at least hold out the hope of real British influence. If we stay on the present path we know exactly what our position will be: at best a very junior partner to whatever party happens to be in power in Washington.

That is not where Britain should be. Margaret Thatcher's first election manifesto in 1979 set out a far better view of Britain's role in Europe, with words that have even more resonance today. 'In a world dominated by super-powers,' the manifesto said, 'Britain and her partners are best able to protect their international interests and to contribute to world peace and stability when they speak with a single voice.'

The ninth lesson

The party should stay on the centre ground and should avoid propounding policies which simply appeal to paid-up members. We would do much better concentrating on local communities than emphasising our misgivings about the European Union.

During the 1980s and 1990s the Conservatives lost their reputation for local commitment. Too often the government seemed to be at war with local councils. The result is that today the Conservatives hold few parliamentary seats in the big cities and in Scotland and Wales. Rebuilding needs to start from the bottom. The need is to engage in true community politics and to show that the party is committed to the local area. We need to demonstrate that we are approachable and offer practical help. Our success in the May 2008 elections provides the opportunity. The Conservatives now control councils throughout the country. Serving the public locally can point the way to serving nationally. Our aim should be to meet the public concerns – north and south – for better education, for more effective action against crime, and for a better living environment. We need to demonstrate once and for all that we have retrieved the 'One Nation' banner borrowed by Tony Blair.

The key players

Humphrey Atkins Opposition chief whip 1975–9, Northern Ireland secretary 1979–81, lord privy seal and deputy foreign secretary 1981–2. Resigned with Lord Carrington following Foreign Office failure to foresee Falklands invasion by Argentina in 1982.

Kenneth Baker Education secretary 1986–9, Conservative Party chairman 1989–90, home secretary 1990–92.

John Biffen Chief secretary to the Treasury 1979–81, trade secretary 1981–2, leader of the House of Commons 1982–87 until sacked by Margaret Thatcher.

Tony Blair Leader of the opposition 1994–7, prime minister 1997–2007.

Leon Brittan Chief secretary to the Treasury 1981–3, home secretary 1983–5, trade and industry secretary 1985–6. Resigned from government during Westland affair. European Commissioner 1989–99.

Gordon Brown Shadow chancellor of the exchequer 1992–7, chancellor of the exchequer 1997–2007, prime minister since 2007.

David Cameron Shadow minister 2003–5, leader of opposition since 2005.

Lord Carrington Leader of the House of Lords 1963–4, defence secretary 1970–74, foreign secretary 1979–82.

William Cash   Tory MP since 1984 and long-established Eurosceptic.

Kenneth Clarke   Health secretary 1988–90, education secretary 1990–92, home secretary 1992–3, chancellor of the exchequer 1993–7. Defeated in three contests for party leadership.

Tim Collins   Director of communications at Conservative Central Office 1992–5, elected MP 1997, shadow minister 2001–5.

Viscount Cranborne   Conservative MP 1979–87. First entered House of Lords 1992. Leader of Lords 1994–7, leader of opposition in Lords 1997–8. Sacked by William Hague.

David Davis   Whip and middle-ranking minister under John Major. Twice contested Conservative Party leadership. Shadow deputy prime minister 2002–3, shadow home secretary since 2003.

Iain Duncan Smith   Elected to Parliament 1992 and a consistent rebel against the government on Maastricht. Shadow social security secretary 1997–9, shadow defence secretary 1999–2001. Surprisingly elected party leader 2001 but forced to resign two years later because of perceived failure to restore party fortunes.

Nicholas Edwards   Welsh secretary 1979–87. Now sits in Lords as Lord Crickhowell.

Fiona Fowler   Wife of author. Forced to put up with a flow of government red boxes through her home 1979–90 and a mounting phone bill as government crises multiplied 1992–4. Two daughters, Kate and Isobel, showed polite interest.

Marcus Fox   Chairman of the 1922 Committee, representing Conservative backbenchers, 1992–7.

Tristan Garel-Jones   Government whip 1982–90, minister of state at the Foreign Office 1990–93.

Ian Gilmour Ministry of Defence minister 1970–74, defence secretary 1974, lord privy seal and deputy foreign secretary 1979–81. Sacked by Margaret Thatcher.

William Hague Welsh secretary 1995–7, leader of opposition 1997–2001, shadow foreign secretary since 2005.

Lord Hailsham Renounced hereditary peerage 1963 to re-enter Commons as Quintin Hogg and contest party leadership election. Took life peerage 1970, lord chancellor 1970–74 and 1979–87.

Michael Heseltine Minister under Ted Heath. Environment secretary 1979–83, defence secretary 1983–6. Walked out of Cabinet in 1986 and in 1990 unsuccessfully challenged Margaret Thatcher for the party leadership. Environment secretary (again) 1990–92, trade and industry secretary 1992–5, deputy prime minister 1995–7.

Jonathan Hill In Downing Street policy unit 1991–2, political secretary to John Major 1992–4.

Douglas Hogg Industry minister 1989–90, agriculture minister 1995–7.

Quintin Hogg see **Lord Hailsham**

Sarah Hogg Economics journalist, head of John Major's Downing Street policy unit 1990–95.

Michael Howard Employment secretary 1990–92, environment secretary 1992–3, home secretary 1992–7, shadow foreign secretary 1997–9. Retired from shadow Cabinet 1999 but returned as shadow chancellor 2001–3, leader of the opposition 2003–5. Resigned after 2005 election defeat.

Geoffrey Howe Solicitor general 1970–72, trade minister 1972–4, chancellor of the exchequer 1979–83, foreign secretary

1983–9, leader of House of Commons and deputy prime minister 1989–90. Resigned from government 1990 in dispute on European policy.

David Hunt Welsh secretary 1990–93, employment secretary 1993–4, chancellor of Duchy of Lancaster 1994–5, Welsh secretary (again) 1995. Left government 1995.

Douglas Hurd Northern Ireland secretary 1984–5, home secretary 1985–9, foreign secretary 1989–95. Unsuccessfully contested party leadership 1990.

Bernard Ingham Started career as journalist in Yorkshire. Chief press secretary to Margaret Thatcher 1979–1990.

Patrick Jenkin Chief secretary to the Treasury 1972–4, social services secretary 1979–81, industry secretary 1981–3, environment secretary 1983–5.

Michael Jopling Chief whip 1979–1983, minister of agriculture 1983–7.

Keith Joseph Social services secretary 1970–74. Stood aside to allow Margaret Thatcher to successfully challenge for the leadership in 1975. Industry secretary 1979–81, education secretary 1981–6. An influential figure in the development of policy for the new Conservative government.

Neil Kinnock Leader of opposition 1983–92. Resigned after the party's defeat in the 1992 election.

Norman Lamont Chief secretary to the Treasury 1989–90. Campaign manager for John Major in 1990 leadership election. Chancellor of the exchequer 1991–3. He was chancellor when Britain left the Exchange Rate Mechanism in 1992. Became a prominent critic of the government and supported John Redwood's attempt to defeat Major for the leadership in 1995.

Nigel Lawson Energy secretary 1981–3, chancellor of the exchequer 1983–9. Resigned in a dispute over the economic adviser to the prime minister, Alan Walters.

John Major Chief secretary to the Treasury 1987–9, foreign secretary 1989, chancellor of the exchequer 1989–90. In 1990 defeated Michael Heseltine for the Conservative Party leadership after Margaret Thatcher had withdrawn. Prime minister 1990–97. Resigned after government's defeat in 1997 general election.

David Mellor Various ministerial positions 1986–90, chief secretary to the Treasury 1990–92, national heritage secretary 1992. Forced into resignation after an affair.

John Moore Transport secretary 1986–7, social services secretary 1987–9. Regarded as future leader of the party but moved out of government 1989.

Peter Morrison Various ministerial positions 1983–90, appointed Margaret Thatcher's parliamentary private secretary 1990. Occupied this post during the leadership contest which forced her resignation.

John Nott An early supporter of Margaret Thatcher. Trade secretary 1979–81, defence secretary 1981–3.

Gus O'Donnell Press secretary to John Major as prime minister 1990–94, Cabinet secretary and head of civil service since 2005.

Cecil Parkinson Conservative Party chairman 1981–3, trade and industry secretary 1983. Forced to resign after an affair became public. Returned to the Cabinet as energy secretary 1987–9, transport secretary 1989–90. Party chairman again 1997–8.

Chris Patten Various ministerial positions 1983–9, environment secretary 1989–90, party chairman 1990–92. Lost his seat in the 1992 election. Governor of Hong Kong 1992–7, European Commissioner 1999–2004.

Michael Portillo   Given first promotion by Margaret Thatcher, who saw him as a potential leader. Various ministerial positions 1987–92, chief secretary to the Treasury 1992–4, employment secretary 1994–5, defence secretary 1995–7, shadow chancellor of the exchequer 2000–01. Stood unsuccessfully for leadership of party in 2003 when Iain Duncan Smith won.

Charles Powell   Diplomat who became private secretary to Margaret Thatcher 1983–90.

Jim Prior   Ted Heath's parliamentary private secretary 1965–70, minister of agriculture 1970–72. Stood in 1975 leadership election. Employment secretary 1979–81, Northern Ireland secretary 1981–4.

Francis Pym   Chief whip 1970–73, Northern Ireland secretary 1973–4, defence secretary 1979–81, leader of the Commons 1981–2, foreign secretary 1982–3. Sacked after the 1983 general election.

John Redwood   Welsh secretary 1993–5. Unsuccessfully contested party leadership in both 1995 and 1997.

Richard Ryder   Chief whip 1990–95, responsible for getting Maastricht legislation through Parliament.

Norman St John-Stevas   Leader of Commons and arts minister 1979–81, when he promoted the select committee system. Regarded as a 'wet' on economic policy.

Christopher Soames   Son-in-law of Winston Churchill. War secretary 1958–60, agriculture minister 1960–64. Entered House of Lords 1978, leader of Lords 1979–81. Sacked by Margaret Thatcher.

Norman Tebbit   Employment secretary 1981–3, trade and industry secretary 1983–5, party chairman 1985–7. Seriously injured by a bomb planted by the IRA in the Grand Hotel,

Brighton, at the 1984 party conference – his wife Margaret even more so. A strong supporter of Margaret Thatcher and a persistent critic of John Major.

Margaret Thatcher Education secretary 1970–74. Stood against Ted Heath for party leadership in 1975 and surprisingly won. Prime minister 1979–90.

John Wakeham Chief whip 1983–7, leader of Commons 1987–9. Entered House of Lords 1992, leader of Lords 1992–4.

William Whitelaw Leader of Commons 1970–72, Northern Ireland secretary 1972–3, employment secretary 1973–4, home secretary 1979–83, deputy prime minister 1979–88. Entered House of Lords 1983, leader of Lords 1983–8. Indispensable minister for both Ted Heath and Margaret Thatcher.

Lord Young Minister without portfolio 1984–5, employment secretary 1985–7, trade and industry secretary 1987–9.

George Younger Various ministerial positions 1970–74, Scottish secretary 1979–86, defence secretary 1986–9.

Index